The
LAW-SCIENCE
CHASM

▶◇◀

Bridging Law's Disaffection
with
Science as Evidence

by

Cedric Charles Gilson

qp

QUID PRO BOOKS

New Orleans, Louisiana

THE LAW-SCIENCE CHASM

Published in 2012 by Quid Pro Books.

ISBN 978-1-61027-144-8 (pbk)
ISBN 978-1-61027-145-5 (eBook)

Quid Pro, LLC
5860 Citrus Blvd., Suite D-101
New Orleans, Louisiana 70123
U.S.A.
www.quidprobooks.com

qp

Publisher's Cataloging-in-Publication

Gilson, Cedric Charles.

> The Law-Science Chasm: Bridging Law's Disaffection with Science as Evidence / by Cedric Charles Gilson.

> p. cm. — (Dissertation series)

> Includes bibliographical references and detailed outline of contents.

1. Science—methodology. 2. Law—evidence. 3. Sociology—theory. 3. I. Title. II. Series.

KF 8962 .G31 G41

364'.168.7—dc22
2012337842

Table of Contents

Foreword.. i

Preface.. iii

Acknowledgments... xi

Chapter I. Introduction and Methods... 1

Reasons for the study 1

Perspectives, aims and questions 2

Methodological considerations 5

Incommensurability: the contribution of epistemology 9

Outcomes and evaluation of outcomes 10

Structure and synopsis 10

PART A. DISPARATE KNOWLEDGES: EPISTEMOLOGY AND
THE CENTRAL PROBLEM... 15

**Chapter II. The Ætiology of Science-law Disjunction in
      Legal Contexts**.. 15

The climate of incommensurability 15

The interaction of science and law in the legal forum 28

The self-representation of science 35

**Chapter III. The Accessibility of Systems: Issues of Closure
      and the Ability to Observe**... 47

Systems as bounded epistemologies 47

Early formative systems theory 48

Modern systems theory and the ultimacy of autopoiesis 53

Teubner's deconstruction of legal autopoiesis 64

The possibility of observation 75

Excursus: Transformable law; transformative law. Fresh debates on law's regulatory role 79

Overcoming disappointments in legal development 81

    A. The possibility of transformable law 81

    B. The possibility of transformative law 86

PART B. TRANS-DISCIPLINARITY: CREATIVE SOLUTIONS OR RECREATED PROBLEMS?.. 95

Chapter IV. Portable Decision-making and the Problem of Evidence... 95

Trans-science: exporting science into law for decisions 95

Quasi-legal procedure in resolution of problematized scientific knowledge 103

Evidential standards of science in the legal and quasi-legal forum 107

Law takes charge as tyro in trans-scientific issues 120

Law takes charge as expert: its very peculiar discretion in medical negligence 122

Negotiating the meaning of science: the exemplary procedure of the American Food & Drug Administration 127

Providing assurance in regulatory decision-making 130

Intussusception of law and science 133

PART C. TRANSCENDENT MEDIATIVE RESOURCES: SURPASSING EPISTEMOLOGICAL SEPARATIONS.. 137

Chapter V. The Possibility of Alternative Rationalities in Resolving the Central Problem.................................... 137

Problems and limitations of the epistemological approach 137

Epistemological collisions in the legal forum: origins in the Kantian philosophical tradition 138

Repudiating the epistemological enterprise 144

The philosophical shift to a linguistic approach 145

The consequences of the consensus theory of truth 166

Taking stock: towards a common intellectual space for theory and procedure 172

PART D. PROVISIONAL CONCLUSIONS.. 175

Chapter VI. Potential Frameworks for Bridging Law's Disaffection with Science in Evidence....................................... 175

Postscript on Methodology: the utility of the tripartite approach and the lessons of research 175

A new intellectual space for theory and procedure 180

Bibliography.. 195

About the Author.. 213

Foreword

At the time of writing this foreword, the ongoing financial crisis, now in its sovereign debt phase, has succeeded in diverting the media's attention for several years from its earlier fixation with the myriad problems caused for society by a science that was apparently either inadequately regulated or even inadequately understood. Now the lurid headlines proclaiming the imminent onset of a genetically-modified or nanotechnological dystopia are replaced by equally alarming warnings of an inescapable depression arising in no small measure from the machinations of financial engineering. The issues surrounding science have not gone away, however. If anything, they are set to re-emerge with renewed vigour once popular attention is permitted to return to them.

The difficulties that science faces in responding to its not infrequently negative press can be seen as the result of the fact that it represents one of a number of functionally-differentiated communicative subsystems which go to make up modern society. The complex closure which this self-referential (indeed, self-constructing) differentiation represents has, on one hand, allowed the remarkable exponential progress witnessed since the onset of the scientific revolution but, on the other, given rise to the difficulty which science experiences in communicating with other functionally-differentiated societal subsystems, notably politics and law.

Cedric Gilson's book takes seriously the idea of the autopoietic closure of society's communicative subsystems and works out the consequences in particular for science and law. This analysis both lends support to the credibility of the approach adopted and sheds light on the problems and the direction in which potential solutions might lie.

I am delighted to be able to contribute this foreword to a book which represents the culmination of a project which can be traced back to Cedric's initial postgraduate studies and continued through his doctoral research. The current text clearly indicates the depth and breadth of the work necessary to do justice to this complex field and is testament to Cedric's dedication to and enthusiasm for the project. The book consequently makes an important contribution not only to the literature dealing with the relationship between science and law but also to the literature dealing with the application of autopoietic systems theory to tangible concerns.

This book is therefore of clear significance to those continuing to wrestle with the challenges thrown up by science for law and policy even when the spotlight of public attention is directed elsewhere. But given that the spotlight is currently on the "dismal" *science* of economics, it is worth noting that the approach adopted here is of much broader application and significance. The challenges facing society are now so many and so complex that only an *adequately complex* theory will do when it comes to analysing them. In this vital regard this important contribution is more than equipped for the task.

JOHN PATERSON
Professor of Law
University of Aberdeen
February 2012

Preface

As one of a number of digital and print publications under the Dissertation Series by Quid Pro Books, *The Law-Science Chasm* originated in the thesis 'Resources for Mediating the Incommensurability of Science and Law in Legal Contexts', submitted by the author for the degree of Doctor of Philosophy at the University of Westminster, London, UK. This degree was awarded in March 2007. Motivation for the study grew from an earlier interest in medical negligence, initially from the standpoint of dispute prevention and resolution through a course of that name for the degree of Master of Laws at Westminster. Examination of civil cases in medical negligence revealed the reliance of law on medical experts for its conclusions and the difficulties encountered in interpreting their opinions in relation to facts and the weight to give their evidence. The scope of work then expanded into exploration of science-law incommensurability generally and analysis of potential means of mediating the disjunction. The research was conducted within the Anglo-American common law legal tradition, broadly, and the adversarial approach to procedure. Exceptions will be stated. For international readers of this work, the legal jurisdiction in the United Kingdom is divided into that of England and Wales (the 'English jurisdiction'), Northern Ireland and Scotland. Scottish law is differently founded. Latterly, the United Kingdom sometimes has looked to the courts of the European Union for higher appellate adjudications. Predominantly, the discussion here falls within the English jurisdiction but cases and the work of scholars in the USA are informative.

In modern legal contexts, law increasingly depends on science for determination of legal truth, so that its conclusions can be more drawn more securely. In part, this is due to the growing probative power of science itself which, for law, appeals as providing a route to causation and thus establishing legal liability. As examples, in civil matters, actions for harm caused by pharmaceutical products rely on epidemiological evidence of their efficacy and freedom from adverse consequences; in criminal proceedings, the discriminatory techniques of forensic DNA analysis are well regarded for their support in proving causation to increasingly high standards. A difficulty for law can ensue when evidence of fact is unavailable, scant or is in dispute and expert opinion can produce only its best estimate. But law has a high expectation of science and scientists in this regard owing to the objectivity, rigour and precision extolled in its methods. *It is disappointed when its evidence is doubtful, experts disagree or prove unreliable.* Truth also is at risk when experts are pressed by law for firm responses when they are not confident; similarly, experts imperil truth when they forget or disregard their responsibilities to the court and indulge in personal opinion uncorroborated by sound research.

THE LAW-SCIENCE CHASM

Though science and law are differently grounded epistemologically, judges normally are able to decide on the weight to attribute to expert opinion evidence and can direct juries appropriately. Likewise, usually they are able to decide on the evidence to prefer where expert opinion conflicts. Often, judges can evaluate the reliability of witnesses for themselves, such as in a number of past civil cases in the English jurisdiction where an expert insisted that multiple sclerosis was a likely consequence of whiplash injury. A succession of judges simply distrusted him. More difficulty can arise, though, in unprecedented circumstances, such as in the now notorious instances of suspected non-accidental infant death, where scientific evidence concerning cause of injury either was lacking or there was insufficient research to underpin it. Matters also were aggravated in one case by an expert regarded by the court as distinguished who gave evidence from outside his area of expertise, on which an unsafe conviction then was based and successfully appealed. When such predicaments are encountered, the differences between the pronouncements, cultures and practices of science and law are emphasized. The study proceeds on the premise that the conclusions of law must remain paramount in these cases, even when science contributes the major part of the knowledge on which a decision is based.

The central problem of the study, then, is characterized as the juxtaposition of two incommensurable spheres of knowledge necessary for justice, where one is concerned with fact (science) and the other with legality (law). In their incommensurability, since these not just fail to communicate on mutual grounds but 'talk past each other', the search for a means of resolution of the impasse is presaged. Were this readily available, the present study would be superfluous but there are no facilitative transformations, interpretive schemes or meta-languages. The title of the doctoral thesis that gave rise to this book referred to 'resources' ... resources for mediating incommensurability. It signifies finding the directions in which the study should gaze for potential resolution. This cannot be assured but each domain of knowledge—the resource—can be evaluated for the contribution it can make to understanding. 'Mediating' is intended not so much in the usual sense of a negotiated settlement of difference but a possible amelioration of the difficulty. Thus, the research centres on examining various perspectives that offer to inform the problem.

Law needs to understand the nature of scientific inquiry to ameliorate its disaffection with science as collaborator in evidential contexts. Whereas law needs to conclude firmly at a point in time, the assertions of science always are provisional. And certainty cannot be a foregone conclusion. Law should realize that science represents only a system of inquiry: it is not a privileged source of knowledge, however profound this appears from the outside. The design of its research endeavours affirms *certainty of knowledge but not certainty itself.* Put differently, knowledge of the true nature of the world is independent of our ability to know it. Therefore, the elaborate statistical methods employed to attest extremely low error rates in scientific studies and the concept of statistical significance as convincing proof of the research hypothesis, together signal

iv

the dependability of conclusions but only within the constraints of the empirical method. This is not to suggest they are systematically untrustworthy, indeed there is much assurance that scientific conclusions approximate well to reality, or in many ways modern society would not function well; it is just that law needs to be cognizant of their limits.

That science is socially constructed is a matter of which law often is unaware or might find incredible. Improperly understood, counsel could even use it in cross-examination to discredit evidence. However, to reassure itself of the reliability of scientific testimony in the legal forum, law increasingly tends to impose on science the tenets of the philosophy of science, which provides for high methodological standards and good practice. Sometimes, this is formalized through rules for admissibility of evidence in court proceedings but it can cause the anomaly that law then must become even more involved in judgment of scientific practice, rather than finding resources of its own to arrive at its conclusions. It places itself at risk of becoming a hostage to science instead of making science serve law's purpose. Since this thesis was written, a draft Bill has been drawn up for the English Parliament that would introduce rules of admissibility of evidence into criminal courts. Through these, it is intended that law should impose on science further the philosophical canons of science in order to determine the 'quality' of evidence to be admitted. This work is dedicated to locating means of accommodating scientific evidence within law's contemplations, and with improved understanding of what constitutes science, without sacrificing its hegemony over decision-making.

The social construction of science concerns the social attributes of scientific practice—the social conditions under which science is done. These might concern pressure for results and publications, professional prowess, funding issues, loyalties to sponsors, academic rivalry and others. These can affect its value as evidence. Ignorant of these matters, law might place too much trust in expert evidence; forewarned, it might be possible to question the background against which conclusions were reached in case reliability has been impugned. In studying these matters, the scholar is free to choose between Edmond's disillusionment with the social construction of science as undermining faith in its epistemological basis and the optimism of Haack asserting that awareness of the sociology of science is crucial to that epistemology.

The sociology of science is indifferent to the content of research except when attaching social significance to its productions. The *sociology of scientific knowledge*, in distinction, explores the possibility of maintaining that there exist common criteria of rules of evidence for assessing the validity of knowledge claims, applicable irrespective of substantive concerns or analytical approaches. In the context of the present work, it proposes an evaluative function for the productions of science that presents law with the possibility of a closer estimation of the truth and an improved dialectic with science. The sociology of scientific knowledge concentrates on identifying the principles in terms of which scientists' own accounts of action and belief are organized and is an intelligent enterprise. The conditions and influences under which conclusions are reached would be replaced by reasons for such belief that law would be able to interrogate, making the sociology of scientific knowledge a candidate for a framework with potential to mediate science-law disjunction. At the least, it might enable judges to understand why sometimes science stands at the edge of knowledge, rather than taking risks on the reliability of scant or contested evidence, or pressing experts for opinions they have not formed.

From an educational perspective, then, and for the sake of better interpretation of scientific evidence, would it not be more informative and useful for the judiciary to understand not only the fact of the social construction of science but also the way in which scientists organise and confirm their beliefs? Using this more sociological standpoint would provide the judiciary with an overview of the 'industry' that is science, rather than attempting either to understand science itself more deeply, or even the evaluation of scientific productions through statutory rules for admitting expert evidence into court. Then it should be possible to communicate this perception to juries (where a jury sits) and direct them accordingly. Oddly, this notion is not new. Literature on the subject abounds but legal scholars seem to have ignored it; if they have examined but discounted it, evidence of the decision has not been discovered. This work renews the plea for the sociological aspects of science to be taken into consideration in legal judgments and for juries to be directed in how to regard expert evidence 'sociologically' but not as prejudicial to its value.

No theory approaches that of the systems theory of the sociologist Niklas Luhmann for accentuating the categorial disjunction of science and law. This arcane and radical thesis, often dismissed as unrepresentative of reality by legal scholars, nevertheless affords examination of the central problem of the study in a most reductive and clear manner. The descriptions of Luhmannian systems theory characterize the communications of science exclusively in terms of truth or falsity, or the fact/non-fact distinctive code of scientific inquiry, and those of law likewise as concerned only with the lawful/unlawful code in contemplating social actions. In legal arenas, and concerning conflicts of power *en route* to decision-making, when law depends on science for its conclusions, Teubner warns of an epistemic trap for law but develops an argument to show it can be mitigated. For Luhmann, for science to dictate legal outcomes would signify loss of the integrity of law's boundary—anathema in terms of his of his highly conservative theory. Hearing scientific evidence in the setting of a tribunal reproduces the phenomenon of structural coupling, in which the functionally differentiated systems of science and law participate momentarily in the same event. In this so-called congruence of knowledges, structural coupling sometimes is offered within scholarship (sometimes too easily) as a means of evading the consequences of the autopoietic disjunction of systems. However, each system can see the other only in its own normative terms, so law cannot detect legality or illegality when regarding science. Therefore, 'congruence' affords a view for law only of causation through scientific evidence, proof of which might be sufficient to attribute legal liability. So no miraculous transformation occurs, because the stumbling block remains of the assurances of the proffered evidence. Where proof of criminal liability must be determined beyond reasonable doubt, the onus of proof on scientific evidence is correspondingly burdensome.

Neglect of sociology, often disparaged as a 'soft science', is apparent throughout the narrative of this work yet, in its role as the ultimate observer of systems, it can observe the way in which law's conclusions are affected by extra-legal influences. Sociology can observe the conflict from the outside, while law only can internalize its problems with science. It can provide a sociological view of the epistemic trap for law using the distinction autonomy/heteronomy in decision-making. Is this not too important to neglect? Does it not represent exactly the nub of the central problem of this study?

Research philosophy of the kind avowed here must investigate areas of study that self-select from the literature. There is no imperative to find them fruitful, only to evaluate them for their possible contribution to the study. Reflexive or responsive law is a tantalising possibility but the researcher needs to discover how it could operate in the current context. The legacy of a proposed sociological jurisprudence, it seeks a model of law that responds better to the needs of society. It is hailed as a means of relieving disappointments over the social effects of various paradigms of law, for example the crisis of formal law and its limitation in coping with social advances. A *transformable* law (the author's notion) might offer possibilities for improved science-law understanding; a *transformative* law (also coined by the author) causes science and law to understand themselves and each other better. While proponents such as Teubner, Nonet and Selznick, Willke, and Paterson consider ways in which reflexive or responsive law could function, their theories founder on the dispensation of Luhmann in which autopoiesis prevents absolutely the possibility of such a legal paradigm. The question is examined thoroughly as an *excursus* in the main work but is unable to conclude. To be fair, the concept is more appropriate to regulation and the social state and thus might not be applicable to tort or criminal prosecution. Nonetheless, the theoretical exploration is worthwhile. Ultimately, the reader has the freedom of personal choice over the feasibility and utility of the attractive notion of reflexive law.

Some enterprises also are worthy of momentary attention. While not capable alone of resolving the impasse, nevertheless they contain themes, mainly procedural, that could inform the central problem. Some resources have transdisciplinary aspects, or at least attempt to bring science and law together in a joint forum. Attention is drawn to three prominent methods.

1. Wryly in the sense of the present study, resolution of some of the imponderables of science or inquiries too complex or extensive to mount can be allocated to a quasi-legal procedure called *trans-science*. In a specially constituted forum, legal-type conclusions are drawn after the best available evidence and opinion is presented and questioned. The likelihood of the truth of a given theoretical scientific assertion is then assessed using an estimate of its probability in a court-style judgment,

no other being available. This represents legal resolution of scientific uncertainty. While there is a place for trans-scientific pronouncements in
instances of great uncertainty, is not the same function implied when
courts must conclude on the basis of scant or controversial scientific
evidence? Although pursuing liability, by accepting doubtful evidence or
preferring one side of conflicting testimony, are courts not engaging in
their own estimate of truth? In other words, is trans-science often in operation, unacknowledged, in routine procedure?

2. Democratic decision-making and consensus judgments as determinative
procedures when considering scientific evidence are manifested in some
areas of regulation, of which the procedure of the United States Food
and Drug Administration to licence pharmaceutical products for sale is
typical. A committee-style forum comprising the licensing board and its
scientists, expert representation from both the would-be licensee (the
manufacturer) and user groups (target population) is convened. Evidence from the clinical trials is heard and all parties interrogate it.
Propositions arising from the manufacturer's claims in trials are constructed and agreed as the basis of a ballot to be taken on their validity.
The majority decision of the licensing board approves or declines a licence. Deconstruction and reconstruction of claims in this way permits
licensing to be selective in accordance with strength of evidence for a
particular use and the perceived benefits of the product.

3. The Conseil d'Etat is a French administrative court that adjudicates
claims against the state. Whilst inquisitorial in style, it has a unique way
of representing expert evidence. Experts are not heard directly. Instead,
their evidence is reported in successive stages of discussion, revision
and presentation by officials having no competence in the expert area.
At each increasing level of presentation to the court, consideration
moves from expert opinion towards a legal view and a distancing of the
determination both from the detail of the expert evidence and claimants'
particular submissions. Conclusions therefore not only are dispassionate but result from legal interpretation of evidence in relation to administrative law, for instance from the scientific proof of the harm caused by
exposure to asbestos to the responsibility of the state to protect workers
from it. This process is referred to in this work as intussusception—a
'sliding' of one part over another.

Jasanoff asserts that procedural advances represent only incremental means of
solving science-law disjunction. While the above illustrations might appear
idiosyncratic, nevertheless they contain noteworthy insights.

Having analysed and deconstructed the central problem and dallied with
partial perspectives that could mediate law's disaffection with science, the
study must move firmly into synthesis and reconstruction. However, there can
be neither panacea nor totalizing prescription; indeed, it would be misguided
to suggest one. However, the study is tasked with identifying resources for

mediating law's disillusionment with science and to evaluate them in the role. Since the study has exhausted many of the possibilities, an innovative perspective is required. It is not that the work pins its hopes on a particular scheme, only that one might answer more of the questions posed, offer itself as the resource most worthy of examination and round off the study with optimism. An indication lies in the reality that, when issues are brought into an open legal forum, the means by which they are examined, tested and decided upon rely primarily on speech, language and understanding. Expert evidence is given verbally in utterances, statements or assertions, the validity of which must be tested by the recipient, who must possess corresponding resources. *The Theory of Communicative Rationality* of Jürgen Habermas and the verbal characterisations of evidence and examination in court transpire to be commutative. Habermasian philosophy begins with lamenting Kant's responsibility for the separation of science, law and aesthetics via his *Critiques*, for the consequent closing down of the project of modernity and the demise of the epistemological basis of contemplating the world. It is also situated in the need for a new basis of human trust after it was betrayed in the Holocaust. A development in postmodern scholarship has been the turn to language as a means of critical reflection and to emancipate thought from the fetters of modernity. Habermas visualizes rational communication between parties involving agreement culminating in the intersubjective mutuality of reciprocal understanding, shared knowledge, mutual trust and accord. These rely on comprehensible expressions, the innate truth of propositions by which knowledge can be shared, utterances that are right so that agreement can be reached with respect to a recognized normative background and an intention of truthfulness so that mutual trust is assured. Such idealizations can be identified in the linguistic dynamics of giving and receiving evidence and the theory makes provision for 'argumentation' to which recourse can be made if validity is questionable.

Habermas's crowning achievement is to propose a 'tentative notion of a formal unity of reason' in which the argumentation in one sphere of knowledge can be applied to questions of validity in another, while respecting the distinctive logic of each. By relocating the science-law disjunction from that based on epistemological disparity, normative clash or societal division to an ethical, transcendent rationality based on communicative action, a systems-disregarding resolution might be in prospect. Is this a tangible view or a candidate for the sublime? Would courts have time to engage in argumentation to establish the truth, rightness and truthfulness of assertions? Could communicative rationality be systematized so as to be usable in court? If it were to reduce the number of appealable decisions, the extra deliberation would be worthwhile.

CEDRIC C. GILSON
University of Westminster
March 2012

Acknowledgments

A work of this proportion could not have been contemplated without the encouragement of my supervisors and I benefited enormously from the positive guidance of Dr (now Professor) John Paterson and Professor John Flood. Dr Paterson was a source of inspiration for this project, which evolved from my interest in medical negligence and a Master's Dissertation on risk management in the UK National Health Service, undertaken with his mentorship. This was a direct consequence of a module taken in Conflict, Risk and Regulation led by Dr Paterson and Professor Julian Webb within an LLM on *Dispute Prevention and Resolution* in the School of Law at the University of Westminster, London, UK.

This doctoral thesis was written from the standpoint of a person with a scientific background regarding the representation of science from legal perspectives. Dr Paterson's understanding of science and appreciation of how law regards it through his work on risk in the oil and gas industry has been of significant value in building this study. Professor Flood advised me thoroughly on methodology, structure and strategy throughout the study and was most insistent on and concerned for its originality. He has been the source of avenues of inquiry that I found novel, encouraging creative thinking that forges new and interesting connections between theories. Both supervisors encouraged an approach to research that not only would contribute to knowledge but also enlarge the envelope within which it was considered.

I am immensely grateful to Professor Penny Green, then Director of the Graduate Centre in the School of Law, for being on hand to give advice, for always exuding confidence in my ability and showing great enthusiasm for my work. I wish to thank her in particular for arranging an excellent series of seminars for research students given by Professor Julian Webb, Dr (now Professor) Reza Banakar, Dr Simon Mackenzie and Professor Green herself.

Although the emphasis of my study changed slightly after my Transfer of Registration from MPhil to PhD, nonetheless associated studies through modules from the MSc in *Evaluation of Clinical Practice* in The School of Integrated Health, Department of Community and Collaborative Practice, University of Westminster equipped me with a background to research methods in healthcare and evaluation of service that I used to inform my discussion. I am pleased to acknowledge Dr Janet Richardson, Dr. Geoff Wykurz, Mr David Goosey and Mrs Yvonne Connolly for excellent tutorials.

Central Problems in the Philosophy of Science and Social Science was a one-week course of study at the University of Essex at Colchester, UK as part of the 37th Essex Summer School in Social Science Data Analysis and Collection in July 2004. The course situated discourse theory in the philosophical and theoretical problems encountered in conventional social science approaches.

Insight was acquired into the claims of scientists and social scientists to produce verifiable knowledge. Dr Mark Devenney of the University of Brighton, the Course Leader, illuminated brilliantly the thoughts of Jürgen Habermas for which I am especially thankful, the writings of that scholar in Critical Social Theory and the Theory of Communicative Action in particular having seemed inaccessible up to that point.

I remember with appreciation the *Research Student Conference on Risk and Regulation* at the London School of Economics, London, UK in September 2004, ably organised by Dr. Henry Rothstein, then of the ESRC Centre for Analysis of Risk and Regulation at LSE. As well as experiencing a stimulating conference, I gained from him the idea of the coherence or otherwise of trans-science that contributed significantly to debate in Chapter IV.

While considering the nature of institutes of trans-science suggested by Dr Horton in his account of the MMR controversy, I encountered work via Dr Paterson of Professor Ragnar E. Löfstedt of the King's Centre for Risk Management, International Policy Institute within the School of Social Science and Public Policy at King's College, London, UK in communicating risk. I thank Professor Löfstedt for his kindness in forwarding a comprehensive pack of publications under his authorship that informed the debate importantly in Chapter IV.

Mr Giles Eyre, Barrister, led me to cases from his experience indicating how judges decide on the evidence they prefer amidst conflicting expert opinion in medical negligence actions and in particular the distinction of Gage, J in *Swift v Bexley & Greenwich Health Authority* (25th May 2000, unreported), demonstrating the special logic that judges employ in reaching their conclusions. This was during the course *Giving Medical Evidence* (Professional Solutions and Services Limited) held at the Medical Society of London in May 2002. I am grateful to Mr Eyre for indicating this and for a transcript of proceedings.

I wish to record the patience of Professor Richard Farmer of the Postgraduate Medical School of the European Institute of Health and Medical Sciences, Guildford, UK shown towards my correspondence with him over the ability of judges to assess research methodologies and grasp their significance. This was over *Re The Oral Contraceptive Group*, an action against the manufacturer of an oral contraceptive alleged to cause thromboses in women taking it (Chapter IV). Professor Farmer kindly gave me his view based on his experience of litigation, which was that he considered judges in the UK often were highly capable of understanding scientific evidence and discerning well-conducted clinical studies from others. Also, Professor Farmer forwarded extracts for my inspection from the case transcript where the judge had commented on the evidence of certain expert witnesses.

Dr R W Yates, Director of the Paediatric Intensive Care Unit of the Royal Manchester Children's Hospital, Manchester, UK generously gave his time to consideration of an inquiry I made of him concerning whether the deficient care revealed in *Bolitho* would now be prevented by improved guidelines and changes to professional practice (Chapter IV). The matter was important to me at a time when it was thought medical negligence issues would feature more prominently in my study. That this is not quite the case now does not lessen the gratitude I owe to Dr. Yates for his considerate reply.

Dr Anne Barron of the London School of Economics, London, UK, clarified issues concerning the turn to language in both cultural theory and philosophy that led me to consider the (unanticipated) embeddedness of language in Kant's thoughts that became so important in the later development of my thesis.

Professor Julian Webb, now of the School of Law, University of Warwick, afforded me the strangely conducive space of his kitchen in Warwick for a mock viva. The experience proved invaluable and equipped me to deal with the actual interview, in which I had to provide strong responses to challenging questions.

Professor John Flood, Series Editor for Law in the *Quid Pro Books* Dissertation Series, encouraged me to publish this study, for which I offer him my most sincere thanks. For all its shortcomings, all of which are my responsibility, I remain grateful for the opportunity to avoid the result of five years of study languishing unseen and gathering dust on a library shelf.

The final debt is greatest and is owed to Jean, my wife, who has always given me undying support and encouragement in my work, as well as excusing neglect of many tasks and duties at home and fending off interruptions during my total preoccupation with study.

C. C. G.

THE
LAW-SCIENCE
CHASM

Chapter I. Introduction and Methods

REASONS FOR THE STUDY

This monograph within socio-legal studies analyses the difficulties that law faces in reaching consistent conclusions where science forms an important part of the evidence offered to law. The study seeks frameworks with potential to ameliorate the incommensurability of the two knowledge fields that warrant further examination. In the long view it is anticipated that examination of these frameworks will add to knowledge that can improve coherence among legal decisions and hence justice in law's conclusions.

The Central Problem

Science and law are functionally differentiated. Often they collide in the legal forum due to this and their different constructions of reality, divergent philosophies, disparate epistemologies and evolution. This might be the most acute distinction of knowledge fields in society. The schism is contextualized in the theoretical reflections of the eighteenth century when European society reorganized new central problems of identity and order along the lines of functional differentiation (King and Thornhill 2003: 43), though the systems theory of Luhmann was to organize functional differentiation even more radically (1982: 136).

The present study begins with a fundamental concern: the premise that legal decisions can be caused to err by the poor understanding of science by law amid modern complexity. In turn, sometimes science fails to appreciate that its evidence and opinions are misunderstood by law and often is ignorant of the reasons. Intersubjectivity regarding the productions and expressions of science and law in the legal forum is desirable, but their perspectives are so radically different that formation of a unified view is unlikely.

Currently each talks to the other in its own terms, which goes to the problem of their incommensurability in evidential contexts and law's disappointment with science as collaborator. In its preliminary inquiry, this study found that there exists no universal authority, meta-language, system or super-conception to which appeal can be made that would dismantle the duality of science and law in such a way that would overcome or lessen the difficulties. There is no common rationality of science and law of which legal decision-making involving science could take advantage. Seeking interpretative or deconstructive methods or ciphers to bring science and law into common understandings is likely to prove futile. A dialectic is set up when science presents its evidence to law and moves issues towards resolution—but so disparate is the logic of the two knowledge fields that typically that resolution is by *res judicata* and sometimes is incomplete and unsatisfactory.

With respect to communication between science and law, Paterson (2003) illuminates the difficulty with some well-chosen examples. Regulators in industry or environmental protection use an instrument that respects legal requirements but work with information generated by science (ibid: 526). As examples, safe doses of radiation are the product of a legal process but derived from information produced by science; a judge presiding over a case involving a risk issue exercises a legal function but is confronted with evidence from science; in medical negligence a judge must apply a legal norm relating to the standard of care but on the basis of evidence from the realm of science (ibid: 526-527).

In the legal forum the difficulty law has in understanding science is not that of language but of knowing how to regard the opinions of experts, the weight to put on their evidence, and in trusting that the conclusions reached therefore are sound. Trusting the conclusions of experts is more difficult to learn. As examples, does whiplash injury lead invariably to multiple sclerosis? Did the whooping cough vaccine cause brain damage in children? Are oral contraceptives responsible for thromboses in women that take them? Are certain drugs administered during pregnancy the cause of deformity in children? The opinions of expert witnesses in these legal cases were open to doubt.

For all these and other reasons, this study investigates the nature of the science-law disjunction by reference to their philosophical and theoretical underpinnings, using analytical methods to seek possible mediative resources.

PERSPECTIVES, AIMS AND QUESTIONS

Standpoint

The standpoint of the research is that of a scientifically educated and interested but impartial enquirer concerned over decisions by law in questions involving science. The researcher is not a lawyer but one seeking means of ameliorating the central problem through the broad vision of socio-legal studies. Incursion into legal studies themselves is not intentional but can be necessary when individual cases must be examined to demonstrate the way law reaches its conclusions in matters. Points of law and legal argument therefore will be discussed only to illustrate salient features of legal decisions that bear on the central problem and its possible resolution.

Instead, the resources to consult and explore reside chiefly but not exclusively in philosophy, the philosophies of science and law, their respective epistemologies, the sociology of both knowledge fields, and sociology itself. Legal procedures that bring science into the legal forum or that are intended to interpret its meaning are examined, and so the interfacing of science and law becomes significant for study. The standpoint is from such a distance as not to become involved in legal intricacies but to exercise critical concern for the nature and relationship of science and law, so that the offering of potential resources for mediation of their incommensurability will be objectively informed. This will not be a privileged account but one synthesized from information obtained from a dispassionate external viewpoint.

Aims

The aim of the study is to engage with the complexity of the social systems of science and law and provide an adequately complex account of the central problem of the study. A more satisfactory map of the landscape of science-law conflict is required that will define problems and clarify the causes of misunderstanding. Better conceptualisation and description of the problem sometimes provides clues to finding solutions. Frameworks for examination are a necessary preliminary to identifying resources. The exploration must be of complex theory with a view to finding what will emerge so that any resources discovered with potential to ameliorate the central problem themselves are adequately complex. The study aims at reaching provisional end-points for the mediation of science-law incommensurability and estimating the prospects of its resolution. The themes these adduce will provide the basis for further research.

Research questions

The principal research question consequent upon the title of the work is, 'What knowledges as partial perspectives can contribute to ameliorating law's disaffection with science in evidential contexts?' This overriding interrogative can be divided into a series of challenges. Potentially the list could be long but the following are suggested as corollaries of the main question. 'Can science and law that *talk past* each other be made to *talk to* each other—and, if this should fail, what are its reasons?' 'If science and law talk past each other in the legal forum, what mediative agencies, vehicles and other resources are available to ameliorate their incommensurability for the benefit of security in and coherence among legal conclusions?' 'Is relief for the incompatibility of science and law in evidential contexts more likely to be found externally to their own knowledge systems?' 'Is there some form of meta-critique?' 'Is the potential for mediation of incommensurability more likely to be sourced through theory or concrete resources?' 'Is there any kind of rationality that can make representation of the truth in science and law a universal?' The study moves forward to examine these questions by means of the approach, structure and categorizations that will be seen.

An important perspective of the inquiry

As an observation on research method, this study is concerned with two disparate knowledge fields between which concurrence in a single forum is desirable, naturally requiring that their separate principles, structures and operations be scrutinized. In the quest for means of determining truth, a pivotal issue in this study, a choice must be exercised as to which is to be the final arbiter. Perhaps this predisposition could be seen as limiting freedom of inquiry, though not due to prejudice or bias but rather necessity.

A thorough examination of science and a correspondingly deep inquiry into law represents a large task. The central problem of the research concerns representation of science to law and it is not envisaged as a consequence that the institution of law should be so reformed that the social function expected of it in maintaining order should change.

A question for society therefore is whether law should continue to be allotted the rôle of final arbiter of truth. Literature reveals the tendency in modern society for science to be considered determinative of the ultimate truth, raising the question of whether society could tolerate a scientized approach to all aspects of life. Naturally, freedom of opinion can be allowed on such a question. But this study needs to establish a baseline belief so that other factors then can be compared to its fixed points. In regarding the relationship of science and law as unstable, then their affairs can be examined by assuming the function of law to be acceptably stable and considering mediative resources from this perspective. Prosaically, this also prevents the task becoming disorganized and risking obfuscation of the most useful conclusions. The stance of this study therefore is that law is accorded the rôle of final arbiter of truth over matters within its purview that involve science. This anchors the inquiry in a principle adopted to serve a purpose here. At another time the 'mirror image' of the inquiry—that is, 'What is it about law that makes its understanding of science difficult?'—would be worthwhile and informative, and would form the essential companion to this work.

With law identified as truth-arbiter over matters in contention, it is not as though it is conferred with total immunity from criticism—indeed its processes and conclusions always can be questioned—but the emphasis steers the study into focusing on the way science is represented in the legal forum. Accepted here are the premises that the certainty professed by science is problematic and that neither science nor law is always aware of the limitations of science. For the purposes of law, therefore, the study will devote a significant proportion of its effort to examining means of raising the assurances of science, whether through its increasing reflexivity, more realistic understanding of meaning by negotiation, or submission of its findings to alternative tribunals. This is not to attribute legal misunderstandings unfailingly to science (because law is no stranger to fault), but places importance on its presentation in such a way that law can have increased trust and hence more confidence in its decisions.

METHODOLOGICAL CONSIDERATIONS

Research method

If the incommensurability of science and law ultimately were immitigable, there would be no basis for further research. But a proto-analysis of the central problem discovered concern for it and the desirability of locating solutions; therefore it was reasonable for this study to embark on its own form of inquiry. Mediative agencies or media examined in socio-legal literature may offer successful routes to improving the communication of science and law in legal contexts that would warrant exploration. They must be assessed for their potential as resources in reducing science-law conflict; and a final evaluation will report the provisional conclusions of the study.

The following are the criteria and conditions for selection of resources offering the potential to mediate science-law incommensurability and legal disappointment. They must engage with the difficulty in communicating and understanding between science and law. Before considering their application to the central problem of the study, a critique of the theories chosen for examination must be undertaken for a full understanding of their potential. No resource should be entertained that would transform in any way the innate characteristics of science and law that would subvert their epistemologies or social function. Amid these it is recognized that agency might manifest through theories developed in response to problems other than science-law disjunction so that investigation of their suitability will be required. Some agencies and media function as external observers and might be capable of independent perspectives on how science and law think and work that could illuminate the central problem.

Research will be carried out at three levels. At the first level material will be analysed. At the second it will be evaluated for its relevance to science-law problems. And the third will consist of an evaluation of its potential for success. The selection process therefore involves decisions to accept or reject ideas and refining those that survive.

The study will pursue three categories of inquiry: the epistemological, trans-disciplinary, and transcendental perspective routes. The categories are progressive. The epistemological route intuitively is consequent upon the nature of the central problem. If disparate epistemologies are at its heart, perhaps a solution might lie there too. Connecting largely with procedure as the expression of problems in the legal forum, it also inspects theories that account for incommensurability. The epistemological route therefore is analytical and problematizing. The trans-disciplinary route considers reconciliation of one of the deepest disharmonies between science and law, that of uncertainty in the pronouncements of science. It 'borrows' legal rationality to solve problems in science that transpire in 'normal' legal contexts to be a problem for law also. The transcendent perspective enlists a different rationality to overcome the difficulty imposed by the epistemological separations of science and law. The inquiry progresses along each of these routes and emerges from analysis and restatement of the central problem through vehicles for possible transformation of its decisions to rationalities that do not locate resolution in epistemological resources at all. Along this trajectory several secondary issues emerge that are discussed. The structure gives clear direction to the work, selecting and focusing upon important strands of inquiry among a large and diverse field. From the foregoing the methodology is characterized in the lines of inquiry and there is no pre-ordained methodological style.

The literature review is divided and distributed according to topic because each part needs to be proximate to its argument; therefore it is included, discussed and analysed alongside the structures of the study to which it relates and forms an integral part of the narrative. Similarly, comments and explanations are interspersed among the topics to which they pertain, sometimes helping to justify the stance taken by the study. Examination of specific theories and proposals in detail sometimes imparts an *ad hominem* appearance to the material, referring repeatedly to selected sources, and the account tends to become episodic. No apology is offered for this because it is indicated by the routes of inquiry.

Limitations and circumspection

This study represents only one of many possible stages of inquiry and is depicted as a preliminary trawl through the opportunities that can be seen. It lays the foundation for further research that would be pursued by deepening the critique of potential resources suggested and enlarging the sweep of others. For this reason the methodology is constrained to identifying frameworks for examination and giving outline reasons why they would prove profitable. 'Frameworks' subsist in generally characterized resources and 'resources' indicates where they are located.

It would be a gross overstatement of capacity to represent identification either of frameworks or resources as likely to mediate science-law disjunction in a single move. The ground is prepared by this study for assessment of the effectiveness of these and other frameworks in relation to the central problem. In similar vein a caveat must be issued that looking for a revolutionary solution to science-law problems would be over-ambitious, likely to incur error and unlikely to succeed. A step-wise approach detects deficiencies in newly advanced ideas, discards them, and ensures that chosen frameworks are immunized against failure.

The (doubtful) nexus of legal theory and legal procedure

The present study has elected to examine science-law disjunction chiefly from philosophical and theoretical standpoints in order to provide a basis of observation at a remove from the legal forum and to situate analysis in abstract and general concepts. The study of theory should afford more possibilities to discover mediative resources. This avoids becoming mired in the minutiae of procedure and exemplified occurrences that are so particular to circumstance as to offer no resources generalizable to the world of similar problems. Abstraction can avert such impediments and open conduits to transcendent thought that might permit a more profound basis for resolution of problems.

However, this creates disparity in the work. Inasmuch as science-law disjunction is manifested chiefly in procedure and legal practice, whereas abstracted thought can be worthwhile due to its distancing effects, it is hard to discern the conceptual and processual links between philosophy, jurisprudence, legal theory, legal science and legal practice. Coyle and Pavlakos (2005) explore the relationship of legal science, jurisprudence and practice, offering several models and posing still more questions. Penner *et al.* (2002: 4f) propose a similar theme in that, 'Sociologists and political scientists have things to say about the law, the nature of its authority and its rôle in society, but little of what they describe and analyse refers to law as it is learned and understood by lawyers.' Sometimes it makes attempts in this work at applying 'theory' to 'practice' feel uncomfortable.

The philosophy of law engages with the same contemplations as the whole of philosophy and is grounded in the same traditions (ibid: 5). According to Morawetz, philosophers intend their descriptions to be abstract and general (1980: 7). They inquire about the nature of discoveries, not the discoveries themselves, and what it is like to construct, offer and test a theory (ibid: 6). The philosophy of law is distinguished from its practice by attributing familiarity with legal processes to lawyers but crediting philosophers of law with analysis of law's concepts (ibid: 1). This broad-brush description ignores jurisprudence, which 'explores what is implicit in a lawyer's understanding of law that forms assumptions or beliefs he or she has when "doing law" ' (Penner *et al.* 2002: 4).

Thus far, the explanation is clear and untroubled. 'Doing law' has a philosophical connotation, but Penner and colleagues, while indicating that jurisprudence also occupies a place as philosopher of law, distinguish that the philosophy of law is not the whole of jurisprudence or legal theory; and while philosophers do not make connection with legal practice, jurisprudents do (ibid: 5). Jurisprudence deals with theoretical questions concerning 'the nature of law' to which any lawyer or judge might be expected to provide a reasonably intelligent answer (ibid: 4). But these scholars differentiate further that philosophers of law and jurisprudents resemble each other more closely than do legal theorists (ibid: 5). No clarification is provided of 'legal theorist'. So jurisprudence is accorded an ambivalent position in this literature as neither exactly that of legal philosopher nor theorist but containing something of both. Some of this confusion can be accounted for by the interchangeability of terminology, but it appears at first sight that philosophy, jurisprudence and legal theory are mutually conflated and that any or each may inform lawyers' thoughts and actions.

This kind of dichotomy is less apparent when describing science. Certainly there are far fewer layers of thought, knowledge or doctrine. It is understood that those working in law naturally are aware of its principles, but it is further perceived that procedure itself has acquired almost separate institutional status as an interpretation or representation of law in action. Not only is this study marked by such disparities but also, were it also to claim an ability to apply theory—sometimes arcane, as will be seen shortly—to problems that are almost entirely characterized by procedure, would be disingenuous. This might disappoint a reader, certainly one with a background in science, and the confessed failure of ability to apply the discoveries of theory to procedure in reconciliation of science-law problems would be regarded as a lacuna. An aim more commensurate with capacity would be analysis of these forms of abstracted thought for potential to produce radical frameworks through which overcoming disjunction can be studied.

Amplifying the relationship of philosophical, theoretical and procedural aspects of law meets with increasing difficulty as progressively greater depth is attempted. In science, theory is affirmed by research that impinges on society through technology and fuels a reflexive impulse for greater knowledge. In medicine, theory-laden research emerges as treatment and teaching. Constant enhancement of treatment is sought by further research, thus creating a self-fulfilling prophecy. Law researches actively but the present study casts it as moot whether the interrelationship of theory and legal practice is systematically commutative. Because it might not be, analysis that would run from philosophy and theory to procedure might be precluded. Running the analysis in the opposite direction that would discover the philosophical and theoretical basis of procedure similarly would be closed off. So this debate implies that law-in-action has a different existence from legal philosophy, being tasked with determining solutions to problems while abstract thought is absorbed with the characteristics of law that enables it to deal with them. But since resolution of science-law disjunction is attempted in the legal forum via legal practice, not only can the examiner disregard the principles, processes and dynamics in operation there, but neither can philosophical discourse be regarded as immaterial.

A possible interpretation could be that problems exist at one level and solutions at another—or that in this work parallel narratives must be adopted according to whether the discourse concerns the philosophical resolution of problems or more action-based resources. The problem is refractory. Sometimes the study reveals the possibility of a nexus of philosophy and procedure and is of value even if it serves only to point out the limitation of a scheme. In trans-science, Paterson (2003) finds through legal philosophy and theory that the dichotomy of the facticity of science and the moral compulsion of law is irreconcilable in determinations that use legal procedure to draw scientific conclusions.[1] However, in the formal unity of reason, the idealizations of Habermas not only transcend specializations but also annex sociological theory

---

[1] See Chapter III.

and human speech action in such a way that the present study can visualize their joint occurrence in procedure.[2]

INCOMMENSURABILITY: THE CONTRIBUTION OF EPISTEMOLOGY

Epistemology defined in the context of the study

Inasmuch as the perceived disparity of science and law in legal evidential contexts revolves around their different constructions of reality, this problem is identified in the present study as inhering in the nature of their respective knowledges, the scope of these, and the reliability of their claims to knowledge. Thus epistemology is defined in an ordinary sense but needs to be more specific for the present purpose. In legal disputes, it is the way each sphere comprehends the knowledge claims of the other that assumes paramount importance.

In reconstructing the central problem of this research, such a divergence is perceived as the primary source of conflict and misunderstanding. For legal purposes, knowledge in other spheres is required to be congruent with truth for confidence in decisions, with it being perceived as possessing an absolute and immutable quality. However, estimates of truth in some spheres or, more precisely, the manner of its proof, can be contingent. It is a major preoccupation of philosophy to study how truth is known. 'Scope' implies knowledge is limited, either by the constraints of human inquiry or because there is some natural limit to what can be known. If the reliability of claims to knowledge in each of the different fields partly defines epistemology, then the present study must be concerned with it.

Adopting the above ordinary definition of epistemology is necessary to suit the methods of this research, and then it must be endowed with localised, pertinent meaning. Rather banally, epistemology involves aspects of the theory of knowledge that can render at least a partial account of the incommensurability of science and law in legal contexts. More importantly, though, the present study is concerned with the distortion of meaning that can occur when attempts to transfer knowledge between social systems are made. This has the potential to influence conclusions. Further, the study should explore the relationship between the theory of knowledge and the contingency of asserted truth—and the reliability of its claims requires testing in the real world.

Pragmatically, and as a corollary of the foregoing, epistemology can be regarded as an aspect of the theory of knowledge that, when engaged in assertions of reality, must be subjected to procedures of negotiation and interpretation to assess both its claims and its relevance to socially important decisions. In the context of this research, it indicates significantly those aspects of the

---

[2] Chapter V.

theory of knowledge that lead to explicating the distinction between functionally differentiated social systems.

Therefore, this monograph explores the nature of epistemological contemplation as one form of rationality, and whether amelioration of the central problem will be potentiated there. If it is not, then inquiry must be reconfigured so that epistemology—though omnipresent in all human transactions, communications and experience—no longer is privileged as a vehicle for discovering frameworks to resolve difficulty. Such a strategy would result in deprioritizing epistemological contemplation in order to discover the effect of, and more generally to permit examination of, other forms of rationality. As will be seen in the final outturn of the research, that rationality not centrally reliant on epistemology as the basis of its reason, but rather on the human attributes of sincerity and interpersonal commitment, is chosen as the most favoured mediative resource.

OUTCOMES AND EVALUATION OF OUTCOMES

Evaluations will concern only frameworks with the potential to ameliorate science-law disjunction. An exhaustive evaluation of all the material evinced by the research is not proposed. Sometimes such material provides background information and contextualizes problems but does not constitute a promising framework. Attempts to rank possible frameworks via their evaluations would be spurious and misleading as mostly they offer only partial solutions and there can be no concept of 'best' or 'preferred'. Several ideas, though, emerge more prominently, for instance because they presage improved understanding of the capability of science and reasons for the certainty of scientists that will provide better assurances to law in its decision-making, as well as ways in which law can assess the validity of statements made to it.

STRUCTURE AND SYNOPSIS

The thesis comprises three main parts depicting the three routes of investigation; the parts contain within them four chapters. There are six chapters in all. After Chapter I introduces the subject and outlines the methodology, Chapter II begins with description and moves on to analysis. It situates science-law disjunctions in their encounters in legal settings, whether in litigation, assessment and regulation of risk, the formulation of policy for public safety, official inquiries, or legislation. The central problem is stated as the chief premise on which the work is built. Its ætiology is explored and its consequences explained in these important operational contexts. The study considers the extent to which the difficulty is appreciated in both scientific and legal circles, as well as the way in which current understanding can lead to unsatisfactory legal conclusions and inconsistencies. The problem is identified as rooted in epistemology. The chapter considers the disparate developments of each knowledge field in modernity, the possibility of means of resolution existing in the sources themselves, and the circumstances of their interaction. This defines Part A of the study—the epistemological route—that in the first of its two chapters essentially asks whether there exists in the nature of the problem mechanisms for its own mitigation.

The inquiry continues by reviewing the way in which awareness of incommensurability stimulates reflective thought and the outcomes that are likely. This section assesses the extent to which manipulation of procedural landscapes can succeed in ameliorating the problem as the only resource identified thus far via this route. The fruitfulness of intellectual contemplation of procedure also is considered—and whether it can have substance beyond an ordinary appeal to reason or well intended 'wishful thinking'.

If legal conclusions are regarded as the result of co-construction of realities by science and law for evidential purposes and if law is privileged as arbiter of truth, can it perform this task adequately with only an indifferent understanding of science? The inquiry cannot begin without an examination of the way in which science constructs 'truth'; it proceeds with an analysis of its normative standards and the criteria that scientists use to determine the validity of their assertions. The challenge posed by legal and sociological scholars that science is nothing but a social construction is confronted and an estimate made of social influences on production of truth. The progress from the sociology of science that understands the conditions under which science produces its assertions to the sociology of scientific knowledge by which scientists can validate their beliefs is hailed as significant. The study undertakes a preliminary assessment of this tool with reference to some difficult questions of science.

Chapter III is the second analytical chapter to explore the epistemological route and penetrates deeper into the cause of the central problem in the quest for mediative resources. It forsakes procedure in favour of examination at the level of theory, and examines systems theory first as identifying similarities between knowledge fields (Bertalanffy) and then as a radicalisation of functional differentiation (Luhmann). That the last concretises the fundamentals of the central problem might be thought to finalise the impasse hopelessly. Instead, it has been treated as creating a purity of issues that brook no distractions, from which it is possible to consider afresh on a theoretical basis means of ameliorating the difficulty amid assurances that the functions and normative values of science and law will not be jeopardized. Such a discrete distinction of epistemologies poses a question of whether observation or inter-observation of systems as a route to mediation is possible.

Proposals for averting the consequences of the ultimacy of Luhmann's theory that utilize its very construction are considered and compared with the concessions of Teubner's interpretation. However, this risks law falling into the epistemic trap of which Teubner warns. It transpires to be the essence of the central problem of the present work. Is there a way to avoid or escape the trap?

The study then selects sociological observation as a means of providing an external view of the epistemic trap. Eliminated earlier as a resource in a systems-resembling denial of its ability to observe except by reconstructing the knowledge of systems in terms of sociology, now allusion to Luhmann's desire for an ideal theory of sociology produces a novel way of observing the conditions for the epistemic trap.

Part B considers the trans-disciplinary route. Within it, Chapter IV investigates transcendent vehicles that use procedures external to science to provide conclusions. That these may act as surrogates for knowledge is examined. Using procedures of law to pronounce on science's unanswerable questions raises questions of evidential standards; indeed, the matter already is exposed in 'ordinary' legal disputes that leave law to decide on the basis of misrepresented or uncertain science. Because this permeation is alarming though often overlooked, and trusting its discussion at this point will not endanger the segue of the thesis, a large section of the chapter is dedicated to what constitutes 'good' scientific evidence for legal purposes, the problems of producing it, and the ability of law to recognize it. The section is accompanied by several examples where scant or disputed evidence made law's tasks difficult but also reveals the manner in which law reached its conclusions in such circumstances.

Resuming the account, the remainder of the chapter debates whether transcendent vehicles only reproduce present problems in the representation of science to law. Against a background of incoherence among procedures and conclusions, an idiosyncratic transcendent procedure in medical negligence reveals a surprising logic in its judgments that makes a point for law in deciding where matters of science are involved.

Science improving its self-representation is identified as an important way of lessening tensions in legal contexts and accords with the general principle discovered here that dissolution of problems and not their resolution in conflict is a better route to satisfactory conclusions. Even if decided by scientists, the benefit of procedures to negotiate the meaning of science where this is not conveyed on the face of its findings is an important consideration. In another framework the benefit of a legal procedure that secures disinterestedness in the presentation of scientific evidence is contemplated. Suggestions for agencies able to penetrate science and allay public fears of harm are described, one that would investigate areas of concern and another that would pre-empt the raising of anxiety by improving means of communicating risk.

The search for mediative resources via the epistemological route is thus complete and the account assesses the potential of each introduced measure. Similarly explored, the trans-disciplinary route requires appraisal of its potential success or whether the advantages would be outweighed by its flaws. The nature of its procedures requires scrutiny and the chapter attempts to answer the question of whether the procedures are coherent or unsystematic.

Chapter V opens Part C, the transcendent perspective. So far, the study has searched for a new rationality without reward and the transcendent perspective is taken as a possible avenue to that discovery. A reminder is given that the first reading of Kant's philosophy separating science, law and aesthetics redounds on all attempts so far to resolve incommensurability. Language emerges in two different guises as the rationality substituting for the unreliability of science. The linguistic philosophers and then Wittgenstein perceived it as a means of avoiding the confusions of philosophy, a theme extended in the present work to dissolution, not resolution, of science-law tensions. The appropriateness of Wittgenstein's language-games and 'forms of life' in describing many human interactions is considered for its application to the situations in this study. In a surprising substitution for failed epistemology by rehabilitating the project of modernity through claims to validity expressed in communication, Habermas proffers a tentative formal notion of the unity of reason with potential to transcend the strictures of science-law disjunction. From Wittgenstein's alternative rationality in language the work progresses to one vested in validity claims in statements. This revolutionary proposition requires modification to avoid a circularity identified by Paterson that returns it to Kant's separations of truth and morality by substituting the values of science as morality in the rightness to a validity claim. That the study has provided sufficient grounds for this through its suggestions to improve the representation of science might be a matter of opinion. It is proposed here that sufficient frameworks have been discovered to have made significant inroads.

Chapter VI discusses further validation—through the transcendent perspective of the reliance on language and the right of speech—of a rationality displacing science, a rationality that also accredits Habermas's notion of a formal unity of reason. It involves a surprising recursion to Kant but this time differently interpreted via the second reading of his philosophy that is largely derived from his third *Critique* and its 'emancipatory perspectives'. Kant and Habermas now are seen to occupy the same intellectual space in considering emancipation and the instrumentality of language and communication. Kant never exploited the idea of language as the expression of human feeling but lay open the way for others to realize it. As reimagined from Chapter V, from an impression of him as responsible for making inconceivable the mediation of science and law, Kant now lays the foundations for exactly that possibility.

Chapter VI goes on to evaluate the frameworks offered in the preceding analytical chapters with regard to their mediative potential. On digesting them it is observed that they have achieved a synthesis leading to recurring themes or principles by which the possibility of mediating science-law incommensurability could be considered. Inasmuch as resources give the direction in which to look, further research should focus on those themes or principles and on discovering any further frameworks that amplify them.

PART A. DISPARATE KNOWLEDGES: EPISTEMOLOGY AND THE CENTRAL PROBLEM

Chapter II. The Ætiology of Science-Law Disjunction in Evidential Contexts

THE CLIMATE OF INCOMMENSURABILITY

Categorial disjunction

Science and law are categorially different with respect to their knowledge fields, in their operations, and with regard to their societal function. Yet in the legal forum both are expected to contribute to decision-making as if in some way congruent for law's purposes. However, there are deep, consequential tensions between science and law (Haack 2003: 205). Examining means of their potential collaboration can be postponed while an interpretation anticipating systems theory is received that radicalises their distinction. It offers a 'no margin of error' rendition of the central problem of this work and instructs that to conceptualise solutions would be a non-trivial matter beyond the application of simple logic.

In the evaluation of propositions, law practices the rhetoric of absolutism using the binary distinction or code of legal/illegal. Drawing on the systems theory of Niklas Luhmann that is explored in Chapter III of this work, in its communications law only can regard the propositions it faces as legal or illegal or, as translated into practice, guilty/not guilty. Its knowledge is transmitted through its legal operations. Governance of process is via appeals in which its decisions are reconsidered by a higher tribunal if the procedure in which issues were first heard was flawed.

Propositions in science are evaluated according to the distinction or code of true/false, the equivalent of the legal trial process being research to distinguish between a contended hypothesis (liable) and its null alternative (not liable). In its communications science can acknowledge only truth or falsity, characterized operationally as fact/non-fact. In the evaluation of propositions it employs the rhetoric of provisionalism, acknowledging that science is progressive, although ardent proponents of idealized science object to the contradiction that its 'facts' can be ephemeral. Science is the generator of knowledge and is applied to society through technology. It has its own procedures for self-governance that will be examined soon, but policy and regulation is devised to prevent the societal impact of technological excess. Decisions in the regulatory forum can be appealed and neither regulation nor policy remains static. Public perception of science is that it must evolve for societal benefit.[3]

The principal foundation of categorial disjunction is the non-correspondence of the binary distinctions that law and science each draws: there is no relation between legal/illegal (or lawful/unlawful) and true/false—actually they are distinctions—with neither the possibility of a translatory device nor a meta-narrative that could organize their congruence. The burden of this work is the pursuit of other rationalities that offer frameworks to potentiate resolution of the central problem and in so doing the narrative will disclose the relationship and effect of other sources of science-law heterogeneity.

The apotheosis of science-law disjunction is realized in the legal forum, when law depends on science to assist its conclusions. In part, this chapter will constitute a review of science and law irrelation in legal settings with the scientific expert characterized as an interlocutor with the potential either to ameliorate or exacerbate the disparity. Later, it will evaluate the alleged epistemological superiority of science and examine how science believes. The discussion intends to avoid capture and distraction by the introverted justifications of both pure scientific and legal studies and instead will describe an environment in which science and science-law encounters can be reconsidered. For instance, distinguishing the perspectives of the philosophy of science that emphasizes the cognitive aspects of science and the sociological concerned with science primarily as a social institution makes an instructive beginning (Ziman 1984: 102). Along with other studies, this creates the possibility of considering science and law transcendently in order to gain new perspectives on the dichotomy.

The Central Problem of Incommensurability

The term incommensurable, or the quality of incommensurability—'not capable of being compared or measured, especially because lacking a common quality necessary for a comparison to be made'[4]—sits at the heart of explanations of systems theory and in association with the phenomenon of paradigm shifts in science. It has precise meaning in the contexts within which it is used and is a very apt description of reality. In Luhmann's radically characterized account of systems theory there is no possible means of communication between systems due to their autopoiesis, for example as between science and

---

3 Though this overall assessment can be traced back to a number of authors, I am grateful to Dr. John Paterson for suggesting the basis of this synoptic account in a supervision meeting on 18 December 2002.

4 *Encarta World English Dictionary* (1999) London: Bloomsbury.

law; and in Kuhn's conception of the paradigm shifts of science there is no basis for comparison between a new theory displacing a previous belief and its predecessor, as seen in aspects of quantum theory over classical concepts of the propagation of electromagnetic radiation.

No meta-languages, interpretive frameworks, translatory, transformative or decryptive media, or other interventions, are possible. Philosophy has the exact way of its active depiction that incommensurable bodies of knowledge simply 'talk past each other'. Incommensurability is an absolute term and an attempt to depict it as shaded or contoured not only can meet with theoretical difficulty but also forgoes the advantage of learning that it can convey. Incommensurability is a problem rooted in epistemology that can be studied at both theoretical and practical levels, though the ability of one to inform the other is questionable.

Nothing in the previous statements should be taken to suggest that incommensurability is an absolute barrier to progress in locating resources to mediate science-law difficulties. It does mean that resolution will not be found by denying the characters of science and law that differentiate them but that it might be found by looking in other directions.

It is not controversial that science and law are incommensurable in legal settings. Neither is it a myth nor an apocryphal story. But its substantiation, explication and documentation would rely on innumerable individual instances in legal encounters that embrace disputes, regulation, policy, legislation and public perceptions of science. It is a widespread, general experience in modern life in a 'climate' of awareness as the title of this section suggests, albeit most conspicuous in legal circles.[5] A systematic review[6] of all the ways in which science and law have miscommunicated would be almost impossible. Equally, producing a hierarchy or taxonomy of such findings would be a Herculean undertaking—and even then of limited helpfulness because each instance uniquely would be characterized by its particular science-law difficulty, and the points of law made would be incorporated in decisions that were non-generalizable. There is no standard reference that accounts for science-law incommensurability concisely, but the works cited in the following chapters contribute to that knowledge through describing a variety of problematized interactions and are offered in that spirit.

A theme repeated in this study is that, regardless of the attributions of incommensurability to historical and theoretical origins, it is in legal evidential contexts that it is problematized most acutely. Government as legislator and regulator recognizes this, and its concerns for the political as well as the legal understanding of science and its proper utilization have been raised recently over criminal prosecutions relying on forensic evidence. Its deliberations have had the beneficial effect of underscoring the problems of science for law and

---

[5] *Postnote* 2005: 1: '*How often does science appear in court?*'
[6] Published articles, in which researchers systematically search for, appraise and summarize all the relevant literature for a specific topic.

summarizing them perspicaciously and authoritatively, though the approach of the executive to their remedy predictably is regulative and politically inspired.

Though constrained by official capacity, many government reports usefully fixate upon, concretise and articulate the nature of problems, collecting evidence from witnesses through their preceding inquiries that inform problems knowledgeably and experientially. At first seeming to identify commonality of process, The House of Lords Select Committee on Science and Technology Report on Forensic Science observed, 'Science has this much in common with the law, that it approaches the truth by a process of dialectic in which thesis and antithesis are set in opposition' (1993: §5.15).[7] The Committee then identified the rôle of the expert as interlocutor for science in evidential contexts, was highly disapproving of that rôle, and pointed incidentally to an undercurrent in legal thought that science can take responsibility for decisions away from law. The Report continued, 'In consequence the scientific expert has been given a prominence out of all proportion to the probative value of the evidence he represents, sometimes with disastrous results for the defendant in criminal trials' (ibid). While possibly a reaction to a number of cases lost on appeal involving the (then) new DNA evidence, the reliability of which was placed in doubt, this opinion concerning the rôle of the expert can be generalized to other science-law encounters.

In examining the miscommunications that can occur in practice, it is the function of interlocutor-experts—made paramount by the practice of law in consulting them to assist its conclusions—that has involved a potential source of difficulty. Not only are the two bodies of knowledge incompatible but also the very means law has chosen to resolve the impasse amplifies the problem. King and Kaganas concur that 'law has succeeded in reconstructing as "expertise" any body of knowledge that is not law' (1998: 221). Nelken, who writes on different ways of theoretically formulating or reformulating the problem itself, gives slightly different emphasis by stating that 'at issue here is not the status of scientific truth in general but the particular difficulties of "science-law" conceived as one form of expert witnessing' (1998: 11).

In addition, Phillips (1994: 232) draws attention to the House of Lords' distillation of the fundamental problems posed by the testimony of scientific experts in court. Its wisdom is compelling. The Report articulates succinctly the principal characteristics of the central problem, which are enumerated as follows (1993: §5.14). Deep discord between science and the law is perceived. Questions are posed by counsel who are required to be learned only in the law. Distinction is made in the Report between the understanding of lawyers, juries and scientists about the assurances of scientific evidence. It says scientists' replies to questions are delivered *ex tempore* before juries in adversarial settings that are unlikely to contain anyone with relevant scientific knowledge. Scientists are accustomed to dealing with conclusions that, to satisfy standards

---

[7] Discussed by Phillips (1994: 231).

of scientific precision, are assured only within limits of probability. Though these might have precise statistical meanings they are not comprehended by non-scientists and the values will change with advancing knowledge and technique. That part of the Report concludes that the 'best scientist', implying one who qualifies answers by insistent reference to statistical data, though punctilious, may appear the most prevaricating witness.

Prominent among legal problems concerning science are those depending heavily on forensic science for their conclusions, cases of sudden unexpected infant death, toxic torts and medical negligence disputes. Problems of reliability and the constructions that can be put on forensic evidence were revisited by the House of Commons Science and Technology Committee in its Report *Forensic Science on Trial* (2005). The theme was repeated that interpretation of expert evidence was outside the experience and knowledge of a judge and jury (ibid: §131). Judges and juries may find it difficult to interpret the significance of highly technical evidence (ibid: §164). In it was confirmed that what distinguishes experts from other witnesses, for example witnesses of fact, is their knowledge of specialist matters that do not fall into the realm of the knowledge that judges and juries could be expected to process. With such reliance on expert witnesses, any shortcomings or misunderstandings of their rôle that they may hold assume great importance for legal decision-making. As an example, on the matter of sudden unexpected death in infancy, a report recommending a multi-agency protocol for care and investigation of incidents advises that doctors called as witnesses are drawn into error because they base their testimony on belief not evidence (The Royal College of Pathologists and The Royal College of Paediatrics and Child Health 2004: 4). Judges and juries may not be in a position to discern when a witness is expressing a personal opinion and that it might not have a sound scientific basis.

Medical negligence disputes in the English civil jurisdiction often are resolved by resort to case law of evidence that places deep reliance on the opinion of the medical interlocutor-expert in an area of specialist knowledge denied to judges. In the determination of liability for negligence it relates to discovery of acceptable practice through expert opinion testimony. The actions of a medical defendant to a claim for negligence are compared with that of a 'responsible body of medical opinion', the principle of which was created via procedure in the leading 1957 case of *Bolam v Friern Hospital Management Committee* [8] and is therefore known as the 'Bolam Test'. The 'responsible body of medical opinion' is constituted by medical expert witnesses called by each of the parties to the dispute. It is not possible to provide a detailed analysis here of the significance of *Bolam* for medical law, or its many attachments and consequences, but the type of opinion evidence proffered in *Bolam* will explain the way legal decisions are assisted by means of this procedure.[9]

---

[8] [1957] 1 WLR 582.

[9] General accounts of the legal doctrine of *Bolam* can be found in Jones (1996); Brazier (1992); and Kennedy and Grubb (1994). Much the same process and standard often has

In *Bolam,* it was thought necessary in administering electro-convulsive therapy in psychiatric treatment to use physical restraints strapping the patient to a couch and to give muscle relaxants. These were to avoid physical injury from the violent convulsions that would result. In the case of the patient John Bolam, these measures were not taken, and he received injuries on account of which he entered an action for negligence. In consulting a responsible body of medical opinion it was found that restraints and muscle relaxants were not employed unexceptionally, implying that the practice had been acceptable in Bolam's case, and the decision was for the defendants.

The whole of medical injury is not dealt with under *Bolam*; for instance, an action for product liability concerning harm from drugs is a matter of normal tort. Issues in *Bolam* are peculiar to medical care but seem at first glance to typify the entire science-law 'problematology'. The test does provide fertile ground for exploration of many issues in medical law, not least the question of whether because of this unique situation it is medicine or law that decides cases. Undoubtedly, medical negligence disputes characterize science-law difficulties in that courts rely on medical expertise for interpretations of underlying science and explanations of diagnosis and treatment. Reading cases shows that it can be difficult to disentangle fact and opinion in the complex field of medicine and that some experts fail to make this distinction, as can judges.

Contemplating *Bolam* as the archetypal problematization of science-law disjunction requires caution owing to its important distinctions. Liability is decided predominantly on the basis of medical practice. The rule is normative in attesting reasonable competence conflated with a descriptive one that asks experts to volunteer their views freely on the practice of the defendant by comparison with their own knowledge and the manner in which they would have approached the treatment in question (Teff 1994: 184). Even though medical expert witnesses apprise the court of the scientific basis of illness, diagnosis and treatment, due to the nature of *Bolam* their testimony predominantly is opinion. This differs from cases of non-medical negligence where the House of Lords confirmed that common practice is not determinative (ibid: 184). Were it not for the important fact that expert medical testimony is included in the category of evidence, there might be no basis for offering the Bolam Test as a unique example of science-law disjunction and law's attempt to overcome it.[10]

Though it would be expected that a consensus should be obtainable indicating an optimal method, medical difference of opinion may be entrenched, leaving it to the judge to decide which is preferred. Moreover, a judge may opt for a minority opinion provided it is logical (*Bolitho v City and Hackney*

---

been used in medical malpractice cases and jury trials in the United States, as well as other countries. Its deferential test was rejected in Australia, *Rogers v Whitaker*, [1993] 4 Med LR 79.

[10] In the English jurisdiction, the case of *Bolam* constitutes a rule of evidence.

Disparate Knowledges

Health Authority;[11] Harpwood 2001: 1). To its reputation for idiosyncrasy as a decisional tool therefore can be added that outcomes in cases following *Bolam* can be unpredictable. This could earn the procedure in *Bolam* the soubriquet of incoherence due to an *ad hoc* sense in which conclusions are reached. Inconsistency among decisions over a wide number of cases is one of Edmond's chief criticisms where law is encumbered by non-legal issues in reaching its conclusions (2000b: 216). An advocate of the process might instead applaud the reasoning of judges in sensitively identifying the issues amid complex medical distractions, but it is not consolatory that such decisions rely on a dispute being heard by an understanding judge.

Issues in medical negligence revolve about judgments of clinical care, which are matters primarily of medical ethics until law needs or is asked to intervene. The 1985 case of *Sidaway v Board of Governors of the Bethlem Royal Hospital and the Maudsley Hospital*[12] modified *Bolam*, and distinguished the rôles of medicine and law in drawing conclusions about medical negligence. From that point, decisions regarding the exercise of the *duty* of care owed by health professionals were seen as entirely those of law (*Barnett v Chelsea and Kensington Hospital Management Committee;*[13] Brazier 1992: 117-118). However, decisions on exercising an appropriate *standard* of care were matters for medical practice, medical ethics and professional conduct, though law finally would make its decisions taking them into account. Teff (1994) reveals the panoply of considerations attaching to the standard of care and legal perspectives on the doctor/patient relationship.

The preceding caveats being heeded, the manner in which medical negligence disputes differ from or correspond to other science-law frictions nonetheless is informative. It has been shown that the boundaries of fact and opinion both in the minds of experts and the perception of their evidence are indistinct; this is common to many instances where science is consulted. Worse is the realization by non-scientists that there is conflict of scientific opinion among its communities. This is not cognate with conflicting opinion about medical practice, but both fact/opinion obscurity and divergence of expert opinion are evident in all sciences when petitioned by law to shed light on causation. Prosecutions for sudden unexpected death of infants have revealed all these features in single cases where medical and forensic sciences proffering fact and opinion have converged in criminal proceedings—sometimes with erroneous outcomes that can damage the reputations of both science and law.

The synoptic account of categorial disjunction offered earlier owes its clarity to the sharp distinctions inherent in systems theory.[14] *Alone*, this approach

---

[11] [1997] 39 BMLR 1; [1998] 1 Lloyd's Rep Med 26; [1998] AC HL (E) 232.
[12] [1985] 1 All ER per Lord Scarman at 649.
[13] [1968] 1 All ER 1068 (QBD); [1969] 1QB 428.
[14] Within systems theory, this is attributable to the difference in normative standards in the operations of science and law, on which the distinctions true/false and legal/illegal, respectively, are founded.

gives a highly schismatic view of science and law, and at such a level of abstraction that it can make the prospect of mediating incommensurability bleak. But the same account also discloses pragmatically the operation of science and law in society, thereby creating a different kind of distinction in lay perception.[15] In respect of science, these can occur along a range of possible understandings. At one extreme the lay perception of science, that includes the public and any non-scientist such as a lawyer, is that of an intellectual field espousing strong normative values and conforming to idealized conceptions of practice, suggesting that its conclusions should be received as purely achieved. Ziman defines the realist standpoint as one who seeks to describe a world independent of the acts of perception (1984: 34). The 'Standard View of Scientific Knowledge', according to Mulkay (1979: 21), is that the natural world is to be regarded as real and objective and that those who observe it cannot determine its characteristics by reference to their own preferences or intentions. In the 'Standard View' these characteristics can be more or less faithfully reproduced in conclusions (ibid). Chinks in the normative armour are revealed by Mulkay, beginning with the assessment that judgments of observational adequacy vary, as does the meaning of propositions, according to the interpretive and social context. Recapitulating Mulkay's position, contrary to the Standard View, scientific knowledge is neither stable in meaning nor independent of social context and not certified by the application of generally agreed principles of verification (ibid: 59).

The factual content of science should not be treated as a culturally unmediated reflection of a stable external world (ibid: 119). In *What is this Thing Called Science?*, Chalmers (1999: xxi) postulates that scepticism towards knowledge claims is based on analysis of the nature of observation and the nature of logical reasoning and its capabilities.

Views that are more liberal accept the notion of provisionalism, with probability substituted for certainty, and acknowledge the cultural dynamics of scientific communities supporting the idea that science can be socially constructed. Legal scholars with a positivist preference of science distrust the liberal characterization for its contingency and provisionalism.[16] Sociologists find the positivist perception unlikely through its understanding of human agency as at the root of all society's productions. A problem for law is that these distinctions may be indifferently understood and for some jurists the social construction of science represents flawed methodology that can give rise to disappointed legal expectations of scientific expertise.

A more productive awareness of the relationship of science and law would result from deeper understanding of these different characterizations of

---

[15] Again, in systems theory, such an understanding is closer to the concept of cognitive openness, in which law is aware of its environment. Legal autopoiesis comprises both normative closure and cognitive openness.

[16] For an elucidation of the epistemological character of scientific positivism, see Ziman (1984: 34, 39).

science, which glib statement underlies the central problem of this study. Resolution cannot be contemplated by de-privileging either positivistic or liberalistic characterizations. Law requires an uncritical education in the limitations of science, but appreciation of the sociology of science and the sociology of scientific knowledge is illuminating for law in the way it considers and uses scientific expertise to reach its conclusions. There is insufficient space here for a critical exposition of the philosophy of science but perspectives on the nature of science are helpful.[17]

Casti (1991) attempts to crystallize public understanding of science. Though not a principal concern of this work, nonetheless it facilitates questioning the nature of science. These insights are simple and at this stage in the narrative it cannot be presumed that law's expectations of science are different. Equally, exposure of the extent to which scientists subscribe to these perceptions or recognize themselves either in depictions of practice or the kinds of criticisms recently suggested is important to the ensuing discussion.

Science is characterized as a set of facts and a set of theories to explain them (a deconstruction of causation), a particular approach known as the scientific method (systematic research pledging objectivity), and institutions carrying out scientific activity (in which is rooted a mystique of intellectuals producing arcane theories) (ibid: 11). The riders in parentheses are the present author's. Public misunderstanding of scientific research gives rise to subsidiary misconceptions or fictions that Casti enumerates but dispels philosophically, advocating that research involves ideas not answers; that deep understanding of a question is preferable to insistence on answers but that these will follow as corollaries of well-constructed questions; and that it is important to understand why an answer is possible and the reason it should take a particular form (ibid: 12).

According to Casti, scientists consider their practice to be free from ideology, which the present study assumes to mean that it is insusceptible to nonscientific interests such as those of politics or business. Instead it is posited that science subscribes to an ideology of its own created from logical, historical and sociological ideals about its operations (ibid: 13). This ideology can be demonstrated most clearly by the natural sciences but, without engaging in the turbulent debates that are held over the unity of natural and social sciences, let it be assumed for now that all sciences are included. However tendentious, the following explanation should be accepted momentarily for the sake of simplicity.

The logical nature of science inheres in the scientific method which progresses from observations occasioning hypotheses to their subsequent confirmation, denial, or modification by empirical inquiry. In turn these evolve into scientific laws that engender new theory. Claims are verified and accepted into

---

[17] For helpful introductions to the philosophy of science, see Newton-Smith (1981), Ziman (1984, 2000), Chalmers (1999), and Okasha (2002).

conventional wisdom by peer review aimed at the insurance of accuracy, substantiating their significance within the framework of current knowledge, and providing for the repeatability (reliability) of results (ibid: 14). Those practising science would concur that this accords broadly with their own impression of scientific activity. But a non-scientific sceptic would observe that the conventional ideology focuses entirely on the *process* of science and does not recognize the motivation or needs of scientists: in other words, it ignores philosophical, psychological, and sociological considerations (ibid: 15).

Problems for science

'Science, like life in general, involves creating adequate conclusions from inadequate premises' (Wynne 1989: 23). This reference to the apparent frailty of science relates more to the social expectations placed upon it than to limitations of its achievements, real though these are, and for this law as well as society is responsible. Conversely, in modernity, science can assume a position as a privileged source of knowledge when informing about risk (Ward 1998: 255-256), but Beck suggests that, even as the necessity for science increases in this rôle, its sufficiency for socially binding definitions of truth decreases (1992: 156). By this Beck means that laypeople have begun to capitalize on competing knowledge claims and now are able to exercise the kind of methodological scepticism previously confined to internal debates in science (1992: 156; Feyerabend 1978: 96-98).

In the context of regulation of risk, this remark might reflect reality due to the frequent involvement of laypersons in public controversies but not in litigation, where parties would be reliant on a form of 'judicial scepticism' for similar effect. The extent to which judges are as versed in such skills as might be laypersons committed to a social struggle is unknown. Sociologists of science have called into question the existing stereotypes of science that convey unduly idealized versions of it and through this critique have contributed to the development of a well-informed society (Barnes *et al.* 1996: 110). The stereotypes can be recognized in the 'Old Deferentialist' position described by Haack (1999: 190-191). Disarmingly, the impression conveyed by the 'New Cynicism' movement concerning science is that there is nothing epistemologically special about it (ibid: 195). This concurs with perceptions that science is simply a mode of inquiry without epistemic privilege and 'a social institution engaged in inquiry' (Haack 1996: 259; see also Longino 1990).

A serious problem for law that frequently the adversarial system draws out is that experts called to give opinion fail to appreciate that their views, which they consider the corollaries of systematic research, axiomatically are consequences of theories they supposed, possibly unconsciously, in formulating their original inquiry. Later in this work it will be seen that experts sometimes can depart from established knowledge into realms of unqualified opinion that creates enormous difficulty for law. In describing the problems for science the theory-ladenness of research described by Kuhn signifies that no inquiries are undertaken without a concept of what is being sought and reasons for seeking

24

it; this in turn shapes the approach and methods employed (Kuhn 1970: 27-30). 'The most disciplined and objective inquiry is never free of theoretical and interpretive commitments' (Wynne 1989: 23).

Remembering Casti, this implies that theory is the engine of inquiry and none is possible without it. Theory-ladenness therefore directs the form of inquiry and its conclusions inevitably are shaped by its structure. Interpretation of results—assessing their meaning and significance—superimposes another layer of necessary understanding. Opinions over interpretation might conflict. Cartwright identifies with this kind of pitfall in scientific inquiry and considers the possibility of a reliable methodology applicable to any area of study regardless of content (*Cogito* 1995: 209). As instances, these could be applied without background knowledge to social welfare, education or the problem of drug-taking; but for Cartwright there is no 'interesting articulation of a scientific method' capable of rendering the right answer if followed—and it was a mistake ever to have presumed that objectivity, rationality, truth and the possibility of knowledge in science was available through 'moving up to thinking there was a content-free methodology' (ibid: 209). Feyerabend concurs that there is no single procedure or set of rules underlying each piece of research guaranteeing it is scientific and therefore trustworthy (1978: 98). The conclusions of science therefore inescapably are shaped by circumstances perceived as axiomatic. This is not to assert that science systematically is misleading, only that its conclusions inherently are limited by the nature of its inquiry. Experts may not subscribe to the idea or choose to ignore it and law may be unaware of it.

The standards and norms of scientific practice

This narrative has waxed on social and lay perceptions of science. Scholarly discourse, especially law, has questioned its assumptions, methodology and productions. Its epistemic authority has been challenged. A picture has emerged of science wounded by criticism: it appears easier to discuss its limitations or misrepresentations rather than the positive alternative. If the true ability of science to inquire about the nature of the world and the basis of its knowledge were totally discredited, or were humanity to remain indefatigably sceptical, then, intrinsically, the outcome would be ignorance and anarchy. That this is not so is self-evident but law remains troubled by the lack of certainty, provisionalism and the effects of the social construction of science's conclusions. Instinctively recognition must be due to science in the advancement of society but the conditions for allowing dependence should subsist in re-conceiving the validation of its knowledge. These discovered, it should be possible to establish the means by which trust in science can be re-founded, its contribution re-valued or at least better knowing the terms on which such trust is deserved or, as Fuller says, '...the social epistemology of science must ask how science is to be legitimated once social constructivist accounts are widely accepted' (2006: 17). Before embarking on such an investigation a brief inspection of science's own standards must be undertaken, along with an assessment of its conformity to those norms.

In its traditional characterization, scientific practice is regulated by the norms advocated by Merton in 1942.[18] In spite of expectations that would be thought natural for a rigorous intellectual pursuit, these are not highly prescriptive codifications of practice but sociological guidance indicating appropriate conduct.[19] The vaunted 'scientific method' concerns process, includes the design of studies and often intensely statistical methods to attest proof and estimate error. Scientists for whom process is *raison d'être* look no further for assurance of the objectivity of their work.

Merton's norms provide for the practice of science undistorted by behaviour. Concerning ideals extrinsic to the scientific method, scientists refer to them as metaphysical in an understanding slightly different from that of philosophers. Positivists and some lay observers would expect that these norms represent the ways in which science should operate undeviatingly for authority in its conclusions. Briefly, they are as follows and are emphasized by italics.

Communalism locates scientific knowledge in the public domain whereby it creates its context as serious thought (Ziman 2000: 31). *Universalism* relates to the archive that records scientific knowledge through satisfaction of important criteria for acceptance of research claims (ibid: 36). *Disinterestedness* and *humility* governs the style and approach of formal scientific communications (ibid: 38). It emphasizes researcher's detachment from the everyday world and limits immodest claims to personal originality by comparing their achievements to the 'giants on whose shoulders they stand' (ibid: 38). *Originality* signifies contributing something new to the archive in the form of suggesting a new scientific problem, proposing a new type of investigation, presenting new data, arguing for a new theory or offering a new explanation. Originality is such a paramount consideration that it must be proved (ibid: 41). *Scepticism* is the kind of informed criticism that deters runaway claims and is effected through public debate and peer review of communications (ibid: 42).

If this counsel of perfection were the totality of science conceived as an intellectual activity, and assuming similar precision for law, the problem of incommensurability at least could be visualized clearly. This image of the idealized representation of dispassionate, objective science appears problematic (Edmond 1999: 556, 2000a: 2, 2000b: 217). Casti affirms that, regarding the Mertonian norms, 'these prescriptions are violated every day of the week' (1991: 52), attributing an increase in violations of the spirit of science to external forces but continuing to uphold the Mertonian norms as 'the ethos to which the community of scientists subscribes' and that 'form the heart of the code by which the behaviour of scientists is judged by their peers' (ibid: 52-53). With their basis in sociology the norms prescribed by Merton deemed scien-

---

[18] See Merton (1973: 267-278); Ziman (2000: 31).
[19] See, for instance, Edmond (2000: 221).

tists to be members of a moral community conforming to acceptable standards and placed them in high regard as agents for collective or institutional good, rather than individual benefit (Barnes, *et al.* 1996: 114). In a telling account, the failure of Merton's prescriptions is attributed to the fact that they were 'never systematically extended to describe the technical activities of the research itself [n]or the detailed responses scientists made to each other's technical procedures and knowledge claims' (ibid: 114). This rings true to the present author's experience that researchers have never seemed to exhibit 'Mertonian qualities' in executing or discussing their work and in contests over the assertions of rivals, which often are embittered. Fuller (2006: 15) believes Merton simply surveyed the methodological pronouncements of distinguished scientists and philosophers that were akin to constructing a sociology of science from them. Feyerabend adds that standards are developed and examined by the very same process they are supposed to judge (1978: 99).

Barnes *et al.* offer in substitution that sociological trends affecting norms and standards in scientific practice 'emphasize the standing of individuals as agents in order to make sense of their actions or explain their provenance' (1996: 114). Mulkay avers on the basis of his research that little indication is found that receipts of professional rewards are in practice conditional on scientists having conformed to supposed norms in the course of their research (1979: 68). As if to rehabilitate some form of respect for the norms of science, Mulkay considers it more appropriate to treat them as vocabularies employed by members of the community in negotiating meanings for their own or colleagues' actions (ibid: 93).

The preceding discussion suggests that science has two 'faces'. One concerns its cognitive ability, the relation between its processes and the explanation of objective reality. The other is about its ability to continue to work disinterestedly amid strong external influences on its institutions. Scientists are not always cognisant of the effects of such external forces on their work, the way these control their productions, nor that this is discernible in the representations they make of science. For the purist in science adhering to the objective view of practice the idea of knowledge being in any way constructed is offensive (Ziman 2000: 234; Fuller 2006: 17). None of the foregoing describes the way law develops its regard for scientists. While arguably its estimation of witnesses should be based on knowledge of an expert's adherence to norms in the production of facts, instead it relies on personal reputation in the field, which might not necessarily include a presumption of exactitude in scientific standards.

THE INTERACTION OF SCIENCE AND LAW
IN THE LEGAL FORUM

Problems of science for law

The rôle of science in law can be connected intrinsically to larger social developments (Nelken 1998: 11) than may interest them separately, suggesting that persistence in probing this relationship would be informative. Epitomizing the kinds of difficulties brought into the legal forum through incorporation of scientific matters in its deliberations, Nelken considers, first, that in his concept of 'trial pathologies', science is regarded as a normally reliable institution affording true or false answers. He alludes to the notion of the interlocutor in the form of experts called to proffer opinion. These might be unreliable or dishonest in single instances (ibid: 17).[20] Ascribing to law the responsibility for detecting these transgressions, Nelken also recounts where such expertise either can be irrelevant or unduly influential in the legal process (ibid). Scientific testimony can be portrayed as a powerful tool for justice but also as a source of confusion, not to mention 'opportunities for opportunism' (Haack 2004: 15, discussing Judge Learned Hand).

Secondly, Nelken considers law is charged with an even greater task when in borderline cases the scientific status of expertise is at issue, signifying that instead of being offered the certainty for which it yearns, law is called on to adjudicate on matters at the boundaries of science (1998: 17). Ironically in this predicament, law that operates only under legal/illegal codes is pressed for true/false conclusions, which constitutes a serious abuse of its processes. In terms of science, neither is it equipped for this, nor in law's terms should there be such expectation, given that the opinion of an expert specifically is meant to inform tribunals and inquiries so that they can arrive at reliable conclusions. In the event, law has adapted its normal procedure to enable it to test the reliability of experts rather than true/false contentions in science but is still without a universal guarantee of certainty.

From a sociological standpoint, science and law are described as powerful and often rival 'competing institutions' or 'expert spaces' co-existing or collaborating under conditions of 'unstable compromise' (ibid: 15). In this discussion Nelken refers to Jasanoff's conjecture of ideas and truth being co-constructed by science and law in the context of legal proceedings in which the example is used of the opinions of forensic psychiatrists (ibid: 16).

'Incompatible discourses', the third strand of Nelken's analysis, anticipates systems theory that would prevent science and law communicating due to the incompatibility of their codes. However, attributed to them both is the broader societal function of distinguishing truth and falsehood. With nothing to be gained from direct confrontation, law's attempts to reduce uncertainty by integrating science instead is bound to reproduce it if the beliefs of science are

---

[20] See also Feyerabend (1978: 97).

not adequate for legal proofs, claims are not substantiable or are 'stretched' by legal examination.[21] Nelken proposes instead using legal oversight to proceduralize the question of the discourse that is to be prioritised for a required aspect of social regulation (ibid: 18). Proceduralization is offered as one of several possible escape routes from incommensurability.[22] Nelken does not amplify his suggestion. Properly understood, the notion of proceduralizing an issue in science in order to discover the limits of its capacity is suggestive of methods enjoying notable utility that will be explored later in this work. An advantage would be neutralization of any tendency for scientific discourse to overwhelm an argument but an assumption is made here that the 'discourse to be prioritised' does not indicate choosing between science and law as appropriate for a required aspect of societal regulation, or the risk of causing social chaos would not be eliminated.

Law's rôle in settling disputes

In the stance adopted throughout this work of the law as presider in disputes and decision-making, science is cast as standing in the service of law in providing facts and expert opinion. This is because being considered here is the supremacy of law in complex societal matters that include the effects of science and technology. Though of course pertinent, critical examination of law itself in settling disputes belongs to a different study, as would any deep investigation of science by its own exponents. Therefore, only the way law perceives science is deemed relevant in the context of this work. Simply put, law operates with the fact-value distinction by finding the objective facts, in this instance those proffered by science, then deducing their legal consequences by the logical application of legal rules (Wynne 1989: 23). From this proposition emerge two important provisos that certainty would be crucial in the facts science offers to law and that law must be able to comprehend and interpret them sufficiently to found its decisions. This idealistic wish is frustrated by anomalies apparent from the study of both sides of the science-law enterprise. The difficulty for science in providing guarantees of certainty, the conflict of opinion among experts and the conduct of witnesses will be explained but, in a surprising assessment, Wynne considers within the metaphysics of law that while science is reliable there never has been a *scientist* who is (ibid: 54) and that the formal legal process can be described as 'institutionalized pure mistrust' (ibid: 33). This sceptical view may not be held by all analysts and perhaps simply it is a misattribution of the causes of problems for law in coming to terms with the way science is presented. Also it is an unkind way of dispelling the myth of the neutrality of experts.

Judges are not well placed to determine scientific validity without input from scientists (*Postnote* 245: 2). It is difficult at the moment to envisage a

---

[21] See Nelken's allusion to 'junk science' (ibid: 18).
[22] See, for example, Paterson (2003).

change in current arrangements for experts to testify in the legal forum, but perhaps it is the nature of the forum that would benefit from change, as this work will investigate in due course. While inquiring into the possibility of neutrality in expert testimony through conformity to procedural rules, Edmond questions whether, in spite of them, it can still be guaranteed that scientists and judges will maintain similar interests or share the understandings of neutrality in specific instances (2000b: 248). This is attributed to the socio-legal exigencies of the functioning of law and the courts that could also affect scientists' understanding of legal proceedings and their use of scientific expertise.

The misapprehension of science by law and its opposite can have one of several possible provenances. In one, the problem is attributed squarely to lack of scientific literacy on the part of lawyers, judges and jurors (Edmond 2000b: 217)—a common perception. In another, weight must be given to Edmond's thesis that science fails to conform to the espoused norms that judges convey as its epistemic and legitimatory capital, and that law instead is actively implicated in negotiating, recognizing and determining the legitimacy, social relevancy and meaning of scientific knowledges in legal settings (ibid).

Law might expect the epistemic authority of science to be profound and indubitable but in addition to its inflicted rôle of negotiating the meanings of science in evidential contexts, it undertakes that of mediator in scientific disputes as another aspect of its function, possibly unintentional but necessary. In *Science at the Bar*, Jasanoff seeks 'to understand how the legal process mediates among conflicting knowledge claims, divergent underlying values and competing views of expertise in a democratic society' (1995: xiv). Ward (1998: 258) returns the discussion to the provenance of science-law misapprehension through the supposed incompetence of lawyers in science but incorporating the following paradox. Citing Judge Learned Hand (1901), Ward raises the question as to how a judge and jury can be competent to decide between the conflicting statements of experts when it is precisely their incompetence for such a task that makes experts necessary (ibid: 258).

Without further consideration, Hand's Paradox would symbolize a blocked road to the comprehension of science in legal contexts; indeed already it renders a tantalizing account of the difficulty experienced by law. Rescue from the circularity is afforded by the judgment of Finlay, C.J., in *Best v Wellcome Foundation*[23] and raises two important points of significance that recur throughout this study. His Lordship claimed that judges are competent to draw inferences on scientific fact on the basis of 'logic' and 'common-sense' but conceded that such inferences cannot have the same cognitive authority as those made by trained scientists. However, in law the aim is not a scientific truth but a 'just result' to a dispute at a specified moment. This is the best that

---

[23] [1994] 5 Med LR 81 at 98.

law can provide, because science would take too long to produce a definitive answer and there is a need to conclude.

Adherence to Merton's kind of guidance, the possibility of neutrality, and the rigorous application of norms and methods constitute what Edmond calls 'Enlightenment faith in the idealized normative images of science' that it is contended deludes both scientists and judges (2000b: 251). In an extensive analysis of judicial representation of scientific evidence, Edmond contends that the failure to address the discrepancies between philosophical ideals and the vagaries of scientific practice (ibid: 251) increasingly produces legal decisions that can be criticized. According to Edmond, sciences are a diverse set of practices lacking adherence to universal and prescriptive norms and methods (ibid: 249). He bemoans that there are no easily ascertained and applied methods for evaluating the admissibility of scientific evidence (Edmond 1999: 562). It is his piquant observation but made from a realistic stance that if scientific knowledge was not socially constructed but rigorous with regard to method and norm-conformity, then greater consensus of scientific opinion might be anticipated—and, in a consistent but optimistic view, fewer disagreements in legal settings would occur where the 'proper' standards could be invoked to resolve them (ibid: 562).

Situating his inquiry in legal studies, that is to say by examining the way law responds to and uses scientific evidence jurisprudentially, Edmond admits to a critical approach to the apparent inexactitudes of science presented in the legal forum. Impliedly, he is critical also of constructed science as epistemologically inadequate. His prolific scholarship centred on this subject is prominent for documenting the seemingly intractable nature of science-law problems and is in the vanguard of recent analytical effort.[24] For the present study, it suggests the usefulness of 'a critique of a critique' that considers as its alternative the evaluation of constructed science, relocating discussion from predominantly legal studies more firmly into socio-legal and sociological debate. Examination of the process by which knowledge is acquired and transmitted and the conditions under which it occurs appears promising in yielding undistracting analytical frameworks that might better inform the central problem. In other words the attentions of the sociology of science, as the means of finding the conditions under which truth is produced, are recommended to be more fruitful than attempting to discern the extent to which any emergent fact is dependent on adherence to normative standards. Also, as seen previously, the bases of methodological standards themselves have been questioned.

Again, Edmond is critical of the failure of sociologists of science to examine the honesty of scientific 'method-talk' as other than a discourse promoting conventional, idealized images of science that legitimate knowledge claims and reinforce the epistemic status and authority of science (1999: 560).

------

[24] See especially Edmond (2004), which is a publication of the proceedings of a conference in Canberra in 2002.

By a long route, it has now been seen that Edmond wishes the assertions of science to be so based on the procedural application of scientific norms as to eliminate the possibility of conflict over their meaning. From this law would be confident in the assuredness of scientific evidence. The problem of incommensurability would be diminished because no longer would law be obliged to choose the evidence it prefers in drawing its inferences. This would be a partial solution only since adherence to standards is not a guarantee of certainty in findings. All findings in science are provisional, the meaning of results requires interpretation even within science, and it cannot be assumed that lack of expert conflict always will make law's understanding of scientific evidence perfect.[25]

Construction of interests

Jasanoff sees the purposes of science and law united as formal systems of inquiry through recognition that 'each tradition claims an authoritative capacity (through its procedures) to sift evidence and derive rational and persuasive conclusions from it' and that 'the reliability of observers (or witnesses) and the credibility of their observations are of critical concern to both legal and scientific decision-making' (1995:8). From this point, the way that information is used diverges philosophically in that science is concerned with getting facts 'right' within the limits of the existing research paradigm and, though equally concerned with establishing facts accurately, law uses them only as an adjunct to its transcendent objective of settling disputes fairly and efficiently (ibid: 9). In trials, juries are asked to decide whether guilt or liability has been established to the desired degree of proof (Haack 2003: 206), which requires that scientific or forensic evidence must attest causation reliably. This might be in question. Conflicts arise between the adversarial procedures of law and the investigative procedures of science; between the concern of the law for prompt and final resolutions and the open-ended fallibilism of the sciences, and the ever-present possibility of revision (ibid). At the heart of inquiry is how adversarialism, as just characterized, contributes to difficulties in handling scientific testimony and the modifications of that culture that would be necessary to make it adaptive and improve factual accuracy without needlessly sacrificing other values (ibid: 214).

Even simpler expressions of fundamental differences that are both procedural and social are that science seeks truth while law does justice; science is descriptive but law is prescriptive, and science emphasizes progress whereas law emphasizes process (Jasanoff 1995: 7). Lawyers need to understand that science is a social process undergoing constant critical evaluation and therefore is progressive (Wolpert 1998: 289). Drawing further distinctions, Wolpert counsels that law often is concerned with individual events and their causation while science is rarely interested in single events but rather in general under-

---

[25] For an impression of Edmond's work on expert scientific evidence and its understanding by law see, for example, Edmond (1999), (2000a), (2000b), (2004).

standing (ibid: 297). Ultimately courts must make a clear judgment about a case but scientists rarely can give 'black and white answers' and offer instead only a range of possibilities accompanied by a probabilistic assessment (House of Commons Select Committee 2005: §158). In the words of Professor Sir Alec Jeffreys, 'This expresses a fundamental gulf between the philosophy of science and the philosophy of law'[26] (ibid: §158). Epitomizing the central problem of science-law disjunction, this statement, if accepted, would exclude absolutely the possibility of reconciling the two intellectual fields.

Jasanoff explores the opportunities that would be afforded by 'a more reflective alliance' (1995), an estimable wish that requires examination for substance and its potential to reduce tensions without transforming the operations of science and law. Largely her proposals are at the level of procedure accompanied by analysis, comment and awareness of social and political contexts. It opens with the pregnant question of whether fundamental changes are needed in the (American) legal system's methods of dealing with science, technology and social change (ibid: 205).

Incoherent results in the evaluation of technical evidence are attributed to the disadvantages of case-by-case adjudication (ibid: 205). A theme is introduced that will be repeated frequently in this study that law conducts the bulk of its scientific inquiries, 'at the frontiers of scientific knowledge where claims are uncertain, contested and fluid' (ibid: 210). Of course, law might introduce problems for itself when insisting on finality of conclusions by asking more of science than it can give (Haack 2003: 208; 2004: 19). Jasanoff believes forms of guidance more realistically attuned to the indeterminacy of scientific knowledge in litigative contexts are needed that are mindful of the strengths and weaknesses of judicial dispute resolution (ibid: 210).

Jasanoff builds her argument on the premise that there is a mutually constitutive relationship between science, technology and the legal process (ibid: 210). Initially this can be interpreted as a *de facto* description of the forum in which science and law convene but more importantly it describes the interactions and processes that occur. Next it can imply a dialectical relationship in which law uses its forms of logic and reasoning to arrive at the significance of science for the legal issues being heard. It is in these constitutive relationships that problems occur. Jasanoff chronicles judicial accomplishments in contending with procedural, social and political influences surrounding legal decisions (ibid: 210-218), as well as schemes tried in the United States to separate these 'mutually constitutive relationships'. Among these is the attempt to confer legal approval on decisions based on prioritization of science, such as in the short-lived science court experiments (ibid: 219). While problems arise in mutually constitutive relationships, any losses associated with separating them should be considered carefully.

---

[26] Professor Sir Alec Jeffreys (Witness to House of Commons Select Committee) Vol II: Oral and written evidence, Q 415.

In reviewing the proposed remedies for science-law problems then abounding in debate, Jasanoff includes three, which are that courts should defer more to external sources of scientific authority, that the legal system's established mechanisms for dealing with technical questions should be strengthened and that more alternatives to litigation should be sought. The first seems to run counter to legal opinion, would risk conclusions that are more thoroughly 'scientized' than at present and the weakening of law's autonomy. The second is reminiscent of the approach in the United States to formalize the acceptance of scientific evidence through rules of admissibility, while the third appeals to oft-expressed wishes for less confrontational resolution of disputes. As examples of these ideas, regarding the first proposal, law and politics were hostile to the notion of the separatism symbolized by science courts. Stronger mechanisms for dealing with technical questions appear in the notion of teaching judges to 'think like scientists', and the problems of trying to gauge the reliability of evidence through legal rules of admissibility—depicted by Haack as 'an attempt to domesticate scientific testimony' (2004: 20)— served only to confuse legal thinking and produce more uncertainty (Jasanoff : 219). Reference manuals for assessing scientific evidence (which exist) could be criticized because judges might not question the origins and foundations of the consensus that the manual purports to represent (the underlying assumptions). Jasanoff rated as good the prospects of training judges to increase their awareness of the intertwining of normative and technical issues in litigation (ibid: 221). In many respects, attempts in the American legal system to systematize treatment of science introduce as many new problems as they might solve. The English system is more open, pragmatic, and reliant on 'witness demeanour' and judicial reasoning. This is not without its hazards. However the American experience shows that procedural approaches do not necessarily relieve law of the burden of fine judgments where matters of science are involved.

Jasanoff's characterization of procedural solutions is as 'only incremental relief for massive structural problems' (ibid: 222) and gives the appearance of a deeply entrenched predicament and a feeble remedy. However, she perceives advantages in localised, context-specific epistemological and normative understandings not subordinated to inappropriately universal claims and standards (ibid: 222). Also, she understands the deconstruction of expertise that occurs between lawyers and scientists in the legal forum as belonging to the dynamics of a continuing process of contextualized problem-solving that she values as a proper part of law's operations. The assertion of 'only incremental relief for a massive structural problem' is so momentous that it cannot be excused by the description of the advantages of legal process that follows it. It implies that solution to procedural problems is only by recourse to procedure. Perhaps this is the only recourse of lawyers. Any remedies it could effect would take place very slowly. Thus far, the 'more reflective alliance' therefore gives pause for thought but offers no prospect of significant change that would ease science-law difficulty. The reason that procedural solutions, as Jasanoff perceives them, offer so little to alleviate the central problem is that they are inadequately complex. Nevertheless, Jasanoff affords glimpses of schemes that the present study takes up later which have potential to mediate the central problem in different ways. For instance she detects the opportunity for negotiation of the meaning of science in the procedures of the Science Advisory Board of the United States, rather than those of the Scientific Advisory Panel that encourage the parties to engage in aggressive and pointless discrediting of each other's evidence (ibid: 274-275, n.21). Negotiating the meaning of science will be examined in Chapter IV when the licensing procedures of the Federal Drug Administration are considered. She reveals awareness of the value of the sociology of scientific knowledge to be explored soon in this chapter that would illuminate the way in which legal and non-legal actors construct their beliefs about science, expertise and justice.

Missing from these introspective analyses is the fact that law reserves the right to choose whether to accept evidence with which it is presented or to choose the evidence it prefers amid conflicting testimony. It is a matter of the weight to give expert opinion (see, for example, *Maynard v West Midlands Regional Health Authority, infra*, note 132). Correspondingly, in science, standards of good evidence must centre on truth-indicativeness guidelines for the conduct of inquiry but must also focus on substance and significance as well as truth in order to address 'warrant' adequately (Haack 1999: 197). Warrant might be addressed by 'substance' but 'significance' should account for the importance of findings in relation to the question asked. Even though these statements defer the problem of legal comprehension of science, the connection of warrant and significance to evidence would diminish the distance between science and law. Much depends on the way in which science represents itself in the legal forum.

THE SELF-REPRESENTATION OF SCIENCE

Science as a social institution

Examining constructivism situates the practice of science in acquiring knowledge within the ambit of sociological inquiry. Ziman tells of a research programme that influences 'academic metascience' by looking on science as primarily a social institution (1984: 102). Science is practiced by individuals but becomes a social practice through a community of institutions, research groups, networks, learned journals and specialist groups (Ziman 2000: 232). It takes account of the collective labours of individuals (ibid: 237). In a contextual scrutiny of work addressing the interaction of science and law, Jasanoff reports importantly that it has become customary for the boundaries previously comprehended as sharp that divide facts, institutions and social rôles in reality to be subjects for negotiation (1995: xv). 'Science emerges from this analysis not as an independent, self-regulating producer of truths about the natural world but as a dynamic social institution fully engaged with other mechanisms for creating social and epistemic order in modern societies' (ibid). Another perspective aptly describes science neither as sacred nor a confidence trick (Haack 1995). In this reconfiguration legal disputes around scientific facts manifest as sites where society constructs its ideas about the constitution of legitimate knowledge, identifying responsibility for representing nature and estimating the deference that should be accorded to science in relation to other modes of knowing (Jasanoff 1995: xv). This distinction conveys an impression of the empowerment of society, allowing it to audit sources of knowledge, estimate the significance of their productions and to relate them to everyday life. According to the sociological account, the certification of scientific claims that derive from a multitude of informal negotiations between members of relevant disciplines and a complex network of people, methodologies and data, themselves incorporating social conventions, must be harmonized in order to establish scientific claims as true (ibid: 52). This confirms science as a social institution organized to yield a social product (Ziman 2000: 237) in which processing takes place in a social context (ibid: 233). This perspective, however edifying, must be understood in evidential contexts. Some opinion states that the social character of science is one factor contributing to its epistemic distinction; others that it significantly undermines its epistemic pretensions (Haack 1997: 83).

Social constructions of science

The modern readings of science in both the philosophy of science and the sociology of science have converged (Mulkay 1979: 95), a view indebted at least in part to Kuhn's conception of the way in which we are able to discover the nature of science as 'intrinsically sociological' (Chalmers 1999: 238). If science is to be conceived as an interpretive exercise and the nature of the physical world accepted as socially constructed, justification for distinguishing scientific and social thought is eliminated and extends to the exclusion of scientific knowledge from sociological interpretation (Barnes 1974: 67). So radically re-characterized, science is disenthroned from its traditional position of authority. Unless the expectations of science by law in assisting it are to be recreated by another means, careful examination is required of the possible advantages of reconceptualising science in this way. Succeeding from criticism of the nature of scientific evidence and his apparent chagrin over the suggestion of the social construction of science, Edmond (1999) offers an approach described else-where in this work that concedes to law the means of fashioning its own truth from proffered science that is situated in legal procedure. It is notable that the method does not dispossess science of its traditional capacity but, in conciliatory mood, Edmond does approve a metaphysical rôle for the social construction of science in providing a fertile basis for conceptualising scientific disagreements in disputes and in investigating the ways in which fact-finders assess and rationalize their resolution (ibid: 565). This is a possible resource for law, too, in that judges claim to possess clear logic in deciding between conflicting scientific evidence and give their reasons in speeches but a sociologically oriented study would reveal the circumstances in which they reach such decisions and any constructions of reality into which they enter.

As if to maintain a toehold in reality, Wynne asserts that sociology does not say simplistically that scientific knowledge can be reduced to social factors (1989: 23) and that it does have force but its scope and direction is socially shaped (ibid: 53). The argument continues to oscillate: if law operates with a conception of the fact/value distinction by deducing the legal consequences of objective facts from the logical application of legal rules, previously mentioned, (ibid: 23), then the sociology of scientific knowledge undermines that very distinction, providing a more complex perspective on their interpretation (ibid: 28). If that which science offers as fact, ultimately is shown to be a social achievement among scientists, it admits the rôle of interests in the construction of 'natural' knowledge (ibid).

In the preceding analysis construing science as socially constructed provides a useful descriptive tool. The idea is well-founded and acceptable. The appraisal of the provenance and interpretation of scientific pronouncements is honest and clearly provides for transcendent perspectives on the work of science. The understanding it affords is edifying in a variety of social contexts. Its benefit to law would depend on law's appreciation of the effects of social construction and the way in which this could inform its decisions. Scientists may dissent from the suggestion. Law would need not only to recognize this but also learn not to reject scientific propositions on account of their social construction alone and to allot sufficient time to consider them in the appropriate light. For traditional legal procedures this may be to ask too much. In conclusion the idea of science being socially constructed is valid and informative but does not necessarily advance the security for law in taking the productions of science into its decisions. Another means of assurance is necessary.

The sociology of scientific knowledge

The sociology of science and the sociology of scientific knowledge are importantly differentiated studies. The sociology of science focuses on the social attributes of scientific practice. It has concerns for the relationships between scientists, the reward system and institutional affiliations, illuminating the incentives, internal tensions, positive and negative external influences on their endeavours and the manner in which these can control their productions. Scientists may admit, disown or disregard these factors according to their self-view. The sociology of science is indifferent to the content of research except when attaching social significance to its productions. Forming a narrative of scientists' work that locates science firmly in the context of all social activity, it has been shown here that it disabuses the societal impression of science as the unique arbiter of truth about the objective world. The sociology of science substitutes a helpful interpretation that does not discredit science, conveying instead an understanding of how its productions may be regarded. This perspective fuels the opinions of sceptics of science that it is untrustworthy as evidence but for the more accommodating provides a rational basis from which to regard its conclusions.

Scholars with an implicit faith in foundational science find its social construction an empty concept. Haack encapsulates these sentiment exactly in her assessment of the 'Old Deferentialist' position in science that articulates a uniquely objective and rationalist method (1999: 190), versus the 'New Cynicism' that asserts science consists mainly of the social interests of negotiation, myth-making, the product of inscriptions and narrative, and is disparaged as 'nothing but humbug and just politics' (ibid). Intervening, Haack asserts that an account is needed of what sciences know and how they know, that is realistic in the ordinary, non-technical sense of neither under- nor over-estimating the capability of science (ibid). In place of both positions, she proposes a 'Critical Commonsensist' perspective dedicated to 'finding out when and where (scientific) evidence fails (ibid: 197). In not only distinguishing sensible from cynical sociology of science, there is also a need to distinguish the sense in which it is true and epistemologically important that science is social (ibid: 207).

In the Postscript to the second edition of their ethnographic study of laboratory scientists—an 'anthropological study of science'—Latour and Woolgar (1986: 281) questioned the meaning of social construction if all interactions are accepted as social. They imputed that, in its pervasiveness, it was unconnected with the data, inscriptions, texts and elaborations of complex structures in scientific inquiry and preferred to abandon the term in favour of their new interest in 'the construction of scientific facts', which they appended as a new subtitle to their later edition as depicting their study more fairly. In their justification of method, earlier Latour and Woolgar introduced a working definition of 'social' as concerned with 'the social construction of scientific knowledge in so far as this draws attention to the process by which scientist make sense of their observations' (ibid: 32). In a more comprehensive conception, Bloor writes that the work of Kuhn coincided with broad fundamental re-evaluations of the preconceptions of science as having a 'special' character that shifted the focus of the social study of science into the fundamentally social character of the objects, facts and discoveries of science, represented instead by the sociology of scientific knowledge (1981: 173-198). This cultural shift is significant for law's understanding of science. It explores the possibility of maintaining that there exist common criteria of rules of evidence for assessing the validity of knowledge claims, applicable irrespective of substantive concerns or analytical approaches (Mulkay 1979: 50). It is riven by questions of how scientific conclusions can be considered adequate, speaking greatly to law's interrogation of science that seeks to know the basis of assurance in the evidence it is offered.

Notwithstanding any value it has in describing activity, the sociology of science clarifies little about the utility of scientific evidence for law. And if it serves only to convey as disparaging that scientific knowledge is socially constructed, then it is unsurprising that it is attacked by jurists.

Disparate Knowledges

The sociology of scientific knowledge, therefore, seems revelatory and Mulkay's account of it is especially illuminating and useful here. Explanation of the potential achievements for this innovative approach is mandatory given the value to be attached to it by this study but it is remarkable that the informative outlook it can afford has been so neglected.

Against the background of the inability of science ever to be completely certain, knowledge claims are assessed not for their truth but their capacity to meet the requirement of a particular interpretive context. This recommends, *inter alia*, that scientific claims should show evidence of consistency with other claims and conformity to conventional standards of adequacy regarded by members of a research community as appropriate to a given class of problem (ibid: 54). In planning their sociological analysis of scientists' discourse, Gilbert and Mulkay averred that they 'should concentrate...on identifying the principles in terms of which scientists' own accounts of action and belief are organized' (1984: 112). A review of their findings showed that, in spite of high diversity in participants' accounts of actions and belief, they were constructed from recurrent interpretive forms and repertoires that could be identified, described and documented (ibid: 189). Interpretive regularities could be identified behind the 'babble of tongues' with a suitable analytical approach (ibid: 188).

Lest it should be assumed from this discussion that the sociology of scientific knowledge can substitute for science and now is all that is necessary to understand scientific productions, a balanced view of the issue needs to be struck. If a view of scientific pronouncements is purely sociological (that science is entirely socially constructed), then it represents 'bad' sociology (Haack 1996: 260). 'Good' sociology of science includes some grasp of scientific theory (ibid). In her *Sober Sociology of Science*, Susan Haack proclaims that science must accommodate *warrant* as well as acceptance, implying that science must show how it attests its claims for them to be accepted by society (ibid: 259-260).

It is asserted that adequacy cannot be confirmed by learned journals (Mulkay 1979: 54), thereby destroying one of science's greatest illusions that, by itself, publication in leading journals is all that is necessary to guarantee confidence in its conclusions and uphold the reputations of its contributors. At its most reductive and critically observed, acceptance for publication of scientific communications in learned journals may in reality confer nothing more than a hallmark of high methodological standards. Peer review as the gauge of quality is concerned primarily with process through examining the methods and techniques by which contributors reached their assertions. In empirical science the design of a study is critical to minimise distortion of results and avoid false conclusions. Crudely put, this ranges from elimination of possible bias in the design that could skew findings and application of appropriate statistical methods to ensure conclusions that stand out from the background of chance or that differentiate adequately from another possible outcome.

In the harsh climate of modern science, evidence of adherence to good scientific method keenly is sought and represents the basis of defence against
criticism of research. Earlier discussion here has left open the question of the
extent to which norms and standards of conduct are observed and the way in
which they are understood. Naturally 'peers' must be scientists of good reputation, established as experts in the field in which the communication is offered.
With their experience they will confirm the value or otherwise of new work in
enhancing wisdom in their subject area. For Mulkay these all are insufficient
criteria for accepting knowledge, though it is well to realize that publication is
not the whole of scientific communication and that conversations within the
community tend to affirm general beliefs.

Criteria of scientific validity: how scientists believe

It is unusual to discuss scientists as a body or community sharing a faith
and there is no overt agenda in this suggestion to promote a discourse in
metaphysics or religion. Most scientists would decry the need for faith, depicting science as the archetypal 'faith-free' zone where objectivity, evidence and
proof are sufficient justification for acceptance of knowledge. In 'extreme
science' where even the means of obtaining measurements of phenomena
remain to be determined, let alone the appropriate methodology, belief in any
information obtained eventually from experiments would require the firm
conviction that the chosen approach was appropriate to yield what was sought.
Perhaps faith is a term too far as it implies conviction in the absence of logical
proof but there is a sense in which in scientists require belief that what they
know they have reason to know for sure, which is obtained by reconstructing,
challenging and reconfirming the methodology.

In controversial and uncontroversial science, it can be seen that Haack interprets belief as a matter of warrant (2001: 254). The strong indication of the
truth of a claim or theory is part of the reason that scientific evidence has
acquired its honorific use but uncertainty or fragile beliefs confer ambiguity
and the potential to mislead (ibid). Where proof of a theory is equivocal or
elusive, warrant is a matter of degree attributed by the evidence possessed by a
person or group of people (ibid: 256). This can be related to concepts of
justification and confirmation (ibid: 257) and degrees of warrant determined
by degrees of credence. This can then be differentiated into objective and
perspectival aspects in the concepts of warrant, justification and reasonableness (ibid). Warrant therefore has personal, social impersonal, justificatory and
confirmatory elements (ibid: 257ff).

The following cases are chosen to illustrate Mulkay's and Gilbert's and
Mulkay's recommendations for assessment of knowledge claims [27] in instances
of 'extreme science' where standard predictive models fail and, for that reason,
severely test the way scientists decide their beliefs.

---

[27] See pp. 35–39 above.

QUANTUM THEORY

Kuhn described the way antimonies in the cumulative results of 'solving the puzzles of normal science' signalled the need for radical revision of beliefs in order to discover new theories to explain those perceptions (Kuhn 1970). In a reference to the thoughts of St. Thomas Aquinas, Polkinghorne insists that perception of reality in a new theory subsists in intelligibility rather than objectivity (2002: 86), the customary principle of science. Empirical successes are not by themselves always sufficient criteria for endorsement of a theory by the scientific community (ibid: 88).

The twentieth century realization in science of the necessity of quanta illustrates use of metaphysically based criteria for assessing the weight to put on new theories (ibid) and leads to reflexive rationality for belief. Polkinghorne declares human powers of rational prevision are 'pretty myopic' (ibid: 87). In consideration of new theory, scientists should not ask about its reasonableness as if predisposed towards the form that reasonability should take but rather what compels thought that it might be the case (ibid). It is a more open question, not foreclosing the possibility of radical surprise but insisting there should be evidential substantiation for assertions (ibid). For acceptance, new theories should have the properties of scope to make intelligible the widest range of phenomena. They should also display economy and elegance. A theory will enjoy sustained fruitfulness if it proves able to explain or predict new or unexpected phenomena (ibid: 88-89).

The necessity of quanta arose from findings in physical experiments concerning black body radiation that contradicted predictions astonishingly. Any theory-ladenness of the research was rapidly extinguished by remarkable empirical findings. These compelled recognition that no universal epistemology or single sovereign means exists to provide complete knowledge. Quantum theory involves an unparalleled duality in physics of entities sometimes behaving as waves, sometimes as particles, a realization forced on the physics community by the intransigent necessity of actual empirical experience (ibid: 87). In recognizing the epistemic conflict the ideas of particles and waves appear as complementary rather than rival propositions. The theory shows in a systematic and logical way that wave and particle concepts are each used in appropriate contexts and reveal the relation between them (Ditchburn: 1963: 14-16). Quantum theory is incomplete without acknowledgement of quantum mechanics within which it is situated, which incorporates appropriate parts of the electromagnetic wave theory, quantum theory and relativity theory (ibid: 16).

SOLAR NEUTRINOS

The nuclear physics research into the existence of solar neutrinos, rather than being affirmative of anticipated experimental findings, instead was remarkable for educing pronouncements on how experiments were conducted and the way in which theoretical disputes were settled (Pinch 1986). It is not altogether a salutary account of the way science erects criteria for acceptance of theory but affords a perspective on the conduct of scientists that is honest and so warns an onlooker, analyst or this study appropriately.

Detection of solar neutrinos would confirm stellar evolutionary theory concerning the origin of stars that they develop their energy from nuclear fusion. The theory of their existence has been current for some time but the particles are extremely difficult to detect because they react so little with matter. Problems were encountered in experiments conducted in 1967 because far fewer neutrinos were detected than the theory predicted and the discrepancy continued for a decade (ibid: 36). However, over time the account showed an increase in the predicted flux of neutrinos with interest in the problem by scientists—as much dependent on experimental determination as on abstract theory—thereby breaking the link between theory and experiment (ibid: 199) and showed that 'evidential contexts' (theories) were actively constructed by scientists (ibid: 200). The curious upshot of this work was that scientists were contented with a social consensus over the constructed discrepancy between experiment and prediction, moreover a consensus that could change.

GRAVITATIONAL WAVES

Verification of gravitational waves predicted by Einstein as the result of catastrophic events in astrophysics puzzles science. They would travel at light speed and propagate a gravitational field. Unlike solar neutrinos, of which at least some have been experimentally detected, gravitational waves remain hypothetical. In standard science, there is a need for belief in classical theory and to design suitable experiments to confirm it. In the hypothesis of gravitational waves the theory-ladenness of any experiments conceived is undeniable and science has been criticised for this monocular approach. For the physics community debate was necessary not only on the required experimental methods to detect gravitational waves but also on the criteria by which satisfaction with findings could be judged. The community agreed broadly over the requisite observational equipment kinds, the concept of classical physics underlying such experimental tools and the criteria of validity applicable to such theoretical-experimental consonance. Up to that point the approach was that of normal science (Mulkay 1979: 70) but significantly different interpretive positions of the meaning of observations emerged in which the nature of the phenomenon was negotiated by the progress of claims and counterclaims (ibid: 90-91). This exemplifies Mulkay's counsel that scientific knowledge is established by processes of negotiation (ibid: 95).

INTELLIGENT DESIGN

A vexed question of the modern western world epitomizes the conflict between religious and scientific belief. It comprises the neo-Darwinian theory of evolution that attributes the complexity of living organisms to continuous developmental adaptation, versus the creationist-inspired intelligent design proposition. The latter holds that complexity is too great to attribute to any other than a being with the extraordinary capability to have created nature in its original state according to a supreme design. Because the tension is between immanence and observation, the issue may never be resolved but for concerned society the problem inheres in the availability of convincing proof for either theory. Notwithstanding efforts to teach creationism scientifically (Fuller 2006: 175), imposed on science is the double task, not only of providing its own customary proofs, but also of answering the implicit challenge of intelligent design protagonists to show how it regards those proofs as satisfactory. At this stage it only can be reported as a 'work in progress' but persistence of the controversy holds up for scrutiny the fundamental canons of how science believes.

Shanks (2004) approaches the possibility of evolution by the method of comparison with other theories for consistency. Mulkay advocates this as one of the criteria of capacity to meet the requirement of a particular interpretive context. Siting the facts of the complex, structured, highly organized and ordered states of matter in the compass of the second law of thermodynamics, Shanks is able to allocate understanding of these 'curious phenomena' to 'the territory of the self-organizing, self-assembling properties of physical systems driven by flows of energy' (ibid: 93). Shanks also refutes the notion of irreducible complexity advanced by intelligent design which states that a single system comprises several interacting parts, removal of any one of which will cause it to cease functioning (ibid: 161, 225). This is countered by one of the redundant complexity of overlapping and slightly different processes found in biochemical and molecular systems that science can use to demonstrate that irreducible complexity can be explained 'without recourse to designers of unknown origins, using unknown methods and materials for unknown purposes' (ibid: 225).

This 'scientized' justification for acceptance of scientific explanation is undermined by Fuller's assertion that the presumption of the neo-Darwinian synthesis as consisting of well-articulated bodies of knowledge interrelated by rules of logical deduction may be misguided, saying instead that it represents more 'an extended exercise in interdisciplinary diplomacy' (Fuller 2006: 176-177). Arguments about evolution and intelligent design need not be construed as a zero-sum game in which the protagonists of one theory attempt to convert their opponents (Fuller 2006: 176). From the perspective of Science and Technology Studies (STS)[28] Fuller wishes that in university education there were more interpenetration of the two fields of study since they need not be mutually exclusive, for instance there is a common framework in that both presuppose there is an order to nature that needs explanation.

---

[28] Studies in the social and cultural foundations of science and technology.

DIGEST AND CONCLUSIONS

Quantum theory taught that the assumptions of science could be mistaken, reifying scientific realism and challenging scientists' resourcefulness in reconciling an empirical paradox within a two-state solution. For completeness of description and theoretical consistency, acceptance that quantum theory subsists within the continuum of quantum mechanics was necessary. In the solar neutrino controversy where objective determination was elusive, the scientific community agreed that disagreement through social construction of evidence was inevitable, indicating this consensus was acceptable but that it could change if opinion were to advance. That the route to scientific knowledge was through negotiating acceptable claims emerged from the search for gravitational waves. In the study of intelligent design it was shown that conventional science could provide satisfactory explanations for some of its phenomena without recourse to metaphysical speculation but evolutionary theory and intelligent design need not have mutually exclusive objects in the pursuit of knowledge.

The previous far-ranging analysis shows the extraordinary approach of science to its extraordinary questions. It reveals intellectual versatility in conceiving new methods that puts belief in conclusions on a logical, explicable basis where traditional inquiry would be inadequate. Also it is seen to encourage reflexivity by science on the question of how it can trust its own conclusions in situations sorely challenging to its normative standards. Though the cited instances inhabit the region of 'extreme science' that commonly do not impinge either on ordinary society or law, it provides heartening insight into the ability of science to dig deeply into both its philosophy and the sociology of knowledge in order to provide assurance over its explanations. Even though its solutions varied according to the nature of the problem, in the context of the present work it is revelatory that science has resources to improve both its conviction and its self-representation. Haack has shown that it might be more useful for science to use the concept of *warrant* rather than *proof* over its findings, because it is more honest and realistic, and to keep acceptance of a theory among the scientific community to one side as a measure of how justified it is in accepting it (1999: 262).

Were more recognition given to the sociology of scientific knowledge, characterized by the foregoing descriptions, science could offer law a better understanding that could improve its facility. The social construction of science with which law contends that simply explains the conditions and influences under which conclusions were reached would be replaced by reasons for its belief that law would be able to interrogate. That science is social deflects many legal scholars from appreciating any benefits that might accrue from it. Edmond, for instance, deplores the social construction of science and suggests that it devalues the worth of scientific evidence. Jasanoff offers partial resolution of the difficulty through examination of baseline assumptions, methods of sampling and data collection in disputes (1995: 224-225), which addresses methodology broadly. Haack, though, rehabilitates the impeached social con-

44

struction of knowledge by showing that adopting epistemic standards by which the worth of empirical evidence can be judged, which are not peculiar to science and are constituted by academic rigour and thoroughness of inquiry, science can be regarded as epistemically distinguished (1997: 80). The examples in 'extreme science' throw the reflexivity and resourcefulness of science into far sharper relief, making the sociology of knowledge a promising candidate for a framework with potential to mediate science-law disjunction.

Chapter III. The Accessibility of Systems: Issues of Closure and the Ability to Observe

SYSTEMS AS BOUNDED EPISTEMOLOGIES

Systems are legion, acquiring definitions shaped by the knowledge field, function or activity in which they arise. Impressionistically, the term is offered as that applying to a unity of knowledge or operations in a subject area indicated as being distinct from others able to claim the same description. 'Others' form a general background of different knowledges or operations. Advanced social systems theory labels this background the 'environment', connections to which with a system under consideration may be unclear. Once acknowledged, the advanced form of the theory acts as a 'catch-all' and is intolerant of any concept of 'non-system' in knowledge or operations, so that the environment consists entirely of systems or subsystems contributing to the construction of the world. Proceeding with this extemporization, a system must have bounded knowledge or operations so that an observer can recognize its characteristics according to the exercised choice of study, or else the object of gaze must be 'other' system pertaining. Ontologically, systems must involve structures, internal processes and dynamics or they would be unproductive, so intimating animate or quasi-animate properties. The degree of order or disorder of processes can be examined in each instance.

In engineering, system models may entail input of say, an electronic signal, internally processed and consequently modified in output to fulfil a designated purpose. More advanced forms of this system incorporate 'feedback' operating via an inverse circuit loop in which output information governs the input so as to create responsive control. In spite of this mechanistic simplicity, opinion might be justified in asserting that this model is broadly transferable to social systems, though with infinitely more subtlety. For instance environmental regulation can modify reflexively the measures it imposes in response to its observed effects.

Social systems theory is fashionable, by which is meant that it appeals to a modern conceptualisation of the world as well as having real descriptive value in many fields of study. It is predominantly conceptual in that it is theoretically constructed but, because it is informative, and offers perspectives on and representations of reality that are meaningful, with entirely rational precepts, it can function with almost the same utility and credibility as if it had been empirically determined.

Opposition to social systems theory also is understandable from scholars regarding it as too reductive and that confining knowledge within such sharply defined limits does not correspond to their experience of the way life is organ- ized. Rather than imposing rigidity in socio-legal research, the approach helps to distinguish the categorizations inherent in social life, while by no means reducing them to that of mere machines. The precise difficulty confronting science and law interfaced in the legal forum is that both conform exactly to the notion of systems in that each represents organization of knowledge and operations that is focused, self-referential and bounded. Each is founded on its own distinctive normative criteria. The priority in this study is on their colli- sion in legal contexts and whether their apparent incommensurability can be mediated helpfully for evidential purposes. Systems theory offers a useful means of facilitating analysis of their knowledge constructions, their opera- tions, and an investigation of their interrelationships.

EARLY FORMATIVE SYSTEMS THEORY

An earlier form of systems theory was conceived by Ludwig von Berta- lanffy after the Second World War, originally in the form of a logico- mathematical theory to be applied to all other systems (Bertalanffy: 1971), suggesting it was conceived as a critical or analytical tool. It was modified and extended significantly by later students of the theory and deep abstract think- ing has been superimposed on its original concepts, so that scant acknowl- edgement now is made to the originator of the theory in recent literature. Currently, systems theory is perceived as a requirement to simplify complexity in the study of modern society (Luhmann 1976: 511) and so claims made for its abilities are ambitious. Bertalanffy's were less broadly associated, the full impact of increasing social complexity possibly not being realized at the time of his authorship, and initially he saw particular relevance of his theory to science. He conceived for it a way of transcending technological problems and demands by a necessary distancing of viewpoint in what he called a re-orientation of thinking (Bertalanffy 1971: xi). He included within its scope physics, biology, the behavioural and social sciences and philosophy in a 'gamut of disciplines' (ibid). In spite of this expansive claim, it is not abundantly clear from the narrative whether the author conceived society as being comprised entirely of systems or whether there were elements of it that escaped the evaluation as 'not system enough' or belonged to an amorphous background of 'non-system' that was considered irrelevant. Although this is not likely, the individual is free to interpret whether this was intended but merely omitted from the explana- tion.

Pleased with the freshness of his approach, he likened systems theory to the paradigm shift described by Thomas Kuhn in his *Theory of Scientific Revolutions* (1970). It cannot be deduced from Bertalanffy's narrative whether he thought his concept equally deserving of such a radical reputation. Though strikingly innovative, it contains none of Kuhn's principal criteria concerning the non-cumulative effects of knowledge on encountering antimonies and the incommensurability of traditional and revolutionary theories that define such a step-change in understanding the world. Yet Bertalanffy suggests that Kuhn's revolutions in physics and chemistry are descriptive of changes brought about by 'organismic' and systems concepts (1971: 16). It is difficult to conclude on this argument and time spent on it may not be profitable.

Regardless of the value now attributed to it in current theory, any perceived 'skewness' with present-day purposes or the shortcomings of its explanations, Bertalanffy's study provides excellent grounding for the student of the topic away from attachments to more esoteric arguments in sociological and legal fields. The analysis of it presented here also will be informative on account of the points of difference it has with modern theory, which serve better to explain why those features are important.

A reading of Bertalanffy's philosophy reveals themes and counter-themes associated both with the isolation of systems and their unification that are not contradictory. Examination of their expectations—with the latter term used advisedly here—bears comparison with those of modern developments of the theory.

Bertalanffy's account is not as highly developed as modern versions, and present indifference to it might be due to what would now be regarded as restriction of his vision for systems theory. Partly, he saw it having unifying purpose between the sciences through his identification of isomorphisms, possibly reflecting the persistent self-consciousness of science at the time about proliferating specialties likely to cause diffraction of knowledge.[29] This is intrinsic to Bertalanffy's absorption with parallelisms in the functioning of organisms in biological science as seen in the strict analogies between the central nervous system and biological regulatory networks in cells. He comments on their remarkability and that such, 'an analogy between different systems at different levels of biological organization is but one member of a whole class of such analogies' (1971: xvii). Thus his generalizing proposition that systems exist, can be identified and analysed by virtue of their being isolated from each other, was immediately mitigated by the idea that isomorphisms can make them more alike.

Bertalanffy's isolation-unification paradox

The theme and counter-theme of isolation-unification in systems theory resides in Bertalanffy's analysis of the endeavours of classical science that isolated the elements of the observed universe but had an expectation that 'their reassembly, conceptually or experimentally—and whether concerning cells, the mind or society—would result and be intelligible' (ibid: xvii-xviii). This is reminiscent of the Enlightenment spirit that imagined the entire explicable universe would be revealed by means of the new age of unfettered inquiry. Not consciously intended to achieve a comprehensive unification of knowledge, it did suppose that enlightened rationality would make all neces-

---

[29] See Dampier (1961).

sary explanations available. Bertalanffy's theme is that, while an understanding of the elements in a system fundamentally is necessary, their interrelationships are just as critical and here he cites the interplay of enzymes in a cell, of the conscious and unconscious mind and the structure and dynamics of the social system (ibid: xviii).

Bertalanffy's isolation-unification paradox therefore is reconciled through his treatment of elements of the universe as distinct systems accompanied by his contention that discovery of the commonalities that link them adds a layer of knowledge. Examination of the thesis produces conviction that, in spite of a conveyed impression of claims to generality, its real application, and the consequence of the aforementioned perceptual limitation, was to systems already enjoying broad disciplinary associations, such as among those in the natural sciences and separately among those in the social sciences.

Stylistically, Bertalanffy's narrative is not incisive by current academic standards, though becomes more direct in dealing with aspects of the theory expressed through mathematics and logic, and it leaves an impression that opportunities were not taken to hone the message or that the work was not progressed by its progenitor or a successor. In anticipation, later in this chapter describing systems theories that posit them as closed and incapable of direct communication, it is interesting to speculate whether Bertalanffy could have encountered incommensurability by trialling his scheme across more diverse disciplinary boundaries, such as between science and law. Whether isomorphisms in their knowledges and operations could have been shown to exist would have been informative in the task of mediating their problems of communication, though this might have been to raise expectations too high.

The previous discussion suggests reasons for Bertalanffy's reflections to be regarded as not well connected to modern social systems theory, such as those of the chief proponent Niklas Luhmann, whose work will be discussed soon. Interpretation of current literature gives a strong indication that unconcern for his rendition of the theory must be because it is inadequately complex to analyse today's society, yet the impetus of Bertalanffy's prescription is evident in theories developed more lately by, for example, Spencer-Brown, Parsons, Maturana, Luhmann and others.[30] An important departure from Bertalanffy in present thinking is that he values systems theory for its identification of commonalities that actually eschew complexity, while later authors acknowledge complexity as a problem of modernity welcomely, espousing an alienation principle between systems that militates against commonality of their structures, internal processes and, particularly, the possibility of direct communication.

---

[30] See Andersen (2003: Chapter 4).

The General Systems Theory of Bertalanffy

Bertalanffy's abiding contribution was in the form of his General Systems Theory. In it, he combined the correspondences and isomorphisms of systems that indicate aspects of their commonality with an overarching consideration of 'wholeness' that he had attributed previously to the domain of metaphysics (ibid). General Systems Theory is described as a new paradigm with a philosophy re-orientating thought and worldview that its proponent contrasts with 'the analytic, mechanistic, one-way causal paradigm of classical science' (ibid: xix). He recognizes for it several levels of intentionality. As well as seeing 'system science' as that of scientific inquiry and the systems of science as those residing in the disciplines of natural and social sciences, Bertalanffy proffers General Systems Theory as a doctrine of principles applying to all or defined sub-classes of systems (ibid: xviii).

The tenets of General Systems Theory are divided into several categories. First, systems ontology explains what 'system' means and how systems are apprehended at the various levels of the observational world. Integral to this but unstated, are assumptions about the existence of things in constructing the notion of 'system'. Second there are the real entities perceived from observation to have the characteristics of systems, such as galaxy or atom. In the absence of a concise, cogent account of the necessary characteristics, the present study offers its own impressionistic version found at the head of this chapter. The third category acknowledges conceptual systems including logic, mathematics and music, the last of which is cast as a symbolic construct. Fourth is the category of abstracted systems that includes, for example, science as one of its sub-classes. Bertalanffy credits science with belonging to a group construed as conceptual systems corresponding to reality. This approximates to the received correspondence theory of truth and is one of several occasions where Bertalanffy's ideas comply with theories having legitimacy independently of his private constructions.

Proceeding with a critical examination of General Systems Theory discloses underlying philosophical thought that buttresses its legitimacy, grounding and contextuality. It also prepares it for better comparison with recent theory, this revelation arising more from Bertalanffy's method of explanation than any change of belief. The explanation shows the author stumbling into quite advanced philosophical theory ahead of his time, possibly because, as a scientist, he had not formally recognized the ideas he incorporated into his scheme. Moving into more humanistic and individual subject-centred territory, Bertalanffy describes problems of distinction of previous categories, explaining that, for example, an ecosystem is depicted as real only by disturbances such as pollution from which it is implied that 'these are not problems of perception but of conceptual constructs' (ibid: xx). Describing the objects of the everyday world not as the givens of sense data but construed by mental factors, connects the precepts of his theory to the familiar themes of Locke, Hume and Kant. A systems epistemology for General Systems Theory then is advanced on the basis of this understanding in which the analytical procedures of classical science are replaced by investigation of Bertalanffy's conception of wholes. The operations of this reconstituted theory then become interaction, transaction, organization and teleology (ibid).

Cautioning that perception may not be a reflection of reality and that knowledge is not a simple approximation to truth, Bertalanffy ventures into an agent-centred apprehension of the world and appreciation of subjectivity in his impression of the interaction between the knower and the known. He comments that these devolve upon biological, cultural, psychological and linguistic factors (ibid). Continuing this expansion of thought, Bertalanffy submits a 'perspective' philosophy in which, for example, physics would not pretend to a monopoly of knowledge but would become one science in man's total world perspective. Humanistic qualities of General Systems Theory are completed by incorporation of symbols, values, social entities and cultures as 'real' to counter fears of a mechanistically ordered system (ibid).

Sensitive to the socio-cultural factors of sociological study in his treatment of the system concept in the sciences of man, Bertalanffy considers the causal-logical-meaningful characterization of science attributed to Sorokin as best expressed by biological, symbolic and value levels (ibid: 207). Further reference is made to difficulties subsisting in the complexity of phenomena and the identification of entities under consideration, such as when humans are depicted as belonging to socio-cultural organization and living in a symbolically constructed world (ibid: 208). There seems no suggestion in Bertalanffy's treatment that matters in the social dimension are less amenable to analysis by General Systems Theory, only that identification of the domain in which they flourish can be difficult and that their matters are complex.

Bertalanffy's General Systems Theory represents such an advance on his earlier theory concerned with isomorphisms in the sciences that the later sociologically-inclined development seems offered almost in reparation for the narrowness of the past. Significantly for consideration of modern systems theory, Bertalanffy is critical of the functionalist theories of Parsons and Merton, which he relegates to the realms of conservatism and conformism due to their overemphasis on system regulators that are mechanistically characterized, such as maintenance, equilibrium, adjustment, homeostasis and stable institutional structures. His response to these is that they underplay history, process, socio-cultural change and inner-directed development, feeling that thereby social change is neglected and obstructed (ibid: 207).

So as not to lose the point at this stage in the discussion, it can be said that modern theorists also set aside Parsons's functionalist proclivity as well as his ideas of evolution of action relations, though Andersen in his monograph *Discursive Analytical Strategies*, to be included in later discussion, suggests that Parsons's work is subsumed in Luhmann's autopoietic theory (2003: 63). Although it might be interpreted as dismissive, Cotterrell's statement that 'Luhmann's primary indebtedness to Parsons seems to be for the general idea that differentiation of sub-systems in modern society is a fundamental response to the increasing complexity of social life in the modern world' actually is an endorsement of the contribution of Parsons to Luhmann's development of modern systems theory (1992: 66, n.14). Notwithstanding this claim, the theory of Luhmann itself understands social systems operating so as to reduce complexity.

MODERN SYSTEMS THEORY AND THE ULTIMACY OF AUTOPOIESIS

The limitations of Bertalanffy's theory are apparent but his scheme aimed at reducing societal complexity is different from that expressed in Luhmannian systems theory. The purpose of his initial systems theory was at the same time to characterize society as consisting of systems that could be identified in terms of their separate knowledges and operations and that such systems could be thematized by virtue of their isomorphisms. He appeared to have had two principal aims: first, to achieve new illuminations of the structure and function of society by drawing it towards a mathematico-logical construction—a systemization of society—and, second, to unravel some of the mystique of specialized knowledge fields by unifying them around other thematic elements. The concept was more easily applied to the natural than to the social sciences. In his method, it was simpler to view chemistry as a rearrangement of physics, hence maintaining a systems perception of thematically related material. Fewer attempts were made to extend his thoughts to knowledge fields where thematic relations were questionable, for example as between natural and social sciences. Viewed in terms of modern systems theory, propositions seemed directed more towards a levelling of communications between systems. In his General Systems Theory, Bertalanffy permitted human and social values as its elements; indeed he evolved an elaborate stratum of alternative categories as counter to the threatened mechanistic analysis of the world. Nonetheless, persistence with his concept of 'wholes' represented a different analysis of complexity. Rather than separating systems from a complex background, his method continued either to make comparisons between them or to unify them according to external criteria. On reflection, Bertalanffy's approach appears only to have provided enlightenment on the nature of systems and the different ways in which systems can be constructed. In relation to the methods of Luhmann it would not be counted as simplifying complexity and even could be accused of avoiding it.

The work of the present study perceives complexity to be reified in the operations of society. Modern systems theory is contextualized in the complexity of modern society and is represented as a means of examination that relieves this complexity (Luhmann 1995: 25, 26-27; 2004: 88, 94). In conceptualising society, the theory imagines it as a total system, expressed by King (1993: 219) as 'a theoretical approach to the operations of social systems and their relationships with each other and the general social environment'.[31] In this configuration one system, say economics, is situated in an environment comprising politics, sociology, psychology, art, science, law (see King and Thornhill 2003: 3-4), and all other object fields within a gaze that can be identified.

Autopoiesis is a consequence of radical modern systems theory and is cognate with incommensurability. Its contemplation is critical to the present study because it provides the starkest illumination of the central problem. There are distinctions. Autopoiesis denies the possibility of meaningful system intercommunication due to factors ordaining closure; incommensurability implies that systems attempting to communicate have no common basis on which to do so which, in the world of lived experience, would account for law's disappointment with science as collaborator. Autopoiesis is a distinctive theory, the result of convergence of a number of significant related studies, is highly abstract, sustained by a self-fulfilling rationality and belonging to a well-circumscribed realm of esoteric thought. Incommensurability is phenomenological, more generalizable than autopoiesis and by comparison much more prosaic. Its definition evades precision, having shades of meaning that include incompatibility, incongruity and strangeness between principles and ideas. Kuhn (1970) uses it to describe the relationship between pre- and post-paradigmatically shifted productions of science,[32] in that one cannot be mapped onto the other or that there is no basis on which to associate their propositions. Theories are fundamentally incommensurable. The notion of incommensurability also exists in philosophy where the ideas of one scholar have no conceptual nexus to those of another. It is not that they employ different languages because translations can be supplied or that they encrypt their messages because these can be deciphered. There is no metalanguage or unifying mechanism (Cotterrell 1995: 109). The received explanation is that these scholars with their theories simply 'talk past each other'.

Seen from the aspect of this study, science-law incommensurability is concretised in autopoiesis on the basis of a foundational theory that transcends mere experience. It justifies, explains and supports the phenomenon but at the same time problematizes interactions over evidence. Autopoietic theory is resistant to attempts to dislodge it and, though not empirically-constructed, is sufficiently robust in its derivation to reproduce reality in relation to law and other social systems. While affording deeper understanding of incommensurability, it increases its prominence but exacerbates the problem of its own mediation.

The extreme form of systems theory that relies on autopoiesis has been developed extensively by Niklas Luhmann, sociologist. In a biographical résumé, Andersen (2003: 63) recounts the fields of study within which Luhmann has considered systems theory and published prolifically. These are

---

[31] And see Luhmann (1995): 16-17; and (2004): 64-65.
[32] See also Bertalanffy (1971): 15-16.

the systems of science, politics, art, education, justice, religions, love and family, mass media and economics. Earlier reference in the present study to convergence of a number of significantly related studies alludes to Andersen's account of Luhmann's exploration of the systems theories of other writers that he incorporates in his own interpretations, which nominates three main approaches bearing the Luhmann stamp. Andersen cites these as the 'Spencer-Brownian Luhmann', which prioritizes the approach of observation, the 'Parsonian Luhmann' that centres on the relation of system and evolution, and the 'Maturanian Luhmann' with the central concept of autopoiesis (ibid: 64). It can be detected that only one rendition of systems theory culminates in auto-poiesis due to its anchorage in a particularly intractable notion of autopoiesis derived from a field of biological science. Yet Andersen's perspicacious distinc-tion of approaches becomes blurred in commonly encountered explanations of systems theory, and critiques commonly treat autopoiesis as the sum of all connected themes, though Parsons's work is treated more selectively. The functionalist aspect of his work seeks to explain the existence of social struc-tures by the rôle they perform for society as a whole. This is criticised for taking no account of the internal operations of self-production that is autopoiesis but Cotterrell issues a reminder that Luhmann is indebted to Parsons for the notion of simplifying societal complexity through identification of systems (1992: 66, n.14) The involvedness of Luhmann's writings is little relieved by this knowledge but the above categorization of contributions to the theory has the merit of systematizing examination by the student and adding clarity, though inquiry does not necessarily have to be restricted to or conducted under such headings.

Luhmann's theoretical work has the capacity to attract but also recruits its detractors, some regarding it as arcane, lacking sufficient scientific clarity and an example of pretentious jargon, for example Mahlmann (2004: 421-425). One description of it is as 'an exasperating concept' (King 1993: 233). Luhmann's social theory does not conform methodologically to sociologists' expectations of a testable theory, assessment of causal factors or engagement in prediction, but notions of it being mere 'philosophical speculation' are dis-missed (King and Thornhill 2003: 2). The foregoing is a gentle suggestion that Luhmann's theory was not deduced scientifically but King and Thornhill recount the more acerbic criticism of Zolo, who finds that social autopoiesis has no basis in empirical observation or evidence and that it was developed independently of any theoretical tradition (2003: 221). The amelioration they provide is a reversion to the fundamental tenet of sociological inquiry that emphasizes the need for theories convincing of an understanding of the complexities of modern societies and the relationships of people to these societies (King 1993: 222).

For those absorbed by it but maintaining provident analytical distance, the ways in which autopoietic theory suggests reality provide not only intellectual challenges but encourage deep contemplation of the radical effects of its closure, and hence a quest for possible escape routes, the particular instance of autopoiesis applied to law representing a special and complex case involving the most profound attributions of the theory.

A comprehensive exposition of the theory of autopoiesis, its complexity, different arguments and treatments is beyond the scope of the present study. Rooted in investigation of the origins of science-law incommensurability in the legal forum, the resources for and means of its mediation, this work will endeavour to explain autopoietic theory only in relation to the present thread of study and make links and references that are appropriate. This will also direct that the many divisions, topics, arguments and propositions of autopoiesis be dealt with in an order that is natural to the way the narrative of this work is constructed. The approaches of works of reference differ widely in approach in this respect, though in explaining legal autopoiesis a certain regularity often can be seen. Cited sources of reference accompanying this work will assist a scholar seeking deeper understanding.[33]

Social systems

Luhmann characterizes society as complex, inviting social scientists to observe it but urging avoidance of a reductionist account of the social world, the corollary of which would be 'a highly abstract and generalized notion of social events more appropriate to philosophy than sociology.' (Luhmann 1995: 27). Disdaining the possibility of representing society in a single, definitive and exclusive theory, Luhmann admits the feasibility of infinite theories and offers his own that his reviewers perceive as 'a social theory of social theories', considering multiple ways of comprehending society (King and Thornhill 2003: 1). Such description therefore is of a 'theoretical paradigm rather than a unified theory' (King 1993: 218) and a theoretical approach to the operations of social systems, their interrelationships and with those of the general social environment (ibid: 219). Some of Luhmann's critics appear not to have perceived what is expressed in this expansive view of autopoietic theory as a paradigm and are critical of it as theory.[34] More deeply examined, this paradigm theorizes modern world systems as social systems constituted of functionally differentiated, evolving sub-systems with constantly maintained identity, reproducing themselves through internally relevant communications and relating to other sub-systems in their environment (Luhmann 2004: 72-73, 465). This is a perception of society as comprised of autopoietic sub-systems and is the mainstay of Luhmann's theory.

With only this information, an impression of the theory of social autopoiesis can be had that it is reasonable though unremarkable and departs from the systems theory of Bertalanffy only in respect of its adamant assertion that social sub-systems are autopoietic. Progressing understanding of Luhmann's theory involves aspects that make it extremely radical, itself becoming complex

33 See especially King and Thornhill (2003); King and Schütz (1994).
34 See Viskovatoff (1999); James (1992); Neves (2001); Capps and Olsen (2002).

in its ways of describing societal complexity, creating its own paradoxes, issuing cognitive challenges and in the process giving indications for science-law incommensurability that it is a deep-seated problem. Viskovatoff locates the roots of this difficulty in the fundamental differences between systems theory as an abstract concept and empirical science considered in relation to Luhmann's vision of autopoiesis (1999: 492). Only the empirical sciences can provide valid and complete scientific explanations, extending them as far down as possible to link a chain of causes producing an event or phenomenon. Systems theory is likened to the conjectural, abstract realm inhabited by mathematics that is 'free to explore conceptual models without concern for their immediate applicability' (ibid: 493). Luhmann's systems theory also generates a lexicography of terms and expressions that have highly theory-specific and theory-contextual definitions essential to explanation of relations and arguments that need to be understood for deep study.

Advancing his thesis, Luhmann discards a principal pillar of traditional sociology, reconceptualising society within systems theory as comprised not of people, neither groups of them, nor institutions but as communicating elements of a social system (Luhmann 1995: 39, 2004: 73). Luhmann justifies this by confining his selection to the observable in sociology to which thoughts are not amenable but communications are (King and Thornhill 2003: 4). In terms of sociological inquiry, Luhmann's unit of analysis thus becomes not people but communications (King and Schütz 1994: 264; King and Thornhill 2003: 2). Viskovatoff (1999: 492) considers Luhmann to have adopted a model drawn from science that 'respectifies' generalized theories taken as a starting point of inquiry to conform to the social domain defined by its constituent entities, which he estimates to be communications. Though there is no 'centre' in systems theory, because the sociological unit of analysis is communications, not people, Teubner claims that the individual is decentred (Teubner 1989: 732). There is no concept of 'centre' in systems theory, so perhaps this confusing term should be replaced by saying that the individual is 'excluded' or 'displaced' from consideration, though of course communication always is by individuals.

The theory that projects communications as the basic elements on which social systems are built depicts meaning as contingent, or at least that it is dependent on its reception by another communicating system. Luhmann's counsel is that meaning is created in the world by a social system when the meaning it produces is relied on by other social systems (Luhmann 1995: 61-62). This involuted proposition means that a system, for example politics, can recognize another such as religion, or law recognize science, through attribution of meaning for itself. Social systems are thereby constructed as systems of meaning (King 2003: 219), but meaning is consolidated as relational. In active social systems, each system relies on meanings that it attaches to several other systems concurrently, namely those (sub-systems) of its environment so that, for example, politics will recognize the existence and function of law, science, economics, religion and many others in its social rôle. They will be recognized from their communications (Luhmann 1995: 29, 39) but this does not imply a direct communicative ability.

Emphatic distinction between communication and language is drawn that emphasizes why communication must be regarded as the essential basis of social systems. Language is seen as a symbolic construct of consciousness in which even nonsense expressions and conversions from feeling or intuition would have to be recognized and admitted (Luhmann 1976: 511), thereby discrediting meaning wrongly as a prerequisite for communication in social systems. It is possible to amplify here that communications considered thus are not forms of signalling, as they might be if considered purely as language, but instead concern the internal processes of each social system that legitimate it, so that communications about law concern law's operations, science those of science and so on, because this is key to appreciation of communicative difficulties that ensue.

Social systems discourse finalizes the nature and effect of autopoiesis in relations between systems. King's introductory remarks concerning 'The Truth About Autopoiesis' refer to the original conception of autopoiesis in biological science that Luhmann translated into social science (King 1993: 219-220). An account of the development of autopoietic systems in the theory is 'as units repeatedly reproduced from their own elements that in doing so became independent of their environment' (ibid: 219). La Torre (1997: 338) comments that Teubner's description in his treatment of autopoiesis is that social systems, including law, are closed systems that reproduce themselves through internal dynamics, not external stimuli, a simple but excellent encapsulation of the self-referentiality of autopoietic social systems and their imperviousness to outside influences. Cotterrell defines legal autopoiesis as a conception of law as a distinct discourse, possessing its own integrity, its own criteria of significance and validation, its own means of cognition and constituting the objects of which it speaks (1995: 100), and this is generalizable to all systems.[35]

Functional differentiation

In the introductory chapter of the present study, functional differentiation was presented as an historical phenomenon concerning the separation of science, philosophy and law as evolving fields of knowledge and practice in the Enlightenment. The progress of this phenomenon was described admirably by Dampier (1961). Luhmann's more profound theoretical interpretation of functional differentiation sharpens the distinctions and moves them away from a world of mere cultural separation into a new realm constructed by a highly refined vision of autopoiesis, which extends to all systems and their environ-

---

[35] There must be constant reminders that autopoiesis, though normatively closed, is always cognitively open. A fully closed legal system nevertheless needs cognitive 'input', so that it can compare events from its environment with its normative values, that is, in order to decide whether they are legal or illegal.

ments. His notion of functional differentiation is based on communication by systems that express criteria denoting their identity and self-validation using communicative codes (Luhmann 2004: 172ff). It is Luhmann's proposition that the basis on which each social system communicates about events within its purview is in the form of a binary code, so that communication concerning law is based on legality or illegality as one of only two possible and mutually exclusive states (ibid: 174). Put differently, King (1993: 225) states that legal communications occur whenever people express themselves in terms of that which is lawful or unlawful, or legal or illegal. Science communicates by encoding aspects of the world it sees as true or false, medicine as healthy or unhealthy states and economics in terms of profit or loss. These require a little qualification, for instance law uses the legal/illegal code or as guilty/not guilty code in operational contexts. Jurisprudentially law might communicate using a code of moral/immoral or just/unjust when considering natural law, normative/non-normative based if describing positive law. Science communicates on the basis of truth or falsehood in its inquiry into the causation of phenomena and events but rarely can these be represented as absolutes, only as the best approximation that a contingent and provisional science can achieve.

Regardless of such equivocations the notion of binary codes emphasizes that each social system communicates in terms of concepts that are fundamentally different. King and Thornhill also locate the idea of coding and programming in Parsons's 'symbolically generalized media' that parallel Luhmann's binary codes of communication in which each sphere of social activity sees the world in its own terms. Hence, the economy communicates on the basis of money, law on legality, politics on power, science on truth, religion on faith and sexuality on love (2003: 23). Teubner (1983: 270-271) assesses that system conflict is inevitable as a consequence of Luhmann's analysis of functional differentiation that elevates social sub-systems to such a high degree of specialization through identification of binary codes and media. 'Differentiation leads to greater complexity in relationships between the system and the environment' (Luhmann 1989: 139). Although expressed in terms of clashes that occur between many social sub-systems and not just science and law, it emphasizes the very nature of the central problem of the present study. At the same time it both ratifies the central theme of the incommensurability of science and law in the legal forum and grounds it in a theory accounting for incommensurability in a manner far more profound than mere implication of difficulties encountered in procedure.

Andersen uses a sociologically-oriented illustration of functional differentiation from social life that creates a slightly different emphasis. The separation of the social sciences into different branches of knowledge relating to particular societal functions has brought a tendency for them to invalidate each other (Andersen 2003: xi). Attributed to separate discourses, concepts and the limited resonances of each field, systems increasingly are able to communicate only with themselves. He holds that progress in one field can signify retreat in another or that the consequence of one system challenging the validity of another is an impaired emergent field. He cites the topical instance, though within a narrow socio-political arena, of secret filming being associated with political journalism that creates a new genre but in fact disturbs the political process (ibid: xi).

While more accustomed theories of system closure anticipate inhibition of intersystem communication that simply leaves them unable to inform each other usefully, Andersen's point refers to degradations that occur when a system achieving increasing societal influence, communicating only in terms of its own constructs, challenges the validity of another field similarly constrained in its communicative ability. In the present study and in a less narrowly-defined context, an example relied on is that of the interrelation of science and law where science and its increasingly radical productions, especially those affecting human life and moral values, tests law's ability to apply its normative prescriptions to unprecedented phenomena. Any degradation of law in these contexts—Andersen's impaired emergent field—would signify transfer to science of responsibility for social order and determinations of 'right' and 'wrong' courses of action in society's moral dilemmas.

First and higher-order observation

In the subdivision of social sciences into different fields of knowledge, a need arises to question their evolution, communicative closure, reflexivity and attachment with and from other fields (ibid). A new form of questioning then advances from mere questioning of actions to the way questions are asked—a theoretical shift from the primacy of ontology to the primacy of epistemology. Andersen depicts this as a move from first-order observation of 'what is out there' to second-order observation of the point that observations are made from the position occupied when observing 'what is out there'. A strand of discursive analytical strategy attributed to Spencer Brown concerns observation and analysis of form (ibid: 64). It pertains to how systems observe events and operations, amplifying the self-referentiality at the heart of modern systems analysis. Observation also is the raison d'être of sociology. Explanation of the special treatment of observation in systems theory therefore is important and the utility of sociology in this study will be described soon.

Next is a much-simplified rendition of the Spencer Brownian-Luhmannian theory of observation. According to it observation nominated as being of the first order is that which observes a distinction by making an indication in opposition to everything else not indicated (Luhmann 2000: 61). In the case of observing law the following would be understood. The indication would be of law as a system communicating on the basis of a distinction between the codes of legal/illegal. The indication would be of a system operating on the basis of this binary code and everything else not indicated, which therefore is non-law. Everything that is non-law belongs implicitly to the environment of law. Andersen (2003) posits first order observation as relating to any indication of a distinction, not necessarily in the fixed sense of the present study that is concerned only with the systems that fragment society. For example distinction can be indicated in aesthetics as beautiful/ugly, even though these might be hard to define, or moral/immoral when indicating marriage.

First-order observation is indication of distinction but provides no elaboration. It is an indication within a framework of difference and the observation of something in the environment, thereby using an external reference (ibid: 64). Attribution of meaning to events and communications within the distinction is by second-order observation that observes how the first-order observations were observed, distinguishing the event or object from the observation that makes sense of them or between what is being observed and the sense being made of them (Luhmann 2000: 61). Second order observations of how observations are made rely on internal reference (Andersen 2003: 64) and these concern the observation of legality/illegality. The Spencer-Brownian-Luhmannian approach names second-order observation as the basis of systems theory (ibid: 64-66). Second-order observation therefore is the observation of first-order observing systems. Sociology makes second-order observation of how the first order observation—the distinction— is made. Later in the discussion it will be seen that in the area of risk, sociology makes second-order observation of how the distinction risk/danger is made.

Paradox and tautology

For Luhmann, codes signify the way in which systems distinguish themselves from their environment, that is, from all other social systems, and organize their operative closure (Luhmann 2004: 183). When considering codes in respect of law, this entails acknowledgment that recognition of matters as either legal or illegal is the prerogative of the legal system and no other, while simultaneously accepting that that system is the sole arbiter of the difference between legal and illegal (Luhmann 1989: 139).[36] This represents the so-called paradox much emphasized in legal autopoiesis that it is only law that can make the decision. The paradox also incurs a tautology because (it is posited that) law could not possibly be anything but lawful (Luhmann 1995: 361).

King and Thornhill intimate its relief under special conditions from the exclusivity of distinction accorded by this version of systems theory. 'Relief' is a construal of the present study. Citing observation of the political system, they report that the distinction government/opposition prevents simultaneous accounts of events from a non-political perspective (2003: 19) but that this could be achieved by indicating a further distinction encompassing non-political aspects. In carefully considered circumstances, indication of a further distinction allows a re-perspectivization of observation. For example, indicating law through the further distinction moral/immoral could permit observation as if from the standpoint of natural law. The possibility then can be imagined that indication of a social aspect of law, say contract, can be distin-

---

36 Compare also King (1993: 225), regarding Hart's secondary rules of law.

guished further as trust/distrust or the law on abortion on an aspect of women's rights, such observations acting as perspectival stand-ins more akin to those with which social studies often are concerned.[37]

Structural coupling

Previous characterizations of autopoietic systems signify that, when systems interact, for example as occurs between science, law, politics, economics or permutations of these and other systems in performance of societal function, the communications of one are perceived by the others on their collision as 'noise', 'interference' or 'perturbation'. One graphic description refers to it as 'hammering' (Teubner *et al.* 2002: 919) or as 'irritation' (Luhmann 1992a: 1432). In this absolute expression of the theory, whichever term is preferred, social systems mutually perceive communications as unintelligible. This is a reminder that systems recognize each other only from their communications but that direct communication is impossible (King 1993: 220).

Experience brings into question how the previous suggestion is evidenced in reality, since the interplay of different fields of knowledge is observed to be an essential part of societal organization. The theory insists that each and every social system is autopoietic. Structural coupling indicates only that, in their encounters, each autopoietic system reconstructs the other in its own terms. So, science will reconstruct law with the understanding of law by science; correspondingly, law will reconstruct science with the understanding of law. There will be no transfer of understanding. Each system simply includes the other in its environment (Luhmann 1992a: 1419-1438). Discursive closure and all that it entails therefore precludes the possibility of any form of intercommunication based on commonality, putting great distance between this theory and that of Bertalanffy. Commentators on autopoietic theory have pointed out that in their discursive closure, social systems nonetheless do not behave monadically (Teubner 1989: 740). 'Monadically' is taken to be a reference to Leibnitz's 'windowless monads' as solitary units of existence by which 'nothing could come in or go out'. Autopoietic systems are not depicted as incapable of any form of communication, that is, 'hermetically sealed' (King and Thornhill 2003: 26) but that meaning is contingent and relational.

The danger of de-differentiation

Law cannot produce scientific findings nor science those of law (King 1993: 26). Using this science-law relationship as an example, the principle of structural coupling would inform that law reconstructs science within itself in

---

[37] See Luhmann (1998b: 158-160) for a discussion of eighteenth century movements introducing concepts of freedom, democracy, and a constitutional state. Legal/illegal distinctions could then be replaced by those that set legal decisions against the values of universal morality or natural law, or in politics against those of democracy, freedom *versus* state control, public requirements or national interest.

terms of the understanding of science it achieves by observing science's communications, and vice-versa in the case of an understanding of law by science. This does not produce a scientifico-legal discourse of law because that would be defeated by factors underlying the phenomenon of noise, perturbation or 'hammering'. Were such a discourse possible it would result in de-differentiation of systems with pernicious effects on their validity, authority, meaning and ways of assessing the value of information (ibid), to which Luhmann's conception of functional differentiation is fundamentally opposed.[38] Under these circumstances, the desirability of a common discourse would need newly to be questioned if the aforementioned sacrifices incurred were to be so great. In the case of law its ability to stabilize normative expectations over time would be lost, which refers to the understanding that law's conclusions will, on average over time, conform to the standards that society requires of it (ibid: 40, 52-53).[39] Even more pertinent is the question of society's intention when for certain purposes one social system resorts to another to assist in its conclusions, as does law frequently in relation to science over legal decisions involving scientific evidence, or politics in relation to science over regulation, informing policy and so on. An ordinary understanding would be that if one system cannot reach a satisfactory conclusion using its own judgment criteria and methods, lacks the requisite information or cannot adjudicate on a matter outwith its competence, recruitment of other relevant knowledge systems is axiomatic for the establishment of truth. In autopoiesis correctly understood, this presumption is rendered naïve, ill-informed and improbable. The theory of legal autopoiesis asserts that law constructs its own reality (Teubner 1989: 730) yet a single reality is sought or even expected by attempts to interpolate the findings of different systems in a decisional forum. This cannot possibly reduce a potentially multi-path decisional process to a single conclusion without sacrificing the integrity of the social sub-systems concerned, which is a loose way of describing the perils of de-differentiation. To the extent that society believes different social systems do collaborate successfully in decision-making, disorder is prevented only by virtue of the general acceptance of one social system as final arbiter. Law will use its ability to close an argument, conclude because of limitations of time and exercise its privilege to 'have the last word' and politics in the form of government will decide on issues of policy and regulation because it is constitutionally ascendant. However, in situations of conflict, law's curtailment of proceedings sometimes can prevent recognition that de-differentiation of systems was potentiated. The conclusions so brought about are not necessarily synonymous with decisions that transpire to be impervious to challenge, as the central problem of the present study reveals.

---

[38] See King and Thornhill (2003: 40-41) regarding Luhmann's normative theory of law.

[39] This counsel is from an unpublished translation by the authors from Niklas Luhmann (1993) *Das Recht der Gesellschaft*, Frankfurt am Main: Suhrkamp, p.125.

The early introduction of the topic of de-differentiation in this exploration of autopoietic theory indicates its criticality to the present discussion and the risks it would entail. Also it explains the reasons for its improbability as a solution.

TEUBNER'S DECONSTRUCTION OF LEGAL AUTOPOIESIS

Luhmann and Teubner: 'hard' and 'soft' interpretations of autopoiesis

Cotterrell's view of legal autopoietic theory as developed by Luhmann is that it renders a form of legal closure, the result of extreme functional differentiation, 'as radical as any to be found in the literature of legal philosophy' (1995: 105). It can be conjectured that if there is power inequality—and in this study it is asserted law has a presiding rôle due to its societal function—structural coupling is a preferentially-disposed process with law's reconstruction of science assuming the ascendancy but with science protesting at law's conclusions. The extent to which this is true is critically important to arguments in the present study. On it hinges much of the debate on the issue of science-law incommensurability in evidential contexts. Also, if it is permitted to suspend the literal contradiction momentarily, it is possible to ask whether autopoiesis is mitigable.

In seeking the truth or otherwise of the notion that science-law incommensurability is absolute it would be necessary to consider the following critical issues. First, whether conclusions in the legal forum emanate inevitably from an entirely self-referential system as imagined by Luhmann with respect to law and, if they do not, where the power behind decisions resides. Second, the benefits or otherwise to decisions of structural coupling that reconstructs but does not recreate science within law's ambit. Third, whether law's recognition of the communications of other systems has a deleterious effect on law's autonomy and ability to produce decisions that are purely legal, or instead become a matter of mere social adjudication. The outcome rests largely on the choice between acceptance of Luhmann's strictured autopoietic theory and the more adaptive belief explained by Teubner.

The epistemic trap and science-law tension located in issues of power

Teubner views power relationships in the legal forum as constructivist with sociological inclinations. His conceptual strategy is one in which amelioration of the rigidity of Luhmann's theory is taken so that law can retain the momentum to fulfil its function to the satisfaction of society, not to just that of law itself. A course is steered through the intellectual labyrinth of autopoiesis by his rational argument in which the effects of law's autonomy, structural coupling, cognitive openness and enslavements of non-legal systems by law are examined. Advisedly, Teubner problematizes tensions between the normative closure of law and pressure to recognize the contribution to decisions of other systems in its environment that overshadows law's operations as potentiating an 'epistemic trap' (1989: 745).

Teubner develops his argument using science as particularly challenging to law's operations, which is reflective of societal concerns in modernity. Science also has a clear rationality of its own that is different from that which law enjoys and therein lay the seeds of difficulty when the two fields collide. Teubner identifies science as the cognitive system most influentially placed to challenge law's epistemic authority in the need for law to reconstruct non-legal communications for its recognition of truths. Juridical constructs are exposed to the constructs of other discourses in society, particularly the constructs of science (ibid). Of course, this is the nub of the central problem and Teubner has detected it astutely. *Science is not privileged epistemologically* (ibid: 744).[40] The notion of 'power relations' emanates from impressions of lawyers and scientists that each has the other in its thrall.[41] However, there can be a pseudo-effect of privilege for science in legal matters because, if law is too dependent on science for its conclusions, it might fall into the epistemic trap of giving true/false decisions for which it is not competent. This can give science cause to claim 'superiority'.

Typical problems for science and law in modern complexity manifesting in institutional and procedural frameworks are those of Gulf War Syndrome, the risk to health of children's vaccines (MMR and Pertussis inoculations), Rape Trauma Syndrome, Sudden Unexpected Infant Death (or Shaken Baby Syndrome), the link between Bovine Spongiform Encephalitis (BSE) and new variant Creutzfeld-Jacob Disease (vCJD) in humans, tobacco litigation and continuing issues in medical negligence. Scientific opinion in some of these instances is uncertain, qualified or contested. It is more certain in DNA profiling leading to criminal convictions and in proving causative links in asbestosis/mesothelioma litigation and some other instances of industrial injury. In the area of defective products liability there have been class actions for the harmful effects of thalidomide, *Opren*, *Bendectin*, the oral contraceptive and litigation over silicone breast implants. Concerning environmental risk, the law has considered scientific opinion in the association between the incidence of childhood cancer and proximity to nuclear fuel reprocessing plants, the effect of pesticides on human health, the toxicity of food additives produced on cooking and the harmful effects of living near high-tension electricity cables, among others. Currently it is confronted by the problems of assisted voluntary euthanasia, stem-cell research, gene therapy, genetically-modified products, and other issues posing legal, ethical and moral dilemmas.

---

40 Author's emphasis.
41 Possibly, these are delusional.

Denial of the immutability of autopoiesis is germane to Teubner's conception of the epistemic trap. Recognition of non-legal communications in law's operations imperils the exclusivity of Luhmann's theory of autopoiesis, accentuating that Luhmann's perfected concept of legal communication is theoretical while Teubner's is concerned more with action as constituting its observable features.

Once the epistemic trap has been identified, issues concerning the balance of power of legal and extra-legal communications in the legal forum require examination. In cognitive matters, Teubner is able to posit the advantage of science over law because it specializes in such procedures customarily, whereas law does not (ibid: 745) and can be seen in the reliance of law on science for explanation of events for which law lacks its own means. Of course, science frequently is unable to affirm causation of an event with a certainty sufficient for law's satisfaction but, barring egregious errors, in principle the cognitive opinion of an expert in proceedings would render a legal decision unsafe were it ignored. With regard to epistemic authority, though, Teubner acknowledges that science and law can lay equal claim to it, while commenting that the 'facts' they recognize depend on guarantees of truths by formalized procedures of factual inquiry that are significantly different (ibid: 744). So, in his perception of science-law conflict, Teubner sees no justification for privileging either epistemology. No superiority of scientific over legal constructs can be claimed because procedures and conventions of factual inquiry both lead to empirical statements about reality so that, for instance, fact arising from scientific research and the fact of a legal duty should not be regarded differently (ibid).

Res judicata and revising decisions

Teubner depicts *res judicata* as the arbiter of truth (ibid), referring to law's ability to accept or deny extra-legal truths, for example scientific ones, in reaching its conclusions. He characterizes this as a situation to which law and perhaps the whole of society is resigned and in it lays the basis of the central problem of this study. In one view, it could amount to law exercising options through its authority but, even if based on blatant errors in extra-legal evidence or its interpretation, its decisions are rarely overturned. Recourse usually is made to appeals and reviews that consider whether there were errors of procedure. In that sense, hardly ever are legal decisions themselves judged wrong but subtly they can be reversed by referring to the way they were reached. This has been known to reveal shortcomings in disclosure of evidence, as was revealed in the appeal of Sally Clark against her conviction for murdering her two children where a forensic pathologist decided for himself that some findings were not relevant to the case.[42] Teubner's point appears to be that decisions based on evidential errors can be rectified but must also be that

---

[42] [2003] EWCA Crim 1020; [2003] 2 FCR 447; (2003) 147 SJLB 473 CA (Crim Div), Digested CLY 04/73.

avoidance of the implied unpredictability of *res judicata* should lie in improved legal understanding of science. Under Luhmann's conditions this is prevented precisely by the conditions of autopoiesis. Perversely, that law should be influenced by extra-legal matters invokes the conditions of the epistemic trap according to Teubner and nothing but a circularity of argument remains for which some kind of escape is necessary.

In declaiming conditions for the epistemic trap, it can appear that Teubner dismantles Luhmann's insistence on the autopoiesis of law. The suggestion will divert the present narrative briefly but essentially. Lest the statement be considered an over-dramatization of Teubner's 'softer' treatment of legal autopoiesis, in one sense it is shown to have come about through his contextualization of legal discourse within society. He says that, regardless of its proclivity for closure and self-reproduction, unavoidably legal communication is *social communication*,[43] so that a communicative event in law is always represented by two discourses—the specialized institutionalized discourse of law and diffuse and general societal communication (ibid: 745). The ability of Teubner to reconcile these arguments is hard to accept. Is depicting law as social communication an attempt to undermine autopoiesis, or is it a different concern? To be precise, does 'the specialized institutionalized discourse of law' emanate from legal autopoiesis, or is it a discussion of law's operations that, somehow, does not refer to its normative standards? Moreover, is 'diffuse and general societal communication' nothing more than a kind of unstructured 'social chatter' about law? Teubner does not amplify. The message could be that communicating with society does not involve law's internal operations. It could be so but it does not improve understanding of how autopoietic closure can be compromised. It will not be adequate to explain Teubner's position on autopoiesis by reference to reflexive law, exploration of which will be made later in this chapter. Reflexive law is difficult to conceive when set in autopoietic theory, because it challenges law to go beyond mere acknowledgment of the cognitive openness required for its autopoietic operations. Here, too, Teubner's seeming dissension from the stringency of autopoiesis manifests in his proposition that law can be semi-autonomous, that there can be degrees of closure when there is reliance on interference and a desire to bring ostensibly separated systems into dialogue.[44] The dichotomy is perverse, especially when the reality of the epistemic trap for law must be admitted.[45] While leaving the situation in suspense, perhaps it is best in the interim to accommodate the

---

[43] Author's emphasis.

[44] See the discussion under the heading 'Arguments for the Premise of Reflexive Law', *infra*.

[45] The epistemic trap is sprung when law tries to make decisions, founded on its own distinctions, on the basis of communications from other systems (exemplified by science) with different distinctions. A necessary cognitive openness to its environment is implied but reference to the 'wrong' normative standards for its decisions produces inappropriate conclusions. There is no possibility within autopoietic theory for aversion of the epistemic trap by erecting a false notion of compromised system closure.

challenge to autopoietic theory by depicting this argument as one of locating the limits of semi-autonomy, degrees of openness and the extent to which systems can be brought into dialogue, until more satisfactory explanations of Teubner's intentions can be deduced.

Returning to the deferred main narrative, at this point the onlooker will wish to know whether the legal communicative event as a decision is precisely one of law, corresponding to Luhmann's conservative autopoietic view, or if it reflects the cognitive reception of science or any other system of knowledge; in other words, the extent to which a conclusion evidences law as having fallen into the epistemic trap. Further, unless the onlooker is an ardent disciple of autopoietic theory, a question would arise whether such an influenced decision is acceptable to society. If the epistemic trap for law cannot be avoided because of its need to rely on science, society would need to know how to value law's conclusions. Affirming structural coupling, Teubner is certain that in this situation interference will have occurred in which information is constituted anew in each discourse but he continues that it adds nothing but the 'simultaneity of two communicative events' (ibid).

The burden of both science and law is shifted from their traditional responsibilities to provide conclusions corresponding with a reality that transpired to be fictive, to that of a test of social coherence (ibid). Teubner volunteers no more information on the meaning and effect of 'social coherence', so it is assumed that it describes situations in which legal conclusions involving science are reasonably systematic, adhere to some kind of rationality and comply with the expectations of society. It is difficult to determine whether 'social coherence' has been used disparagingly. In one respect it sounds like the least worse scenario, where stability in decision-making provides compensation in which the conditions of the epistemic trap are unavoidable. It would be an advance on mere social adjudication by law in matters of science. Perhaps the notion of a 'test' need not be interpreted too literally—there is no immediate form it can take—but the assumption from it that society is watchful over legal conclusions involving science is comforting. King describes how the law develops in different areas of the social environment and the relationship that evolves between law and other social systems (1993: 230). He locates evaluation of law's expectations according to external criteria derived from social scientific expectations in the socio-legal paradigm of study (ibid). Social coherence may be part of such an examination.

King describes the 'enslavement' of one system by another when reconstructed in its own terms, taking the stance that power relationships between social meaning systems are not equal, for example as between economics, politics, science and law (ibid: 231). Teubner indicates that, in legal institutions, it is considered law enslaves the cognitive aspects of science according to normative context and institutional purpose (1989: 745) and, with respect to remarks made previously here about law's obligation to conclude an argument, this perception seems accurate. Employing an example of the enslavement of experts in proffering opinions in legal proceedings, Teubner recounts 'the poverty of psychiatry' (ibid: 749) in which forensic psychiatrists regularly are required by law to distinguish guilt from causation in the action of a person when, for scientists, determination of guilt must be a matter of trans-science.[46] It can be seen from recent criminal prosecutions in England and Wales that medical experts' proffered opinion on the multiple occurrence of sudden unexpected infant death in a single family as unlikely to have been due to natural causes, also might subsist in trans-science for them as scientists but they have not shown awareness of this. Their apparent alacrity to offer such unqualified opinion can be countenanced as a 'voluntary enslavement' of science to law in making its task simple, but no expert should assume law's rôle in this manner (Ward 2004: 328; *R v Clark*;[47] *R v Cannings*[48]). Enslavement of cognitive operations, according to normative context and institutional purpose, usually subsists in a claim by those engaged in the practice of law. Teubner insists, instead, that legal communication is forced to reconstruct science's construction of reality within its own, therefore exposing juridical constructs to those of science (1989: 745). King suggests that, while enslavement does not necessarily indicate total domination of one meaning system by another, weaker systems must convince society that their constructions of reality should be preferred over more prevalent systems (1993: 231).

Case study: structural coupling and mediation of the epistemic trap

Smith illuminates issues of structural coupling applied to an acknowl-edged problem in society, drawing useful conclusions based on Luhmann's comment that not all legal communications, even though falling within the legal/illegal code, are equally significant in law's operations (2004: 322). She observes that, for law, communications concerning post-adoption contact and parenthood do fall within the definition of legal/illegal according to law's code. However she distinguishes legal institutions such as the courts that are obliged to produce binding decisions and what she calls 'contact zones' that occur 'peripherally' between social sub-systems, such as politics and law. She asserts that structural coupling in these circumstances produces intelligibility from the resulting interactional 'noise' but in this characterization politics and law are structurally coupled via the 'peripheral' nature of legislation (2004: 323). Smith's percipience with regard to legal autopoiesis in relation to law's treat-ment of post-adoption contact between children and their birth parents supplies a context in which the epistemic trap—'a challenge for law's author-ity'—is potentiated (2004: 330).

---

[46] See Weinberg (1972) and Chapter IV of this study.

[47] [2003] EWCA Crim 1020.

[48] [2004] 1 All ER 725.

In providing a reminder that structural coupling describes the reconstruction of the communications of one system within another in terms of its own operations—the usually received view in systems theory—Smith makes insightful distinctions that re-render this reasoning to exemplify the epistemic trap in a real situation. First, she clarifies that social science communications are relevant to law only if in a particular context they are legally relevant to its operations (ibid: 322), citing parts of child protection legislation as instances.[49] From the various explanations of structural coupling in the literature at large, it appears that the communications of one system need to be reconstructed within any other on their encounters in order that meaningful operations can occur. This question of the necessity for law's attention to its environment as sketched by Smith appears to have useful bearing on its operations. In social science context, communications concern the social, emotional, psychological and relational issues of post-adoption contact. Politics communicates in the same context about events connected with the family as a site for producing socially, psychologically and economically competent citizens, so that it concerns law only if resulting in legislation. Thus is a picture painted of each system—political, social and legal—thinking differently about post-adoption contact and interacting 'peripherally' in contact zones according to Smith's earlier assessment but influencing directly in disputes requiring binding decisions.

The normative closure of law and the challenge of the need for cognitive openness

In a paper highly critical of autopoietic theory, Capps and Olsen attempt to impeach the integrity of normatively closed law by accusing it of inconsistency in decision-making (2002: 557). They contend that decision-makers in a strictly normatively closed system constantly would produce identical solutions to identical problems if there were no recourse to external reference. The fact that this is not seen in legal outcomes is ascribed to use of external references or influences consequent upon the cognitive openness of law. This reductive and mechanistic view of the workings of law could be criticised by interjecting that identical problems facing law that could have identical solutions are unlikely but perhaps that is petty. Instinctively, it seems that, in their criticism, these authors fail to appreciate the fine but necessary relationship of normative closure and cognitive openness and that different discretions are exercised in making choices over the weight to ascribe to external considerations. Nonetheless, if their argument is specious it is essential to determine the reasons because, at first sight, their theme would appear to coincide exactly with the perception of the present study, namely that law's decisions involving science as an external influence are inconsistent; indeed this proposition agrees in

---

[49] See also Teubner (1989): 745-746.

spirit with that of Edmond (2000), though he suggests carefully that this is due to inadequate or improper understanding of science. So, the notion of Capps and Olsen could be taken to enshrine the central problem of the present study. Developing their proposition to the other extreme would suggest that law is so open to the persuasions of other systems that, with regard to decisions, de-differentiation of law's function might be complete. Such anarchy has no currency in autopoietic theory. It does nothing to dissuade the opinion of this study that law should continue to occupy the position of final arbiter in law-science system conflict, assuming that the reconstructions of science in law's terms lead to 'appropriate' decisions. Cognition provides the material that is compared with law's normative standards. If law understands the legal implications of that material sufficiently, its decision as final arbiter will be legally secure and there will be no destabilization of law's processes by other systems.

Luhmann clarifies the seeming mystery of meaning attached to normative closure and cognitive openness which, when properly appreciated, should deter any skewed interpretations (1987a: 20). Normative closure concerns its self-continuation in difference to the environment by bestowing normative quality on its elements, while cognitive openness serves to determine whether in the reproduction of these elements certain conditions have been met (ibid: 20). Law therefore compares its response to challenges from issues arising in its environment with expectations emanating from its normativity. In modern society law thus can consider whether its operations remain intact, for instance when pressed for opinions over 'right to life', 'right to die', and other ethical dilemmas.

Case study: normative closure and cognitive openness in issues of death and dying

Preceding parts of this study reveal the vicissitudes in legal decision-making in matters involving science created by structural coupling, potential de-differentiation of function and the need for law to remain cognitively open to its environment. The last of these appears particularly challenging due to a general sensation that law must change according to circumstances surrounding it and difficult decisions with which it is faced in a rapidly changing society. The following analysis of a legal dilemma typical of modernity attempts to capture the essence of the relationship in a real situation of law's normative closure and the way it uses its cognitive openness (ibid). Also it endeavours to show through the particular example whether law truly changes in response to external influence, whether its decisions remain entirely those of law and whether it is able to accommodate issues in its environment without sacrificing its normativity. In view of the exceptional opinions of Capps and Olsen discussed above, this clarification is essential to avoid wrong assumptions concerning law's ability to cope with issues of science in its decisions.

Technology in modernity challenges legal and social norms potently. In the American jurisdiction, issues of death and dying and the ability of medical science to prolong the life of very ill patients quickly transcended scientific fact-finding and medical judgment. Medicine appealed to law for clearer articulation of patients' rights and to redraw the boundaries of responsible and irresponsible medical decisions (Jasanoff 1995: 185-186). As pressure from the onslaught of new cases obliged the legal system to medicalize 'end-of-life' decisions, these becoming too substantial for case-by-case resolution (ibid: 186). Law was made to refer to its foundations to consider the values of autonomy, privacy and dignity in human life, with the institutional duty of the courts identified as safeguarding the patient's rights and interests (ibid: 190).

The autonomy of state law in the United States created different state-by-state solutions that could be compared, so a legal debate was afforded of a kind that could not be reproduced elsewhere. At first conflicting and confusing rules emerged from the different jurisdictions but Jasanoff records that, on balance, the social impacts of life-sustaining technologies were dealt with by the courts in ways that furthered collective norms, and new institutional arrangements were introduced with respect to death and dying (ibid: 202). Between 1976 and 1985 new state statutes giving legal force to advance directives and a number of 'natural death' acts provided a recognized legal means for patients to refuse life-sustaining treatment, though some of them brought problems of interpretation (ibid: 197-198). After the precedents of leading cases were set, courts were able to delegate 'right-to-die' decisions to local ethics committees for micro-management. With state legislation in place courts no longer needed to 'tinker at the frontiers of the common law' (ibid: 203) and judicial decision-making could concentrate instead on resolving ambiguities in state enactments, for which courts institutionally were better adapted (ibid).

Life-altering medical technology challenges that which law's standards can regard as lawful or unlawful. Cognitive exposure to forces in its environment requires law to reconsider how it would regard acts arising from resolution of ethical dilemmas. Traditionally in medicine, withholding treatment from a patient by a physician, even though it might concur with the patient's or relative's wishes, would attract legal penalty. A lay perspective might be that these important matters of humanity and modern medical science are beyond the capacity of law to decide.[50] It then suggests a new social order, one that is closer to human circumstance and experience. It might even be contended that the new rationality in such cases should no longer be that of law but of *ethics*.[51] Those encountering mental difficulty with the concept of legal closure, would hold that law could not remain obdurate in the face of major social upheaval and apparent shifts in morality over the social expectations of medicine. Ethical dilemmas constitute no lesser predicaments for medicine and law. In end-of-life decision-making, law is implored lately not to apply legal penalty to withholding treatment where it is deemed futile. Ostensibly, cognitive open-

---

[50] Remembering that a 'layman', in the context of this thesis, is any person without training or qualification in the law.

[51] Author's emphasis.

ness in this situation asks nothing more than that law should apply its legal norms to events in its environment. However, these events potentiate radical change via the social expectation of law. In removing the penalty from doctors who withhold treatment, from the outside, it can seem as if law's normative standards themselves have been changed. In this instance they have not: law always stays more or less the same but certainly the challenge it faces in modern times exercises its discretion severely.

Outcomes of the end-of-life decision controversy in the United States can be analysed in a number of ways. Total legal closure would disbar advance directives, rendering clinicians and sometimes relatives responsible for death through conscious neglect. At the other extreme, a hypothetically complete legal openness would allocate to law no rôle in deciding whether a death brought about by a patient's or relative's wishes was the result of a responsible decision. It would not be known whether the caring clinician could be held liable, producing a kind of anarchy in which other patients might be placed at risk. Although there might still be contention about its effect on law, a putatively proper analysis would include both legal closure and cognitive openness in which law could rely on its normative reference in remaining cognitively open to events in its environment.

In the exigent circumstances described, a possible conclusion could be that, in giving ground to strong social and moral arguments, some state law in America changed that which its operations *no longer would consider illegal*.[52] In systems theory though, it might give the false illusion of moving end-of-life decisions from one side of a distinction to the other. Such a radical change could be interpreted as a fundamental modification of law's operations and its societal function, a dangerous impression to have. At times when there is pressure on law to concede to adjustment in societal values, it is important that the rôle of law is distinguished. A different analysis would be that this showed accelerated development of legal norms due to pressure of cognitive communications. But law did not abdicate its responsibility totally in this instance, setting up instead mechanisms for delegated decision-making to take account of individual contexts and utilizing the common law to deal with problems of statutory interpretation. For the purist in legal theory, it is not law that changed in this instance but *the law*.[53] The enactment of law then might represent the effect of mere structural coupling through the polity of social and legal interests. Law could maintain its insistence on the rhetoric of absolutism, treating legislation as occasioning only transient changes.

The question now is whether law does or does not change according to the problems with which it has to deal. The situation in the preceding analysis has

---

[52] Author's emphasis. Whether the subtlety of this semantic manœuvre is convincing, rather than the usual recourse to the legal/illegal code, can be decided at another time.

[53] This difficult expression means that law as an institution does not change but its operations—contained in '*the law*'—do. The author offers this distinction only in this special discussion.

already been considered by Luhmann that he interprets in relation to complexity and the rate at which law must change in response to external influences. Asserting that it is always too slow, he issues a typically classic statement that '...the law, despite its accelerated tempo of change, remains by and large the same' (1989: 148).

Cause célèbre: the autonomy and heteronomy of law

Teubner's description of the epistemic trap when law consults science for assistance makes it an inescapable consequence. Whereas Luhmann's conservative and positivist systems theory supports law's autonomy entirely, Teubner's admits to heteronomy in its conclusions. This has not been treated here as a conflict in itself because Luhmann's theory can be admired for its exquisite depiction of the operation of law, even if it seems for the meantime in legal academe as if it cannot be used in real situations. Teubner recognizes the problem in considering action expressed through communications that legal decisions often are heteronomous as law recruits other social systems to its assistance. Escapes from the epistemic trap therefore are desirable, but Teubner's account demonstrates that many routes are obstructed through realization of other consequences (1989: 746-752).

Nevertheless, one possibility holds promise. Throughout this study and particularly in Chapter II it has been made manifest that the ability of science to construct a reality corresponding to the truth is problematic. While it attests attenuation of errors in the scientific method, its normative standards have been found lacking or based on the wrong precepts, so that its guarantees of certainty cannot be accepted. As mentioned earlier, correspondence theories of truth have had to give way to consensus and coherence theories, as Teubner asserts (ibid: 752). Let it be supposed that for the benefit of society and so that decisions under *res judicata* need to be challenged less often, law should retain its autonomy. The condition for this could be that courts would abstain from a material construction of reality and adopt instead 'proceduralization' of the legal solution in which attention is focused on the procedures that dictate the premises, content, and consequences of institutional constructions of social reality (ibid).

There is no single form of proceduralization. It can be applied successfully in regulation where delegation of epistemic authority, responsibility for risk, defining procedures and methods, allocating the burden of proof in evidence and responsibility for error can be distributed among the multiple agencies concerned (ibid: 751-752). Often it is tantamount to law taking a supervisory and indirect role, and this is evident in the two case studies incorporated here, where legislation and the courts make provision for legal acts but law does not necessarily pursue substantive legal decisions in individual instances. It distances itself from decisions but is prepared to intervene where necessary; where it does so it acts autonomously and so preserves its autopoiesis.

In post-adoption contact, law refuses to, or cannot, incorporate social scientific issues into its decisions and diverts the issue of contact away from law into the realm of trust (Smith 2004: 338). Here Smith invokes Luhmann, who says that law could refuse to incorporate certain cognitive questions into its legal/illegal code and refer them instead to science or philosophy (Luhmann 1987b: 340). Centring the security felt by a birth mother in the trust she may have for adoptive parents, family courts avoid making their conduct the subject of legal coercion, instead relying on moral agency and their willingness to engage with others in anticipation that they will act in a beneficial way (ibid: 338). It can be recorded in decisions that making a contact order was deemed unnecessary. If such relationships fail, law can impose its normative expectations and authority on social scientific communications and grant applications for contact orders by birth parents (ibid: 339). Smith comments that law is more comfortable in dealing with broken promises than dealing with contested social scientific evidence about children (ibid: 340). In end-of-life decisions in the United States, law averted the epistemic trap by delegating individual decisions and the conduct of patients, relatives and carers in arrangements respecting patients' wishes concerning dying to local ethical committees and interested groups, even though it was statute that provided the means. Law could then reserve for itself issues of statutory interpretation for which it was better suited (Jasanoff 1995: 203).

THE POSSIBILITY OF OBSERVATION

A rôle for sociology as a privileged observer of society

The proposition of a meta-theory, meta-language or universal authority existing to which to appeal can be made to reconcile the incommensurability of science and law in the legal forum is shown in the present study to be facile. In these circumstances it is natural to seek media of engagement that would support the kind of inquiry able to report on disparate knowledge fields from an external perspective, such engagement aspiring to new insights on the operations of the fields being observed and especially knowledge previously undetected by those fields themselves. Hope is held of revelatory and impartial information that can guide future action. In its traditional rôle, sociology inquires into all fields of social activity in a society composed of individuals, groups, structures and institutions of which those belonging to science and law form part. It gives the appearance of a versatile research medium, non-preferential with respect to the field of activity into which it inquires because of the generality of its ability to investigate social groups and structures of which all are composed—an overarching kind of social science. Research questions in sociology in the context of the present study therefore could be framed around the interplay of individuals, groups, structures and institutions when law is required to produce decisions in matters concerning science, where science forms a critical part or is required to inform the process. Ostensibly, this unique capacity of sociological inquiry would enable comments and conclusions to be drawn about a wide spectrum of social phenomena but examination reveals a number of limitations. These are revealed in the views of a sociologist of law and show a strong relationship to the nature of systems theory and autopoiesis.

Conventionally understood, sociology is the systematic study of individuals in groups or social formations so that its observations can be used to organize socially desirable changes and improvements. An ideal conception of sociology from the point of view of this study would be one of a medium of observation that comprehensively could explore the focus of its attention without becoming involved in its arguments and operations or distracted from its own purpose. This idealization is a reworking of Luhmann's mourning of 'the lack of an adequate sociological theory of law able to take full advantage of an external description, which is not bound to respect the internal [legal] norms, conventions and premises of understanding, while not losing sight of its object' (King and Thornhill 2003: 42).[54] This is regarded by him as accomplished in his reconfiguration of sociology through systems theory in which the unit of analysis becomes not people nor groups but systems, and in turn systems consist not of people or groups of people but communications (King and Thornhill 2003: 2).

The limits of sociological observation

Cotterrell suggests that the findings of sociological study become 'mere sociological data' as gathered according to its precepts and methods. According to that proposition sociology subverts the object of its study, which becomes instead purely sociological construction (1995: 62-63). On its face, that surprising presumption would de-legitimise the entire sociological enterprise, so it is impossible to proceed without clarifying Cotterrell's intention. Elucidation is available through Cotterrell's conception of an active sociology. He envisages a more incisive rôle for it in his study of law and sociology than expressed by the previously benign requirement for a passive observer. Submitting a description of sociology as a general science of social life he positions the knowledge claims of other fields of activity within the subject matter of *sociology itself* [55] so that power relationships and structures can be examined. 'Sociology builds itself a necessarily subversive or revisionist attitude to the knowledge claims of other disciplines' (Cotterrell 1992: 16-17; 1995: 63). This finds a place for sociology not merely as observer but as analyst, critic and transformer. At the same time it challenges the assumptions and conclusions of the body of knowledge it observes, making the 'subverted or revised knowledge claims' part of its own existence. It is another way of saying that sociology can become a surrogate for a necessary understanding that the systems observed do not appreciate.

---

54 Taken from King and Thornhill's unpublished translation of Luhmann (1993) *Das Recht der Gesellschaft*, Frankfurt am Main: Suhrkamp, p. 14.
55 Author's emphasis.

The previous analysis is not due to systems theory but resonates with it strikingly. Systems theory would regard sociology as one of society's autopoeitic subsystems able to observe the inputs and outputs of other systems in its environment but blind to their internal operations. Following Luhmann's construal, each autopoietic system can only construct its own meaning of a system it observes in its environment and Cotterrell's characterization reproduces this at least in outline. Sociology becomes a construction of its own observation. The sociological route to a possible mediation of the difficulties of science and law would seem barred in keeping with the general account of social systems theory that permits little dynamism between subsystems, but encouragement is found for seeking a rôle for sociology through evidence of successful interpretations that re-conceive observation. Luhmann shows this can be achieved in his treatment of the sociology of risk, the rationality of which will be explored soon. In progressing the study, sociology therefore will continue to be interpreted via Luhmann's theory of systems. Within the triad of categories framing this study (see Chapter I: p. 5), the systems approach conforms thematically to the epistemological heading through knowledge embedded in communications.

The pursuit of a rôle for sociology sometimes can be difficult. King and Thornhill provide an encapsulation that appears at the same time to consign the capacity of sociology to minor significance and conceal its considerable potential. 'All that is possible for sociology is to describe and analyse how communications are organized functionally within social systems' (2003: 211). Certainly this accords with the doctrine of systems theory but appears to be acceptance of the *status quo*. What this research should seek are means to discover the potential for resolution of science-law problems, by taking clues given by Luhmann in his own application of it to social systems, and generating hypotheses from them that will create frameworks for examination.

The accommodation of sociology within systems theory

Through autopoiesis, sociology should be no more immune from the doctrine of systems theory than any other system but it is difficult to indicate the distinctions of its operations. Certain and obvious, perhaps trivial, would be the distinction social/non-social, that is to say it can distinguish social encounters from the non-social, like those of the natural sciences, such as physics and chemistry. It would permit observation of economics, for example, which, though displaying characteristics of a science, nonetheless rely on human judgment and action in its productions. But that is not a sufficient distinction. In sociology, in its traditional guise, the distinction society/state also would be among those valid but would arise from a particular focus of its inquiries. Uniquely, its *modus operandi* is observation of other systems and, though again obvious, indicated would be the distinction observable/non-observable that, coincidentally in Luhmann's terms, subsists not in people or groups but communications. This proposition has the satisfying appeal of completeness but does not move the question of distinctions far from its starting point. In accepting the conservatism of autopoiesis, countenancing a social subsystem with unclear parameters for its own first-order observation is unsettling. In Luhmannian terms it would be as if asking 'what are the operations of sociology that give meaning to its communications in society?' and 'is sociology not reflexive?' and not being able to answer.[56] It would be absurd to impute that it has no internal operations of its own but, because of its methods, sociology appears resolutely as an interstitial medium that takes its distinctions from the fields it observes. For example, in Luhmann's conception it is able competently to observe risk—environmental, health, economic, business, research and others—via the distinction risk/danger. Luhmann defines risk as 'loss which social processes attribute to decisions' and danger as arising in cases where 'future losses are not seen at all as the consequences of a decision that has been made but are attributable to an external factor' (Luhmann 2005: 101-102).[57] Risk is available for wide study by accommodating a plurality of distinctions (ibid: 16). Rather than a distinction through first-order observation as either 'negative' or 'positive' (risk/security), risk is constructed as a phenomenon of multiple contingency offering different observers different perspectives (ibid).

Such perspectives are those of the domains with which sociology is concerned that in turn indicate its distinctions. 'For autopoietic sociologists, social communications are explained in terms of the identity, function and code of the system which generated them' (King and Thornhill 2003: 224). Luhmann's aims for sociology are then well-met in that it can enjoy an abundance of opportunities for second-order observation. In the present study, sociology therefore emerges well from this assessment. Not only is its fundamental capacity undisturbed in systems theory but its rôle as observer of others is confirmed and strengthened.

Now it must be discovered whether in this revised perception of sociology a framework for examining mediative resources can be offered. Luhmann's clarificatory prescription for indicating distinctions that confers on sociology its ability to perform second-order observation of other domains is promising inasmuch as this is precisely what is required to examine science-law difficulties. A sociology of interactions would not advance knowledge greatly since, in social systems, it would belong to the stratum of societies, organizations and interactions, a level of operation examined previously where procedures, professionals and institutions merely concretise the incommensurability problem and through which remedies at best can be only incremental. The heart of the matter is the inconsistency among law's conclusions where it takes in matters of science. Avoiding further circumlocution, sociology essentially would be required to observe the functioning of the epistemic trap for law. 'Law

---

[56] But compare Luhmann (1995: 432): 'Sociology, too, operates as a self-referential system'.

[57] See Luhmann (2005: 18-28) and King and Thornhill (2003: 184-186), for lucid discussions on the advantages of choosing the distinction risk/danger over the normally perceived risk/security.

is forced to produce an autonomous legal reality and cannot at the same time immunize itself against conflicting realities produced by other discourses in society' (Teubner 1989: 745). The distinction of legal/illegal in law's operations that an autopoietic sociologist of law would indicate and the second-order observation of how that is observed and, likewise, the true/false distinction of science, together enshrine the epistemological difficulty encountered in the legal forum that obstructs reconciliation. Even observing how those distinctions are observed adds little to the usefulness of knowledge for the purpose of the present work: it simply reconstructs the origin of the known difficulty. Secondary observation by a system can be of only one system. Each system we need to examine must be separately observed. Apart from some commonality in what it means to observe, no new information can be discovered about either system. Required in the current context is observation of the relationship of science and law in legal decision-making.

A sociology of law's epistemic trap

Imagined in a scheme of observing the epistemic trap, these disparate distinctions would not be brought into play but instead would be concerned with law's oscillation between autonomous and heteronomous conclusions.[58] These belong to areas of concern for the proper operation of law when stressed by other discourses. Indicating the distinction autonomy/heteronomy in legal decision-making would overtake the divisive indications of fact and legality in the systems of science and law respectively.

A systems-oriented sociology of legal decision-making under conditions of science-law tension would observe observation of the distinction. Autonomy is the positive operation of law when concluding entirely on the basis of legal rationality, or when 'working properly', heteronomy its negation when conclusions are contaminated variously by other discourses, such as when 'scientized.' Suggestive of Luhmann's wish for an adequate sociological theory, observations of the theories, concepts and beliefs used to understand events, attribute causes and make predictions would pertain to how conclusions are reached in science-law debates that sometimes are constitutive of imperfect legal truths. This signifies observation of the way the epistemic trap is sprung.

EXCURSUS: TRANSFORMABLE LAW; TRANSFORMATIVE LAW. FRESH DEBATES ON LAW'S REGULATORY RÔLE

In this work, stress is given to the understanding that science has of its own productions, the consequent representation it makes to law and the meaning of science that law takes for itself in reaching its conclusions. The misunderstandings that can occur in each of these areas of cognition have the

---

[58] See Teubner (1989: 730).

potential to affect legal outcomes. A decision was taken in the present study to confine itself to this, the 'representation of science' argument, and for now to resist the implicit 'obverse' examination of what it is about law that makes such misunderstandings possible. It ordains a simpler methodology, presages clarity and leaves the opportunity for the implied complementary thesis for another time or to another author.

The present work is charged with exploration of resources that engage with the central problem. Because of the previous explanation and contentions for the special rôle of reflexive law, this is now to form part of that interest. Importantly for the discussion, by contextualizing its study in legal evolution, disappointments with the social effects of successive paradigms of law have been revealed. Examination of the subject reveals that reflexive law manifests as a means of *relieving such disappointment*.[59] How it might achieve that is germane to the incommensurability problem and thus it emerges as a resource for consideration. This is indicated both by the literature and the author's experience.[60]

The nature of a possible reflexive law is considered generally in two related ways as a helpful resource. Either it would need to be a form of law capable of adaptation that could more readily accommodate the productions of science within its ambit—a transformable law,[61] or one that could create a forum, at least conceptually, that could influence the way in which science and law understand themselves and respond to each other in regulation—a transformative law.[62] These two categorizations will be prosecuted in the following account, in order to conserve the essence of legal development that could be responsible for a better understanding between science and law.

The metamorphoses of law intimated here are considered in two main ways. Some accounts are evolutionary, sociological and historiographical—the effect of changing society, developments of law already undertaken and surpassed and the employment of history in rendering the account. Others are ideological and radical—belonging to systems theory and showing resistance to adaptation on the same terms. In the following, there are arguments supporting and denying the possibility of transformable and transformative law in turn. Effort will be made in the following description to distinguish between evolutionary and ideological accounts. Whereas the evolutionary-sociological-historiographical version can demonstrate a basis for transformable and transformative law without incurring onerous theoretical objections, the ideological-radical version has no equivalent. It must appeal to the strictures of its own radical being for opportunities as transformable or transformative law. Though

---

[59] Author's emphasis.

[60] Reflexive law as an aspect of responsive regulation was described in the Option Module *Conflict, Risk and Resolution* in the course leading to an LLM degree in Dispute Prevention and Resolution at the School of Law, University of Westminster 2000/2001.

[61] One that adapts itself to its social environment.

[62] Ultimately, law that can effect change in other social systems via regulation.

prohibited in Luhmann's strict prescription, such petitions are by no means unheard if the reasoning of Teubner, Willke, Paterson and others are acknowledged. The ensuing description is aimed at sufficiency for evaluation of transformable and transformative law in relation to the central problem of this study, but no more than this. The evaluation proceeds via a condensed review.

Arguments for the premise of reflexive law

The catalyst for debate over the need for and possibility of a new type of social law is provided through the exigencies of three socio-legal perspectives. The debate is depicted here as residing in the disappointments of legal development for modern society. The first relies on an evolutionary legal, sociological and historiographical standpoint that enunciates the crisis of formal law, deplores the bureaucratization of social life, the materialization of law and the inception of the interventionist state. The second articulates the need through social, democratic and technocratic viewpoints for a social or responsive law and studies the changes of which law might be capable. Thirdly, there is a passionate debate between the ideological insights of systems theory and the more liberal perception of social systems over whether reflexive law is a possibility, spurred by a self-conscious compulsion among some socio-legal scholars to 'find Luhmann's theory useful'.

OVERCOMING DISAPPOINTMENTS IN LEGAL DEVELOPMENT

A. THE POSSIBILITY OF TRANSFORMABLE LAW

Evolution of law: a resource for legal study

Evolution of law commands attention in its own right as an informative source for studying legal development and explicating present controversies in law. It is empirical in that it is described by the archive, but no advances in any theory are detected here. Nonetheless, consideration of reflexive law in this *excursus* depends on an account of legal development situated in society and the changes it has undergone in the last two centuries. The description was of an iterative, open-ended process, the pace of which accelerated with social change but in which problems for legal theory and doctrine multiplied, rather than diminished.

Some of the principled objections to reflexive law present exquisite challenges to legal theory. In the evolutionary account, reflexive law emerges as a progression from previous forms of law and their limitations in coping with social advances.[63] It shows the decline of many features of the formal law paradigm and the adoption of substantive forms of regulation. It reaches the possibility of reflexive law in the present day that, again, is the source of dilemma. Teubner (1998) recognizes this evolutionary description but, crucially, he contextualizes his arguments for reflexive forms of law in the fault of what he calls the juridification of social spheres (Teubner 1985a: 3-9), a modern effect that, at this early stage of the discussion, can be characterized simply as bureaucratization of the social world (ibid: 389). In rendering this entire scenario as a struggle with an historical basis, he compares the effects of these evolving paradigms of law.

Legal paradigms and their societal effects: formal, substantive and instrumental

Sources abound that may be consulted for a detailed history of legal development and description here will be restricted to that necessary to structure the debate.[64] With the formal rationality of law, the legal system creates and applies a universal body of rules. It relies on a body of legal professionals who employ peculiarly legal reasoning to resolve specific conflicts. This model of law was the basis of classical civil law in the nineteenth century. In a liberal attitude to society's affairs, governments relied on the contractual basis of private relationships and maintained a policy of non-interference, the so-called 'invisible hand' mechanism (Teubner 1983: 254).

Modern theories of an evolutionary approach to law are united by the common theme of the crisis of formal rationality (ibid: 242).[65] Substantively rational law is law seen instead as instrumental for purposive, goal-oriented intervention (ibid: 240), developing in the context of the social state (Teubner 1998: 403). Instead of delimiting spheres for autonomous private action (ibid: 397), the law directly regulates social behaviour by defining substantive prescriptions (Teubner 1983: 254). From the current political instrumentation of law, geared to the political intervention requirements of the modern welfare state, emerges a new social function. Law is orientated towards material

---

[63] An account of legal development that supports this part of the present study is given by Jürgen Habermas and contextualized partly in social history, in Habermas (1996) Chapter 9: 'Paradigms of Law', 388-446.

[64] For instance, see Reiner, R (2002) 'Classical Social Theory and Law' in Penner, J, Schiff, D and Nobles, R (eds), *Introduction To Jurisprudence and Legal Theory* (2002), pp. 255-258.

For a history of development of law from the 19th century liberal to the welfare state that is relevant to the present study, see also Paterson, J (2006) 'Reflecting on Reflexive Law' in King, M and Thornhill, C (eds), *Luhmann on Law and Politics* (2006), pp. 20-21.

[65] Weber's categorization of types of law is used as the basis of description in many accounts of legal development. See Weber (1978).

outcomes, hence the process understood as the materialization of law[66] (Teubner 1998: 401).[67] Material law is designed to produce social effects (ibid: 405) and legitimates itself by the social results it achieves through regulation (ibid: 402). The re-materialization of law is an inherent part of the programme of the welfare-regulatory state (Teubner 1993: 240) and Teubner asserts that the juridification of the social world is described by the relation between law's structures and functions and this emergence (1998: 397f). The juridification process should be analysed in terms of the specific conditions of the modern social state as the interventionist state, in which the wider historical context of juridification becomes clear (ibid: 397). It signifies a development in which the interventionist social state produces a new type of law—regulatory law (ibid: 405). Characterized by material rather than formal rationality, it is geared to the guidance requirements of the social state. (ibid: 399, 405).

Teubner contends that such strategic models of law represent 'internal models' of law in society, their main function being to use the self-identity of law to produce criteria for its own transformation...the ability of legal theory to produce normative criteria for a conscious self-transformation of the law (1985b: 303). This goes to the heart of any attempt at transformable law.

Teubner's narrative of the evolution of law and its effects continues with an account of the shortcomings of the substantive paradigms of law. As a control mechanism for the welfare state that is aimed at producing social effects, law can resort to modes of functioning, criteria of rationality and forms of organization inappropriate to the 'lifeworld' structures of the regulated social areas. (ibid: 389). He locates this principally in Habermas's perception of responsibility for the destruction of intact social structures, which is that the benefits of social modernization are sacrificed by subjugation to the logic of the system (ibid: 389).[68] Paterson comments that democracy demands that societal norms must emerge from open and inclusive processes but, in modern techno-cratic society, such norms are based on expertise (2003: 530).

The problems for law and modern society do not end there. In Teubner's estimation, further mutually detrimental effects emerge. Politics can fail to achieve the relevance criteria of law and modern legislative decisions are inadequate for litigation, so that political guidance of law produces an over-abundance of legislatory signals of direction that 'no longer appear on the internal screen of the legal system: they vanish without trace' (Teubner 1998: 409). This is a problem of mutual indifference between politics and law. While social security advances the condition of the underprivileged, bureaucracy and payment of legal benefits impair their social status, self-image and relations

---

[66] That is, to produce *material* results, not that law 'materializes'. A confusing term at first.

[67] Weber refers to this as the re-materialization of formal law. See ibid: 333ff.

[68] This is a reference to 'colonization of the life-world' in Habermas's estimation, which is described in Chapter V of this book in respect of 'expert cultures'.

with their social environment.[69] The corollary is social disintegration through law. In the juridification of society, the internal structures of law are appropriated by the autonomous logic of the regulated areas of social life that law cannot evade, giving rise to legal disintegration through society. These (emphasized) experiences that exist on the frontiers of law, bordering politics and areas of social life, constitute Teubner's regulatory trilemma (ibid: 406-414).

A socially responsive law

A socially responsive type of law [70] should be considered as an offered means of overcoming the disappointments of earlier paradigms, but the consequences of a possible damaging of law's autonomy or integrity should be held firmly in view. The idea would take law away from its exclusively prescriptive rôle towards Pound's concept of a 'sociological jurisprudence' aimed at enabling legal institutions 'to take more complete and intelligent account of the social facts upon which law must proceed and to which it is applied' (Nonet and Selznick 1978/2001: 73).[71] Proposals for the way in which this can be achieved without sacrificing law's important tenets follow.

Predominant rule orientation, or formal law, is being increasingly overlaid by an instrumental orientation. In Selznick's perspective, 'sovereignty of purpose' is visualized as the main feature of a responsive law, which can only develop in the context of the social state (ibid: 78). In their prescription for a purposive law, Nonet and Selznick perceive that a responsive institution would preserve matters essential to its integrity, while acknowledging new forces in its environment. Such law would not perceive social pressures as threats, but rather as sources of knowledge and opportunities for self-amendment (ibid: 77). It would assume that purpose could be made sufficiently objective and authoritative, so as to control adaptive rule-making (ibid).

Herein lays cause for the kind of concern articulated at the head of this section. Nonet and Selznick show their awareness of it. In conjecturing such a more purposive and open legal order, they declare that advocates of responsive law opt for a high-risk perspective, as opposed to those adhering to autonomous law with its low-risk perspective towards institutions and received authority (ibid: 77-78). The high-risk option would confirm all the worst fears for the autonomy of law and the basis of judgment, but the issue is retrieved in

---

[69] Again, this is described by Habermas and a selection of his material can be found in the bibliography accompanying this thesis.

[70] Though 'responsive law' is a category of law proposed by Nonet and Selznick (1978/2001; see also Teubner (1983)), the term is used here to depict generally a form of law that is responsive to its social surroundings and their requirements. Reflexive law, then, is treated here as a type of responsive law with specific characterizations. Nonet and Selznick's intention for responsive law is as purposive and instrumental, which Teubner says stimulates a different discussion.

[71] Nonet and Selznick (1978/2001), citing Pound, R (1959) Part I, Chapter 6 'Sociological Jurisprudence'.

the following vital amplification. Responsive law searches for *implicit values* in rules and policies. As these are articulated, they offer *authoritative criteria for criticizing existing rules, generating new rules and guiding the extension of due process (of autonomous law) to new institutional settings* (ibid: 79).[72] As seen elsewhere in this research, resources are to be found in evaluative concepts like these, rather than through scrutiny of form, substance or process.

The extent to which responsiveness occurs in real situations, and upon which modern socially-oriented law increasingly is asked to embark, is revealed in a number of illustrations. Perhaps it is not really so recent a phenomenon or has gone unrecognized. In the following description, responsiveness is depicted both positively and negatively. It demonstrates that new standards are necessary if law is to survive without abdicating its rôle.

ILLUSTRATIONS OF RESPONSIVE RATIONALITY

'Generalization of purpose' is cited as a key source of flexibility in modern organizations where, for example, a university moves towards responsiveness when learning to distinguish the requirements of higher education from its assumed traditions and routines of teaching (ibid: 79-80).

In the interpretation of rules, legal norms, such as liability for negligence, only set a standard and leave much room for autonomous judgment in deciding how to comply (ibid: 88). A special case from the present study can be included here. In the Bolam Test of medical negligence, a matter of case law cited frequently in this work,[73] the duty of care is decided by law and usually is uncomplicated, but in the standard of care, doctors are called to advise the court on matters of acceptable medical practice. By this reckoning, law can be construed as responsive, firstly, in that it recognizes extra-legal issues that must be taken into account in deciding the outcome; secondly, that *Bolam* simply sets the standard by which negligence should be judged.[74] The court decides with the help of doctors whether there has been compliance.[75]

With the need for increasing legal discrimination in criminal law, it is pressed to look beyond the punishable acts in which it is competent to judge, to contexts that imply the erosion of rules. This incurs a multiplicity of justifications, growth of the complex doctrine of responsibility and the corollary risk of excessive reliance on psychiatric and social scientific expertise (ibid: 89).

The way for representation of social interests is opened in class actions in torts for defective medical products (ibid: 97).

---

[72] Emphases in the preceding text are the present author's.

[73] *Bolam v Friern Hospital Management Committee* [1957] 1 WLR 582.

[74] It asks only for the opinion of a responsible body of medical opinion to represent such a standard.

[75] See the main discussion of *Bolam* in Chapter IV and its occasional mention at different points in this work.

Enlarging the scope of legal inquiry to include new constituencies brings added energy to legal institutions, in that the strength of industrial interests is balanced when a policy of environmental protection is vigorised by the ability of regulatory agencies to rely on pro-ecological constituencies to generate complaints or mobilize interests. Regulation then becomes more 'self-administering', less dependent on imposed official prescriptions (ibid: 97-98).

PRESERVATION OF VALUES IN RESPONSIVE LAW

In responsive law, there is no derogation from the 'master ideal' of legality on which autonomous law stands, but it is conceived more generally to be cured of its formalism. That achievement requires institutions that are competent as well as legitimate. If there is a paradigmatic function of responsive law, it is distinguished as *regulation*, not *adjudication* (ibid: 108), which places it firmly within the purview of the present study.[76] Also, it is characterized as clarifying the public interest and portrays law as a problem-solving, facilitative enterprise (ibid: 108). Surely, these new perspectives do not constitute a reduced rôle for law or a threat to its integrity but an improved, more understanding, socially relevant function?

B. THE POSSIBILITY OF TRANSFORMATIVE LAW

METHODOLOGICAL NOTE

Explanations in the remainder of the *excursus* will be by reference predominantly to systems theory. Initially, this is for methodological adequacy, given that the nature of incommensurability already has been examined from this perspective. It would be instructive to discover by this route whether reflexive law offers a potential for its resolution. More importantly, Teubner and Paterson, sometimes with differences in approach, consider the possibility of reflexive law within this framework and examine ways in which Luhmann's seminal theory of systems can permit or prevent it.[77] For the purposes of the present study too, systems theory purifies issues and elucidates brilliantly the conditions under which a transformative type of law could be conceived. The correspondence between the postulate of a transformative law and systems theory caused by the notion of reflexive law stimulating reflexivity in other systems is not by chance. It is seen as the only way in which Teubner and Paterson can conceive its success, given the strictures of Luhmann. Cross-talk between the ideas of transformable and transformative law ideas can occur, though. For instance, in order for law to be transformable, it needs to be able to

---

[76] Emphases are the author's.

[77] These authors have published both separately and together on topics that impinge on the issue of reflexive law. See, for instance, Paterson, J and Teubner, G (1998) 'Changing Maps: Empirical Legal Autopoiesis', 7 *Social and Legal Studies* (4): 451-486.

learn from its social conditions; to be transformative, it uses this learning to understand the reflexivity of other systems.

The chief application of reflexive law in the present study is to regulatory law. It is because the area of regulatory law commonly includes several systems that interact with law in their operations, be they politics, economics, science or others. In such study might be found ways in which reflexive law can communicate meaningfully in resolving problems of incommensurability.

Evaluation of the new paradigm: identification of standards in reflexive law

EVOLUTIONARY PERSPECTIVES (REVISITED)

In systems theory, the evolution of law is characterized more particularly via Luhmann's conception as situated in a transition from a stratified to a functionally differentiated society (Teubner 1983: 244). Both positive and substantive forms of law were thought inadequate to deal with its complexities (ibid: 244). In considering the development of law, there was a need for higher abstraction and functionalist thought and understanding of the place of self-reflexion[78] of the legal system (ibid). In current legal theory, there is a contention that this aspiration could be fulfilled by reflexive law, with its obedience to a logic of procedural legitimation (ibid: 270). In considering the appropriate direction for law in contemporary conditions, Paterson reminds us of the Weberian categorization of law and the ensuing evolutionary changes, as depicted here previously, in which he situates the development of reflexive law (2006: 20-21).[79] The Luhmannian and Weberian accounts are not incompatible, because each offers its own historical perspective of the same events, one through examination of society and the other through the evolution of law in society. For explanation of reflexive law via systems theory though, it is important to view events via the perspective of functional differentiation.

SOCIAL KNOWLEDGE, LEARNING AND SOCIALLY ADEQUATE COMPLEXITY

In considering substantive, materialized law as instrumental and a means of social guidance, this model aims to have influence outside its own operations. For this it needs to gain social knowledge (Teubner 1998: 404). The requirement for law to begin making reference to systems in its environment therefore is heralded and it is intimated that it should learn how to learn from them.

---

[78] 'Reflexion' = 'reflection'. Some authors use one spelling and some the other. It is assumed there is no semantic difference between the two.

[79] For a detailed account of the inadequacies of autonomous (positive) law in a highly differentiated society and the disappointment with substantive legal rationality, see Teubner (1983), especially the discussion at 270-273.

Positive law hinders the emergence of a socially adequate learning law but, in the operative dimension, 'proceduralization is offered as a formula for the rôle of law in protecting and setting up of 'social systems with a learning capacity' (Teubner 1985b: 307). What is missing, according to Luhmann, '...is a conceptual system oriented towards social policy which would permit one to compare the consequences of different solutions to problems, to accumulate critical experience, to compare critical experiences from different fields, in short: to learn' (Teubner 1983: 264).[80] In such claims are represented Luhmann's fundamental objections to the possibility of reflexive law, but Teubner and Paterson find it is not so fixed. As the discussion unfolds, the theoretical basis of the way in which they perceive reflexive law to be possible will be seen. The legal order in post-modern societies must have mechanisms that allow it to operate in a complex environment of functionally differentiated, semi-autonomous systems, for which it needs to be socially adequately organized (Bechmann 1992: 426). A post-modern legal order must be orientated toward self-reflective processes within different social subsystems (Teubner 1983: 246).

LAW AND ITS ENVIRONMENT: REFLEXIVITY MEDIATING AUTOPOIESIS?

The positivity of law that emerges from the account of formal law is of no avail in producing the transformations required for responsive law, and in fact precludes them (Bechmann 1992: 423). Autopoietic theory also curtails this capacity absolutely. Positivity not only implies that law cannot be reduced to applicability theories, conventions or responsible decisions (ibid). Within the framework of a general theory of autopoiesis, positivity of law indicates recursive self-reference to the unity of the legal system (ibid). With regard to closure, autopoietic systems cannot draw from their environment the requirements for their own self-reproduction as an entity (ibid). However, autopoietic systems are '...likewise open systems in that they may only execute this self-reproduction within an environment', (ibid) indicating that, for law (or any system), the environment is indispensable. Law therefore is seen as one functioning entity among many within the *unity of the social system*. Law in fact requires there to be an environment for the act of distinguishing it to be possible. In systems theory, it owes its identity to that. In such a sense, there is an implied relationship with the environment. If a transformative kind of law is feasible, the possibility and manner of its relationship to systems that it must influence must be discovered. This is not straightforward.

Teubner sees it through almost a duality with which he characterizes autopoietic systems, and he capitalizes on a capacity that he thinks arises from self-reference. This and similar development of ideas mark his difference with the ideological prescription of Luhmann. The choice for the student lies between a classicist conviction that autopoietic theory is immutable, reflexive law there-

---

80 Citing Luhmann (1970) 'Evolution des Rechts', 3 *Rechtstheorie* 1.

fore being infeasible, and persuasion by the intuitively appealing arguments of Teubner, rooted in legal experience, which assert the contrary. 'Self-referential systems, being closed systems of self-reproducing interactions, are at the same time necessarily open systems with boundary trespassing processes...the linkage between internalising self-referential mechanisms and externalising exchange mechanisms make the concept of self-reference fruitful and complex' (Teubner 1985b: 309). This reiterates and reinforces the need to identify the concrete mechanisms of self-referential closure and openness, and the linkage between them (ibid: 314). Self-referentiality is always in danger of self-closure and self-referential systems need outside support to develop certain externalizations (ibid: 316).[81]

PROCEDURALIZATION AND SELF-REFLEXION

In describing the shift in law since the nineteenth century from formalism to that of social practice, Wiethölter (1985: 225) observes that legal programmes increasingly have been oriented towards proceduralization. This is aimed at neither social guarantees, as in rights to freedom, nor at provisions, as in political administration, but at *the conditions for the existence of such guarantees and provisions.*[82] In understanding what these conditions are in relation to their own self-referentiality, Wiethölter characterizes such systems as 'reflexive' learning systems (ibid: 226). Teubner describes proceduralization as representing society's response to the needs of self-referentiality, which are autonomy, externalisation and coordination (Teubner 1985b: 310), under which the legal system concerns itself with providing the structural premises for self-regulation within other social systems (Teubner 1983: 274). This not only guarantees the autonomy of other social subsystems but also Habermas's concept of the democratization of social subsystems, which, with its stress on procedural legitimation, shows the direction in which reflexive law can develop (ibid: 274-275). By 'proceduralization of the law' may be understood the transformation of a social context of legal freedoms (linked without rule-exception, interest reconciliation and decision-making patterns) into a system of justification of the respective new contexts of 'ideas' and 'interests'.[83] Such new creations—as stable change in permanence—are compelled by the state of socialization (Wiethölter 1985: 246).

The concept is that of a sort of forum, before which negotiations on transformations of society go on reconstructively and prospectively (ibid: 247). Proceduralization fosters mechanisms that systematically further the development of reflexion structures within other social subsystems (Teubner 1983:

---

[81] For example, political and economic systems can operate too selectively and neglect problems of their social environment.

[82] Author's emphasis.

[83] See also Habermas (1997), Chapter 9, Sec 9.3: 'Crisis Theories and the Proceduralist Paradigm of Law', 427-436.

275f). The law is relieved of direct regulation of social areas and instead tasked with legal regulation of self-regulatory processes (Teubner 1985a: 8; 1998: 420).

REGULATION OF INTER-SYSTEM CONFLICTS

Reflexive law is imagined to deal with inter-system conflict, but its problems are accentuated through autopoietic concepts. If there were no parallax in perception of reality between systems and no closure due to intra-system self-reference, the requirement for responsive forms of law would not exist. But the idea of a regulatory mechanism to perform such a function is important to the present study, and the manner in which it might carry out its operations interesting. Some kind of inter-system adjudication might provide the key to incommensurability problems.

A concept of a legal programme has been developed by Willke, aimed at the regulation of inter-system conflicts through a specific 'procedural regulation', called the 'relational programme' (Teubner 1985b: 319). Programmes concentrate not on the internal relations within each system but on the interrelation between them. For instance, though law cannot intervene directly into the economy, legal access subsists in *the relation between law and economy*. Relational programmes regulate internal processes only indirectly by concentrating on the relations between systems. In the interaction of law, politics and economics, the requirement for law's cognitive capacity (to understand each system) is reduced. No longer is an attempt made to influence economic action but only 'concerted action', whose internal structure is much more transparent (ibid: 320). Sounding initially like structural coupling, relational programmes perform a weak, though interesting function. If they were to constitute a 'grand jury' to which appeals could be made in resolving inter-system problems, then relational programmes would be hailed as very useful. However, their influence would be indirect, dealing only with relationships, and not approaching the nub of conflicts, for which they would be incompetent.

INTERMEDIATE ASSESSMENT: THE ACCOMPLISHMENTS OF REFLEXIVE LAW

Reflexive law is described as a new means of control for other social systems that solves the problems of both formal and regulatory law (Bechmann 1992: 423). Reflexive rationality involves the stimulation of changes in social subsystems by influencing them to institutionalize environmentally appropriate reflection processes (Teubner 1998: 428). More adequately, 'control thus proves to be a combination of the self-reflexion of the system and of reflexion of self-reflection of other systems' (Bechmann 1992: 422),[84] but it restricts legal performance to more indirect, more abstract forms of social control (Teubner 1998: 274). So, what is the value of encouraging reflexivity in other systems

---

[84] Citing Luhmann (1992b).

and what effect is it likely to produce? The decisive point for Teubner and Willke is structural correspondence of legal standards and of social situations requiring regulation, but Bechmann claims 'this is what regulatory law already did' (1992: 424). He develops themes that are more successful by locating the problem for society in ensuring common order in increasing functional differentiation or, as he portrays it, unity that still is required in conditions of diversity. Teubner and Willke say it is by reflexion (ibid: 425-426). Reflexion takes the place of social integration mechanisms, especially if subsystems develop conflicting orientations (ibid: 426). It mediates between the functional perspectives of the system and its contribution to other systems. By 'learning' to attune its self-selectivity to those of other systems, it contributes toward the production of the unity of society by making it compatible with their own set of rules (ibid: 426). By development of reflexive structures, the legal system brings itself into a position where it is socially adequately organized (ibid: 426).

IDEALISTIC, REALISTIC OR UNSETTLED? THE TANGIBILITY OF REFLEXIVE LAW AS A CHOICE BETWEEN RIVAL ARGUMENTS

In legal academia, reflexive law has both its protagonists and antagonists. Since the possibility of its reality and operations is restricted so far to theoretical discussions, a thorny dilemma is precipitated by contrasting views. It crystallizes via systems theory but this provides the best means of testing the concept. The question of the possibility of reflexive law within the constraints of systems theory is answered differently by its supporters and detractors, leaving belief in it for the inquirer or observer to be a matter of choice. Arguments on both sides are compelling and the researcher is obliged to evaluate them. They are not schismatic or polarized, though the debate often is fervent, but the result of different theoretical perceptions of the problem. In the sociological language uncovered during the research for this thesis, an intellectual space has been opened up by healthy discussion and for trialling the themes that deep consideration affords. It has been stimulating to observe these debates. It is interesting to reflect that the present researcher may have witnessed the naissance of an innovation in legal development. Although still the product of evolution, this emerging paradigm will have been developed consciously and intelligently to overcome the limitations of its predecessors. Unlike them though, its precepts should be shaped other than by pure circumstance, the result of social change or political interference.

CONDITIONS FOR REFLEXIVE LAW TO OPERATE

The issues are put succinctly by Paterson in *Reflecting on Reflexive Law* (2006) and importantly revolve around whether reflexive law can be consistent with autopoiesis. A crucial question over reflexive law is whether it is capable of steering other systems.[85] Translated into concrete situations, this tests whether some form of social engineering is possible. Teubner and Paterson consider that it is, while Luhmann asserts the opposite. 'This is no throw of the dice: if Luhmann is right, then reflexive law proceeds from false premises' (ibid: 15).[86]

The social requirement of a new paradigm of law would need to be consistent with that pertaining to law generally, namely of stabilizing normative expectations over time (ibid: 14). Within the compass of systems theory, such law would need to maintain its deparadoxifying strategies (ibid: 22, 33)[87] and operate within the constraints of structural coupling (ibid: 22). For reflexive law, it would require an orientation of law that was aware of the double contingency of the situation it finds itself in (ibid: 22).[88] Programmes define what is 'correctly' legal and 'incorrectly' legal (ibid: 18).

ARGUMENTS ON THE PREMISE OF A THEORY OF REFLEXIVE LAW

In the turbulent debates surrounding reflexive law, it is easy to lose sight of reasons for attempting its prescription. Fascination with its possibility, especially when acknowledging the strictures of systems theory, tends to distract attention from visualizing an overriding purpose. Paterson has exactly the way of it when advising that, through contemplation of reflexive law—and even though he says that outcomes may not be predictable—it might be possible to improve law's performance (King 2006: 42f).[89] Is this not an estimable desire in overcoming not only the disappointments of other paradigms of law but also the problems of understanding that exist between science and law? Optimism for this capability is justifiable, though its reasons need cautious evaluation.[90]

In a very modest claim for the utility of Teubner's reflexive law, Paterson explains that it models science and law as 'discrete communication systems' (2003: 537). This is plain enough in systems theory but it 'allows an examina-

---

[85] For discussion of the ability of law to steer other systems, see Paterson (1997) and Luhmann (1997).

[86] Adopting a Habermasian perspective here, the sense of 'right' or 'wrong' in theoretical discussion proceeds from the willingness of those engaged to be persuaded by the better argument. Only time will tell whether a particular argument achieves consensus. When that happens, the argument will be socially accepted as 'right'.

[87] The paradox produced by autopoiesis was described earlier and arises from law's legal/illegal code. Paterson asserts that law conceals its paradox so that it appears its operations are not in fact based on self-reference (2006: 18).

Deparadoxification also is explained usefully in Luhmann, N (1988); and see Luhmann, N (1992b).

[88] Double contingency is explained very cogently in King, M and Schütz, A (1994) at p. 272.

[89] In a critique of Paterson's chapter in the same work: 'Reflecting on Reflexive Law'.

[90] The whole of Chapter 2 in the above work (King and Thornhill (2006)) is devoted to discussion of arguments for and against the possibility and use of reflexive law, chiefly through the works of Teubner and Paterson.

tion of how each reconstructs the other and offers scope for a more adequately complex account of the generation of knowledge and of norms and of the constructive misunderstandings that arise when the two systems communicate' (ibid). By itself, this is helpful enough but the thinking of Teubner and Paterson has advanced beyond that, especially more lately in the interpretations of Paterson. In perceiving law's function in response to risk in society, Paterson drew attention to the task of reflexive law in encouraging reflexivity in other communicative systems, saying that law was not reduced to a passive rôle (ibid: 541).

King observes that Paterson draws for his material in *Reflecting on Reflexive Law* on Teubner's 'highly complex account of how law might understand science' (2006: 43). This is an apt approach for the purpose of the present study, though really the problem is a more general one of how systems in society can improve their understanding of each other. Though King's critique at times is acerbic, it is significant for arguments concerning the premise of a theory of reflexive law that he admits there are instances where Paterson's proposals do not contravene autopoiesis, even though this may have occurred in a manner not envisaged by Luhmann (ibid: 4). This reveals possibilities for scholars to discover ways of developing reflexive law, seemingly denied by autopoiesis, into concrete proposals for a successful and settled model of reflexive law by accommodating its precepts.

Teubner also sees opportunities in Luhmann's account where reflexive law might be possible, in that reflexive law seeks a way of enhancing the structural coupling of law and other subsystems. While perceiving the advantages this would bestow, Paterson warns of the risks of exceeding the boundaries of structural coupling in a concrete programme and thereby re-confronting the regulatory trilemma (ibid: 24). King detects in Luhmann's theory the possibility of a combination of structural coupling and programmes of one system being able to influence the self-steering of another (ibid: 44). Such an achievement, developed to its ultimate extent, would visualize law influencing science to reconsider its normative values and attesting such standards in its communications. Perhaps legal rules for the admissibility of evidence in court already attempt that. Certainly they impose on science its own philosophical (methodological) standards and require assurances in the self-representation of science that, together, constitute criteria for reliability, though these rules are criticised.

The prospect of reflexive law always returns to the theoretical question of the immutability of autopoiesis. The present study frequently refers to the dilemma caused by Teubner's insistence that law can be semi-autonomous (ibid: 30) and that there can be 'degrees of closure' of systems when there is reliance on interference (ibid: 30-31). King remarks on what seems an inconsistency in Teubner's stance that he insists on the radical separateness of social systems and yet wants to bring them into dialogue (see Campbell 2000: 442). As mentioned elsewhere in this work, Teubner appears able to regard social systems as affirmedly autopoietic and simultaneously that legal communication, ergo communication by all systems, is social communication (1989: 745). This acquires for law a kind of uniformity with other systems that is hard to accept.[91] Meanwhile, if the possibility of reflexive law depended on no other factor, it would be reasonable to state that the realization of reflexive law is brought closer by Teubner's more 'liberal' or 'social' interpretation than by Luhmann's ideological prescription. But it would be facile to opt for any solution because the path to it seems less obstructed. Subsequent attempts to concretise arrangements rapidly would expose specious arguments for reflexive law that abstract or theoretical debate, if utilized, would have revealed.

The narrative would not be complete without including the views of this subject's detractors. Perhaps they serve to justify the improbability of successful reflexive law—the 'pessimistic' view—or to reconfirm the shortcomings of more ambitious schemes—the 'optimistic' view. Nonetheless, they are equally valid in an intellectual discussion that is open, honest and dynamic.

Luhmann articulates the problem of law's cognitive competence in taking into account autopoietic systems in its environment. Armed with only its legal/illegal code, it is impossible to know the extent to which law can impose its insights on systems in its environment (1992b: 4). He asserts further that the only reflexive law is self-reflexive law and can thus 'only reinforce the self-sensibilization of law to the facticity of its social conditions'. As Bechmann puts it more finally, '...by recognizing and reproducing its own reflexivity, it merely sensitizes itself to its social conditions, nothing more (1992: 423). Luhmann concludes: '[T]his reflection confronts the system with the paradoxicality to which it owes its existence' (1992b: 20).

Paterson has shown that it is possible to conceive premises for reflexive law without necessarily contradicting the autopoietic attribute of law, so the present author recommends that such an approach in research be taken and is the basis for optimism. It might presage answers that will prove more reliable in a discussion that will not conclude for some while.

---

[91] Or even isomorphy?

PART B. TRANS-DISCIPLINARITY: CREATIVE SOLUTIONS OR RECREATED PROBLEMS?

Chapter IV. Portable Decision-making and the Problem of Evidence

Trans-science: exporting science into law for decisions

The term 'trans-science' was coined by Weinberg in response to public anxiety about the risk of radiation from nuclear power (1991: 10) in which the indicated experimental science would involve such large numbers of tests to determine the probability of biological tissue damage as to be impracticable. He considered the feasibility of other topical projects that then were outside the scope of human undertaking (1972: 210-214), including those in the social sciences that were distinguished as 'researchable' or 'not researchable' (ibid: 212).

Society could not 'shelve' such problems and was anxious for answers, some of which concerned issues of public risk. And progress could not be postponed until science was capable of resolving its own difficult questions. Weinberg considered that resolution lay in the use of a formal or quasi-legal adversarial procedure in which the proponents of opposing views, as surely there were in the scientific field, could be heard before a body or individual empowered to make a decision (ibid: 214). In other words, it was an emulation of a legal dispute but without binding legal consequences. It would evince a determination through consideration of conflicting opinion, indicating the best knowledge available in circumstances where science was unable to conclude. Weinberg called this procedure 'trans-science' and questions are referred to as 'trans-scientific' when they are acknowledged to be beyond the capability of science to answer and are subjected to the procedure that provides a quasi-legal resolution.

In its prospective rôle, trans-science would contend with hypothetical questions, for example concerning near-space travel, the risks of which at the time of Weinberg's writing were unquantified. Procedures in trans-science were envisaged as being comparatively innocuous and rational. Weinberg glimpsed difficulties to be encountered in allaying fears about the harm of radiation. Conflated with psychosocial and political influences, the answers of science no longer might be perceived as the whole truth. The illustrations to be used in this work to evaluate trans-science show societal concern for risks they might encounter in ordinary life from advancing technology and policies beyond their control. Weinberg's reasoned vision has now been tipped further towards demands placed on science by a concerned society to give account of modern phenomena that, due to their complexity and uncertainty, are not easily explained; nor is research that might assuage anxiety simple to undertake.

Similar concern to that expressed by Weinberg over radiation risk was demonstrated in assessment of risk of childhood cancer in the proximity of nuclear fuel processing plants, public anxiety being such that the scientific community could not ignore (Crouch 1986). An official inquiry pronounced that the cancers could not be accounted for by the low levels of radiation involved (ibid: 202).[92] These findings were thought to have been educed by the established canons of science but were later discredited through discovery of methodological flaws (ibid), It was realized that scientific evidence could not be offered with confidence and that significant subjective expert judgment had been used to bridge gaps in knowledge, instead of being able to follow 'the logic of an ineluctable mathematical rationality' (ibid: 211). The policy analysts' view so formed was that the matter of risk assessment in this situation was entirely trans-scientific inasmuch as, having proved unequal to the task of establishing causation by 'standard science', experts had ousted positivity and substituted uncertainty. Instead of providing the necessary public reassurance, the question the inquiry should have satisfied remained open and continuing but no further means existed at that time for providing definitive answers.

The foregoing instances two manifestations of trans-science that may have been inadvertent, which the present study has seen occur frequently to the concern of both scientific and socio-legal fields. Albeit complicated by flawed methods, the first exemplified that association of an effect and a conjectured cause was beyond scientific means. Involving a psychosocial, environmental or even political element, the second went beyond the capability of science due to external pressures. Perhaps the latter phenomenon should be termed 'extra-scientific' as belonging to the requirements of systems other than natural science but in which it is held responsible for explanations.

It has been said here that Weinberg's examples endow trans-science with a prospective quality. That rendered by Crouch is retrospective and also embodies a distinction in that the term 'trans-science' is used to describe the material of the research, whereas its conventional meaning is that of recognizing that proof of causation was beyond the scope of scientific inquiry at that time. While the admission that science was unequal to the task of proof was honest, (and it is tempting to label the substitution of subjective judgment a deception or, accommodatingly, that the conclusions were 'extra-scientific'), it does serve to

---

[92] *Investigation of the Possible Increased Incidence of Cancer in West Cumbria, Report of the Independent Advisory Group* (1984) Chairman: Sir Douglas Black. London: HMSO.

illustrate problems for science in the service of society over complex issues. It suggests too that evidence has differing qualities, whereby it can be unclear whether the issues for decision in different instances reside in science, trans-science, elements of both or conflations of the two. A final clarification concerns use of imprecise terminology in that trans-science refers to resolution of the questions of science that are unanswerable by science, according to Weinberg, which attaches the term not only to the problem but its particular form of resolution. In Crouch's example it can be seen that failure to admit the inability of science to conclude has been labelled trans-scientific, as often it is in legal disputes, as will be seen soon. Usually, if uncertainty masquerades as positive science, it is not trans-science but an aberration of science.[93] Scientific evidence on which a legal or quasi-legal forum concludes or attempts to conclude but which is inadequate for proof could be awarded the soubriquet 'sub-scientific'. Inquiries that incorporate decision-changing opinion affected by externalities such as economics or politics therefore are 'extra-scientific'. In modern developed society, because issues that cause public concern tend to be technologically based, can be large in scale and effect and incur potentially significant risk, it is difficult to separate social, economic and political influences from both the scientific debate and the quasi-legal conclusion.[94]

The preceding discussion might appear pedantic and the purpose of the several levels of distinction unclear. The reasons are that frequently it occurs in the legal forum that science presents such poor evidence that, if undetected, can cause law to commit an error. When doubtful science is introduced into a dispute, sometimes it is called 'trans-science', especially by legal or socio-legal analysts, as evidence insufficient to prove what is contended, of which sometimes science itself may be unaware. If law adjudicates where this evidence is sufficiently important to influence the conclusion, inadvertently it may have engaged in trans-science. The position taken in this study is that the decision resulting from the procedure, not the evidence, is trans-scientific. The term 'trans-science' has been preserved in this work for the deliberative procedure that uses adversarial methods to conclude on questions of science that science cannot answer, rather than a loose description of inadequate science presented in the legal forum. The point of the foregoing discussion will be seen in the evaluation of evidence in legal disputes such as toxic torts, where proof that a substance or preparation has caused harm is notoriously difficult and where law is exercised vigorously for its conclusions.

Contemporary crises of science in society

Controversies in the public domain concerning science persist, some remaining unresolved, though interest in others has abated. A list was provided

---

[93] It will be shown later, that scientific findings can be misrepresented due to 'the social construction of science'.

[94] See Cotgreave (2003).

in Chapter III of which the following few are a reminder. These include the debate over the MMR vaccine and its relationship to autism and bowel disease; the existence of Gulf War Syndrome; New Variant Creutzfelt-Jacob Disease (vCJD) that arose from Bovine Spongiform Encephalitis (BSE) and the possibility of human transmission of it; the association of childhood cancer and nuclear processing plants; danger of intracranial tumours from microwave radiation in the use of mobile telephones, the possibility of cancer in children living in proximity to high-voltage power lines and, most recently, new and conflicting evidence concerning so-called Shaken Baby Syndrome (Dyer 2005: 1463).

These questions are of potential social impact and reliant on conclusive scientific evidence for determination of their inherent risks. Few so far has succeeded as the cause of action in a legal dispute, though not in every instance because a case could not be prepared. None has been submitted to a single systematic inquiry but some were put to a number of individual boards where over time repeated and rearranged consideration has produced a 'default' consensus of scientific and governmental opinion that the public can accept or reject. The debate over the MMR vaccine is typical. Undeniably, these phenomena currently are beyond the ability of science to provide the assurance of certainty, so experts are called to render the best current scientific opinion. This represents a weak consideration of issues that could be submitted to procedures in trans-science but that sometimes are made less exhaustive and less democratic by resort to the inquisitorial procedure of institutional inquiries.

Among communities such as those of science that promote systematization of knowledge, systematic reviews of published literature can gel into a general consensus of findings, epidemiological studies in particular being unified by this method (Bastide, Courtial and Callon 1989). Often such agreements will stand *pro tempore* as the derived 'right' answer to a problem, but then this represents agreement among a community only, not necessarily having exposed it to the probing of a tribunal for a purpose outside that community. Weinberg's prescription for exposure of complex issues in adversarial settings that reach more than provisional outcomes therefore is born more of hope than experience. Identifying a forum or tribunal with a sufficiently broad remit, political and scientific neutrality and adequate knowledge to be able to hear complex issues can be difficult. Institutionally, for some purposes they may not exist. Consequently, Weinberg's visualization is of a counsel of perfection, the extent to which any adopted procedure can approximate to this ideal becoming important if tasked with the ultimate resolution of uncertainty.

Trans-science in its social setting

Using an example of an hypothetical society far less complex than today's reality, Weinberg imagined a scenario in which science and politics could collaborate over policy formation but in a compartmentalized way so that

science would provide all the necessary objective evidence for political decisions without issues in the one becoming conflated with those of the other
(Weinberg 1972: 209). He observed further that moral and political issues
invaginated into science in modernity meant consequently that conclusions of
social importance could not be reached via this simplistic model, that science
neither operated in isolation nor could be exempted from social and political
implications; equally that politics was unable to claim simply to be 'informed
by science' and acquit itself from the social consequences of the advice taken.
This *ad hominem* prescription includes two of Weinberg's perceptions of the
social aspects of science. In the first, Weinberg depicts science according to the
foregoing as charged with social responsibility but unable to respond to such
demands through an unsuitable ethos; in the second, he characterized science
as expected to provide answers to socially important but imponderable questions, for which its methodology was inadequate. He was concerned with the
problems that arose when scientists could offer only answers that were trans-
scientific in response to matters of policy in which science was consulted (ibid).

Weinberg's schema also suggested that society has formed such an impression of the achievements of science, especially physical science, that it
confers upon it unlimited ability to explain all the complex issues of the world.
A common perception of physical science is that the inferences it makes from
the particular to the general imbue it with accurate predictive ability (ibid:
212), a quality that, if true, would render it of great social utility. This fails
when problems become impractically large in respect of necessary data vol-
umes, time-scales and resources, when great uncertainties of knowledge
remain irreducible or externalities inhibit research. Such predictive characteristics of natural science applied to other knowledge fields like social science can
induce mistaken aspirations (ibid: 210-213). The human selection of *worthwhile problems of science*[95] often entails political motivation, where the truth
of science can become secondary to the use to which it is put. The problems to
which attention is directed are guided by public policy, aesthetics and moral
values, and the choices exercised thereby are matters of philosophy, not science
(ibid: 213, Weinberg 1993: 11).[96] In these categories, Weinberg counsels they
are matters not of science but trans-science, though the present study would
reserve for them the category that it perceives to be more accurate of 'extra-
scientific', because they pertain to matters external to science. The present
inquiry is concerned with the extent to which Weinberg's characterization is
understood in scientific and socio-legal circles and the possibility of trans-
scientific issues being mistaken for the productions of true science by society.
Further, it is evident that trans-science is not a single phenomenon but can be
viewed as a spectrum of problematized scientific knowledge for legal or quasi-

---

95 Author's emphasis.
96 See also Weinberg (1991): 10.

legal resolution, the boundaries of which may be both wider and more blurred than previously assumed.

Transcendent vehicles like trans-science are quasi-legal when their procedures are not held under legal auspices such as courts or in regulation and policy-making. They do not operate procedurally 'in the shadow of the court' as does arbitration, for example. From the resources consulted, the extent to which quasi-legal procedures operate 'in the shadow of the law' is not apparent. The consequences of this are crucially important if resolutions in trans-science are to have societal effect. In Luhmann's systems perspective, taking disputes away from the courts not only is detrimental to law but also to society. In his explanation, it would reduce law's ability to stabilize normative expectations over time (1987a: 27). In disputes, this amounts to systematization by juristic skill, comparisons of cases, concepts and a doctrine of 'congruently generalized behavioural expectations' that become experienced as law (ibid: 28).

Impoverished science offered in evidence to law

The notion of trans-science proposed by Weinberg (1972) recounts that scientific uncertainty in areas of risk informing public policy and regulation is such that legal-type adjudication of issues represents the only means of determination. Although an extreme instance of the inability of science to pronounce in its own affairs, it is believed in this study that thought about the special features of trans-science precipitates reconsideration of much scientific representation to the field of law. This is occasioned by critical examination in the literature concerning trans-science that tries to locate the boundary between science and trans-science, suggesting concomitantly that the quality and intentionality of some scientific evidence proffered to law can be questioned.

This revisitation gives rise also to those terms coined by the present study as 'sub-scientific' and 'extra-scientific' that imply misconceptions and misrepresentations of scientific evidence that detract from any surety attestable in its assertions. Such negative *considerata* indicate sometimes that opinions offered to law are based on unsatisfactory or weak science, may transgress the boundaries of true scientific knowledge or even are not sufficiently known to science. Later it will be shown that egregious error can result from legal failure to discriminate between proffered opinions that are genuinely scientific, sub-scientific or extra-scientific.

Examination of trans-science creates a useful platform from which to reconsider these other issues of science presented to law, in which it transpires that the sub-optimal varieties of evidence to be described here abound in procedure more than is supposed because they remain unrecognized. Assessment of risk, individual and mass torts over environmental issues and product liability reveal that scientific evidence sometimes is dubious, the legal tribunal grappling with an amalgam of evidence including sub-optimal and misrepresented science, conflicting expert opinion and the issue of balanced judgment.

In simple language, the following are possible scenarios in the way science is proffered and understood in legal contexts and, when combined, can create a cyclical process of confusion. First, science is not aware always of what it does not know; it might feel it has sufficient for convincing law about its state of knowledge on an issue and therefore offers 'sub-scientific' opinion. Second, experts may feel obliged by law to attempt convincing answers, whereas an admission of ignorance would guide legal decisions better; and third, law may be unaware that science cannot provide certainty always and that it might be being offered 'best guesses'.

The MMR debate: a disappointed candidate for trans-science

The debate over the relationship between the Measles, Mumps and Ru-bella (MMR) vaccine in young children and the incidence of autism and bowel disease has never been brought into a single systematic and conclusive inquiry. Several expert committees were appointed to consider the safety of the vaccine after publication of the research causing the initial alarm. Group actions in tort were contemplated in the UK but did not materialize. The MMR controversy is depicted fully by Horton (2004). Dr Horton edits *The Lancet* and his discourse explains the circumstances surrounding publication by the journal of the initial report that was found later to contain flawed research.

Different types of evidence can be seen in the trajectory of this public health controversy as well as 'sub-scientific' and 'extra-scientific' research findings, according to the definitions tendered by the present study. Until its more satisfactory resolution, the problem resonated strongly with the precepts of trans-science due to the inability of conventional medical science to disprove the alleged association between the vaccine and autism, combined with the lack of safety information from government health departments that could have refuted flawed research and allayed parental fears (ibid: 21, 38)

Epidemiological studies showed a strong correlation between the conse-quent lowered uptake of the vaccine or its substitution by separate, single vaccines and increased prevalence of measles (Kidd *et al.* 2003: 832). It is verified empirically that onset of autism in young children coincides with the age at which the MMR vaccination normally is given (Horton 2004: 19). The associations found in the original study (Wakefield *et al.* 1998) could not be reproduced by other inquiries (Horton 2004: 28-29), thereby raising suspicion that a fundamental norm of research had been breached. Science neither has established the suggested link between the MMR vaccination and au-tism/bowel disease, nor the contention that the triple vaccine overloads the immune system (ibid: 95, 99). Literature now shows that MMR is not a risk factor for autism (Murch 2003: 1498-1499), there is no epistemological evidence for a causal association (Taylor *et al.* 1999: 2026-2029) and a nega-tive association between MMR and autism is concluded (DeStefano and Chen 1999: 1987-1988). The outcome of the flawed research can be classified accord-ing to the nomenclature of the present study as 'sub-scientific.' Conflicts of interest detected in the aims of the original research group disposed it towards a predetermined outcome, introducing an 'extra-scientific' influence to understanding the effects of the vaccine (Murch 2003: 1498-1499; Horton 2004: 5).

It is a matter for science that causation between vaccination and the disease remains unproven. That side effects of the vaccine sometimes are experienced but limited to mild discomfort of short duration is also established through science (Vestergaard 2004: 351-357). At the outbreak of the controversy, reports of severe side effects in their children by parents were, at the least, 'extra-scientific' because the connection had not been demonstrated by science but their opinions were distorted by psychological factors convincing many that the vaccine was responsible. There was a (putatively) trans-scientific component in the controversy in that it could not have been shown whether illnesses would have arisen regardless of whether the MMR vaccination was given, nor that illnesses did not pre-exist the vaccinations but were unnoticed. Studies have shown most recently that the rate of parental reporting of autism levelled from a peak in 1992, suggesting the earlier rise was due to increased awareness of the condition brought about by publicity (Lingham *et al.* 2003: 666-670). This hyperbolic effect also could be labelled 'extra-scientific'. The inquiry would lend itself to trans-science, in that it is not reasonable to conduct controlled studies whereby one group of children is trialled on the vaccine and another on a placebo or alternative preparation, to determine the relative risk of treatment. Anecdotal evidence demonstrating parental fear of ulterior motivation in government health departments' advocacy of vaccination was 'extra-scientific', while the implementation of public policy committed to prevention of serious disease should not have been construed as sinister. 'Sub-science', 'good' science', 'extra-science' and trans-science became conflated. Because some parents remained unconvinced that the government was truthful, and in fact some regarded the instigator of the original research as having saved their children from the adverse consequences of some kind of driven policy (Horton 2004: 33), issues of trust were invoked.

The MMR controversy and others like it often conclude unsatisfactorily in the public view. Sometimes the underlying assumptions are represented by simply 'bad' science but often there is inadequate evidence to be able to attribute or disprove causation convincingly. Ultimately, a more serious crisis was averted in this instance. Without new research findings and the deliberations of several expert committees,[97] it could have achieved the status of trans-science as Weinberg defined it and would have been a suitable candidate for resolution according to his proposed adversarial procedure. This also could have applied to other recent events of public concern that eventually were neutralized by government intervention, policy decisions, use of the precautionary principle and late but more reliable science.

---

[97] For example a Working Group of the Academy of Medical Sciences set up in the UK in March 2001, Chairman Professor Peter Lachman and twelve leading experts in vaccines (see Horton 2004: 187, n.31).

QUASI-LEGAL PROCEDURE IN RESOLUTION OF
PROBLEMATIZED SCIENTIFIC KNOWLEDGE

Trans-science is apparent to interdisciplinary research as a prominent confluence of two disparate epistemologies in an active field of operations. Society looks to science for resolution of socially important scientific issues that transpire to be beyond its scope. Matters cannot remain unresolved, because *a priori* estimates of risk or even simple suspicions are sufficient for concerns that insistently are required to be addressed. Frequently, law is tasked with adjudication of issues in science proffered as evidence in disputes; such has long been its traditional rôle in some kinds of torts. Through procedure, it functions as arbiter of truth and employs mechanisms whereby assertions are presented, challenged, verified or rejected, though determining what the facts say is a process of persuasion in both legal and scientific communities (Jones: 1994: 5). In issues of uncertain science, representations of truth are optimised by evaluation of evidence presented to a tribunal constituted in law or having a quasi-legal configuration. Its conclusions are reached via eclectic choices of opinion evidence and application of reasoning to form decisions. In torts, such legal dispute resolution procedures are standard but in the visualization of trans-science, legal methods are reconstructed in order to offer answers to society for acceptance.

Quasi-legal inquiries in trans-science function principally according to two procedures marked by temporal distinction. In a prospective framework, a party makes a plea to an adjudicator for authorization to carry out an activity, say an industrial process, which either another party resists or over which a regulator requires assurances that the activity is safe. This typifies the adversarial setting where there is an applicant and a dissenter or regulator, both of whom call their own experts to support their assertions. Choo describes adversarial hearings as a contest or dispute between two adversaries before a relatively passive decision-maker, whose principal duty is to reach a verdict (1998: 131). It is triadic in form, given that a third party adjudicates the dispute between the other two. A retrospective framework is instanced in inquiries where it is contended a harm has been caused or a substantial risk is involved in a current activity, the purpose of the inquiry being clarification of issues so that remedies can be applied. In governmental or governmental agency inquiries into untoward incidents or risk assessments, these are inquisitorial in character. Non-adversarial procedures are usually structured as an official inquiry (ibid). Parties do not dispute over an issue in direct confrontation, though the evidence each brings might conflict. The adjudicator calls on witnesses of his/her own choosing according to the expertise required, and considers their evidence in forming conclusions. Procedure to resolve the dispute may be considered monadic as the adjudicator controls the process. Neither is there dialogue between the parties as in dyadic/triadic negotiation, nor a consensus of views sought among them. Under the adversarial system, the two adversaries take charge of most of the procedural action; under the inquisitorial, officials perform most activities (ibid). Extended debates concerning the characteristics and relative merits of adversarial and inquisitorial procedures belong to legal study beyond the scope of this work, and insight may be had by comparing systems of legal inquiry in common law jurisdictions, such as those conforming to the Anglo-American tradition and those of Continental Europe (ibid).[98]

Weinberg cautions strongly that science that is certain should be distinguished carefully from uncertain science and that therefore the procedures of science should determine scientific truths, while those of law (or that replicate legal methods) are employed to seek the truth in trans-science (1972: 215). Weinberg is not speaking in a legal context in offering this advice. His stance is that scientific issues are not necessarily the business of society while science does not involve it in risk, and that therefore no legal or quasi-legal adjudication of issues is required. When this ceases to apply, because uncertainty implies risk, such matters enter the region of trans-science and hence become the concern of society, for which adjudication is necessary. Weinberg's counsel is that, in principle, solving the questions of science should be exhausted before attempting resolution of issues in trans-science as he defines them. Implied in his simple advocacy of science managing its own debates is the concept of a consensus over the truth among the scientific community that is problematic in reality. The prominence of scientific experts in legal proceedings has been challenged, and the notion of the alleged certainty of science dismissed as fallacy (Phillips 1994: 231-232). Therefore, certainty shades into uncertainty that in turn can cast doubt on clear identification of issues as belonging to science or trans-science.

Adversarial versus inquisitorial procedures

This narrative also will treat belief that adversarial procedure is superior in eliciting truth when knowledge of a problem is limited, where experts disagree about causes and are unable to provide unequivocal advice (Majone 1989: 40). The power of adversarialism in determination of facts is attributed to the ability it confers on cross-examination of experts in deconstruction of adversary science as 'the greatest legal engine ever invented for the discovery of truth' (Jasanoff 1995: 52).[99]

In the midst of the uncompromising differencing of adversarialism and inquisitorialism, a finer procedural delineation divides even the Anglo-American adversarial legal tradition in which the concept of trans-science is

---

[98] See also Zander (1996: 284-300); Reynolds and King (1992: 87-88); Atiyah (1987); Jacob (1987).

[99] Cited from *California v Green* (1970) 399 U.S. 149, per Mr Justice White, at 158.
    See also the remarks concerning adversarial and inquisitorial procedure in *The Royal Commission on Criminal Justice* 1993 (The Runciman Commission) §§ 11-15; and Zander (1996: 283-300), for comparison of adversarial and inquisitorial procedures in civil and criminal proceedings.

grounded. This results from adoption in the American Federal jurisdictions of Rules of Evidence that govern admissibility of science into the courtroom—as much due to measures to exclude 'junk science' as the fact that in the United States civil cases are decided by juries that are not expected to possess the same skills as judges in evaluating evidence. English court practice emphasises pragmatism (Atiyah 1987: Lectures I–III, 30-103) and operates on the principle of orality, a principle of English courts relying on the oral testimony of witnesses (Jacob 1987 19-20). 'It is said...that observation of a witness's demeanour provides a good indication of the reliability of his or her testimony' (Choo 1998: 132). Once the judge has excluded irrelevant evidence in case preparation, the court prefers all the issues to be heard openly and permits the contest of the adversarial process to indicate to the judge the evidence that should be preferred.

Reference to legal tradition is not mistaken here even when discussing trans-science, because sometimes it is the lack of consensus among scientists called as experts in disputes that leads to uncertainty in presented evidence and to conflict of opinion that cross-examination endeavours to clarify. So, whereas procedure attempting resolution of issues in trans-science is made to resemble legal adversarial settings, similar questions must arise over quality of opinion evidence, the credibility and competence of witnesses.

Toxic torts constitute the arena for deciding causation of harm in legal contexts and, in this instance, seek redress retrospectively in an adversarial setting. Scientific evidence can be in doubt so that the conclusions fact-finders are invited to draw might wander into the territory of trans-science without the tribunal being conscious of it. From digests of such cases in the United States (both Federal and State), it appears that the 'gatekeeper' function of the Rules of Evidence does not necessarily exclude the possibility of the tribunal being misled—an issue that will be exposed by reference to the *Bendectin* litigation to follow—even though cross-examination of experts is superimposed on hearing the residue of evidence. The value of 'gatekeeper' functions on the effect of different ways of presenting evidence in the American and English jurisdictions warrants separate examination but belongs more properly to legal studies.

These matters trouble law in its traditional rôle when confronting the incommensurability of science and law. A further challenge is issued for law. If it experiences difficulty in evaluating evidence in science in the presence of the safeguards and constraints of the American legal system, how much greater will be its task in less formal tribunals and in the English jurisdiction where such functions are absent, with evidence inherently being uncertain, as will be the situation in hearing issues in trans-science? These issues have attained the complexity of a Gordian knot but legal scholars offer prospects of ameliorating difficulty by counselling that law should acquaint itself with methods of evaluating types of scientific evidence so that at least matters within the realm of science can be kept there firmly for adjudication before venturing into the nebulous world of trans-science.

Selecting the appropriate forum

Trans-science and its attached procedures can be perceived as social expedients—science 'exports' its uncertainties for decision into a legal or quasi-legal forum—but casually footnoting issues as trans-scientific does not address adequately the complexities of establishing the boundaries of scientific research and legal knowledge (Edmond and Mercer 1997: 705-706). In tort litigation, the ambiguities of science may form 'an important site of contest' (ibid: 706), implying that contentment to label issues as trans-scientific may be to apply a legal 'fudge' to circumvent or obscure lack of scientific consensus. The utility of trans-science as a transcendent, mediating vehicle is questionable if it is forced into the rôle of adjudicator in conflicts of opinion within the scientific community, by which is meant that it is drawn into their arguments. Distinguishing matters that are scientific or trans-scientific would assist a tribunal in perceiving which arguments are factually based and which might be hypothetical. Edmond and Mercer suggest courts may be drawn unwittingly into confirming simplistic positivist epistemologies of science in instances of contradictory evidence (ibid). The work of these authors analyses deeply the dynamics of toxic tort litigation but does not set out primarily to scrutinize trans-science. Their analyses embrace types of scientific evidence and the competence of experts that convince the courts of their reliability. Trans-science is thus regarded in their treatment as that which is invoked when scientific evidence is inadequate and they show scant regard for it, their appreciation being that the resolvability of issues should depend upon providing 'good' science and exposing it to legal contest.

The limits of scientific capability sometimes are apparent through esoteric theory that itself gives expression to uncertainty, as in quantum theory. Society's acceptance or otherwise of different aspects of science also defines its boundaries so that a trans-scientific limit has emerged as a 'distinct philosophical category' (Weinberg 1991: 10). Weinberg's term exhibits slight ambiguity and could be taken to indicate either the limits of scientific certainty before its matters become trans-scientific or that trans-science, as a philosophical category, is discrete and therefore identified by society as dealing with scientific indeterminacy. It is supposed here that its creator intends the last interpretation as a manifestation of the problems of science that society recognizes in modernity. It reallocates the problem of identifying the boundary of science and trans-science to the social sphere but understates it with respect both to complexity and effect in relation to Edmond's and Mercer's view.

In conditions of utmost clarity, a two-state situation would obtain as follows. In the first, issues that are undoubtedly scientific would be heard best in scientific debate and in this situation do not require exposure to law or quasi-legal determination. When adduced as evidence in torts and a conflict of opinion is encountered, the argument is won by legal assessment that recognizes 'good' science in Edmond's and Mercer's 'important site of contest' (1997: 706).

In the second, evidence that unmistakably is trans-scientific should be tried by a legal-type procedure (Weinberg 1972: 215). Scientific debate should exhaust questions of science 'before dealing with the trans-scientific residue' (ibid: 216), which is good counsel but is simplistic when compared to that of Edmond and Mercer, because the very nub of the question is the successful identification of epistemological soundness or transcendent indeterminacy that governs selection of the appropriate forum.

The MMR vaccine debate typifies such a deconstruction in that scientifically attestable issues were debated by the medical community in expert committees and via peer reviewed research findings, exemplifying Weinberg's distinction of scientific issues being heard in scientific debate. On this occasion scientific proof, or rather proof of a negative association, was sufficiently robust to dispense with the need for a trial of issues concerning the vaccine, even though societal disquiet persisted in a diffuse, sub-critical fashion. Imagining torts, decisions would rest upon whether scientific evidence was sufficient to prove causation. If expert opinion were to conflict, here the court would become 'an important site of legal contest'. But if science showed an inability to conclude, the issues would become candidates for trans-science and, hence, ripe for determination according to Weinberg's quasi-legal adversarial procedure.

EVIDENTIAL STANDARDS OF SCIENCE IN THE LEGAL AND QUASI-LEGAL FORUM

It would be glib to assert that trans-scientific questions are de-problematized by resorting to legal procedure (that is, exporting the questions of science for determination by law), since that forum, too, must own a standard by which to assess probabilities of causation or risks in a contended issue. If driven by expediency in response to political or economic pressure, conclusions might be reached with science as one but not necessarily the most prominent factor. In such a situation, the term 'extra-scientific' should be applied with regard to conclusions. That this sometimes might be true cannot be eschewed but it could distract the present discussion from examination of science-law interplay and will be merely noted, not developed.

It has been shown here that, even as trans-science represents problematized scientific knowledge, the susceptibility to proof of many questions of science is moot and dependent not only on the quality of presented evidence but the weight accorded it in legal contexts when it is heard. This impinges on two matters now familiar in this work: that the boundary of science and trans-science is not discrete due to the uncertainty sometimes inherent in 'conventional' science, and that legal determination, however informal, must rely on some form of procedural constraint to prevent disorder. The legal forum chosen to resolve a dispute or 'settle' an uncertainty might depend, for example, on whether a binding decision is sought or recovery is an objective of the action, which will decide if the question falls properly within legal procedure. It will also decide the rules of evidence and procedure to be employed—whether they are institutional or *ad hoc*. The last of these can introduce complications of their own.

Standard of proof is crucial to any inquiry and a matter for concern imagined in the circumstances of trans-science is where the basis of opinion must be demonstrated in order for the forum to know how to value it. Adoption of uniformity in procedure among the various types of inquiry possible averts inconsistency of decision-making, or variation in the basis of decisions that science, law and society could not tolerate. Completely locally devised and *ad hoc* rules could label trans-science incoherent and unsystematic. Rothstein (2004) raised a question concerning the coherence of trans-science. The nature of the problem, its societal implications and the institutions within which it is investigated would govern the rules that are dispensed. Because of the complexity of modern society, each emergent issue in trans-science attracts different kinds of concerns that suggest context-specific styles of investigation.

A natural question would be whether trans-science has yet attained the status of a discipline or exemplifies such contingency and provisionalism that it cannot be legitimized wholly by science, law and society. The World Trade Organization (WTO) admits its dispute settlement bodies are not structured so as to offer a stable institutional solution for settling disputes (Walker 1998: 319) and that this can be improved only by a process organised so that global consensus on the criteria for 'scientific plausibility' can evolve (ibid). Without incorporation of rules or guidance and an estimation of the proof standard acceptable to stakeholders, even in conditions of extreme uncertainty, institutions embarking on pronouncement of issues in trans-science amid a perceived or imposed duty to reach decisions in the absence of such rationality, themselves risk being labelled 'trans-scientific institutions' (ibid. 320). Would too strict an application of rules of evidence to material that is already acknowledged to be uncertain hamper the ability to consider the real issues in a trans-science forum?

With so little on record of hearings in trans-science, a conclusion is not easily drawn and thought could be given at another time to the effects of juridification of procedure. Weinberg might have seen objections to this development in his original visualization, or he simply might not have considered it. Drawing this debate to its ultimate conclusion would signify that, with the lack of a preconceived threshold of conclusiveness, the courses open to the forum or tribunal would be to dismiss the issue as indeterminable to any prescribed level of satisfaction, or if the risk is not amenable to assessment and normal management procedures, to default into the precautionary principle so that activity could be proscribed in case a harm not yet understood were to materialize. For policy, the choice could be determined by the likely health impact of the problem concerned. Holder and Elworthy (1998: 130) discuss the precautionary principle in relation to the BSE crisis and the 'pre-scientized'

stage of knowledge that existed, which can be read as a euphemism for ignorance in that information is too scant to be able to assess risk.[100] Deliberate
inactivity counts as the exercise of agnosticism, the antithesis of the precautionary principle, where it is decided that inadequate proof of risk provides no
basis for any form of action. Applied unexceptionally, outcomes could render
legal or quasi-legal fora impotent and irrelevant in resolution of matters of
serious concern to society. That this contention is tempered and contoured in
reality forms the basis of the discussion that follows.

The standard of proof is the legal standard a panel should use to make its
finding of fact and establishes the quality of evidence and degree of certainty
needed before a positive finding can be made in any inquiry (Walker 1998:
290). Among the various standards and expressions of proof, adopting the civil
legal standard of 'more probable than not' or 'on the balance of probabilities',
in decisions involving science and trans-science, tells stakeholders that the
evidence presented in the hearing convinced the forum or tribunal there was a
sufficient basis for belief in the assertions made—and that therefore science
had given an acceptable account of causation or risk. Walker recites this as the
requirement that the panel should base its determination on estimation that
the proposition is more likely to be true than false (ibid: 291). This is the
normally accepted standard (Wagner 1986: 428). Amid several plausible
models of explanation of measures, World Trade Organization determinations
are made on the basis of 'a reasonable scientific basis for the choice' (Walker
1998: 291). In reviewing decisions in appeals, the WTO moves to the descriptive standard of the '*reasonable person*'[101] who would not make a finding based
on inadequate scientific evidence.

The present study favours the 'more probable than not' expression rather
than 'on the balance of probabilities' because it expresses better some kind of
affirmation amid uncertainty. Comment could be made that it is vague because
societal expectations of science are that it should be capable of such certainty
as to leave issues in no doubt. In litigation, a 'more probable than not' standard
would give the benefit to the plaintiff or claimant if there is an indication
through evidence that there is truth in their claim.[102]

In areas of risk and regulation, this standard would imply that scientific
evidence is sufficient to warrant positive preventative or corrective action but
confidence in the outcome is more difficult to imagine in trans-science, where
it is already supposed that proof eludes investigators or that extra-scientific
elements have intervened. The statistical basis of a 'more probable than not'
standard of causation demands a certainty that trans-science is incapable of
producing (Wagner 1986: 436). Traditional science is assumed able to answer
its own questions, even though the uncertainty of some evidence is admitted,

---

[100] See Resnik (2003).

[101] Author's emphasis.

[102] See Redmayne (1999) for a comprehensive analysis of standards of proof in civil
litigation.

but it is shown here that in trans-science it cannot, which places heavy reliance on legal procedure for conclusions. That this might revise the applicability of the 'more probable than not' standard suggests itself intuitively since greater uncertainty in scientific evidence must make clear legal or quasi-legal conclusions difficult. If the assurance of science in an issue was such that there could be confidence in a 'more probable than not' standard, then the issue might not be trans-scientific. However, if a legal type of procedure can produce affirmative outcomes where science is unable, it could indicate such procedures are more effective arbiters of at least provisional truths. While judgment on that presumption must be suspended, it should be considered whether there is a basis for asserting that trans-scientific inquiries can operate on lowered standards of proof because adjudicators can choose to impute that evidence is sufficient to infer causation or risk.

There are always caveats in science: an association between an observed effect and conjectured causation never can be eliminated entirely, for example in the MMR debate it is impossible to discount categorically that some instances of autism might have been due to the vaccination. But these constitute a background level of determination above which research conclusions should rise. Individual instances do not constitute proof. This cannot be achieved without employment of evidential standards or it would have to be admitted that an estimate of chance would be no less likely to elicit the truth in issues of trans-science than a formal procedure erected for the purpose.

According to Wagner, in trans-science the probability standard to prove causation cannot be attained which also eliminates the possibility of establishing the 'but for' criterion normal to torts (ibid: 445). Attempts to modify standards of proof in trans-science attract other problems as Wagner's speculation shows and connote a misunderstanding of the deductions of science. In an endeavour to circumvent the task of attaining the 'more probable than not' standard in uncertain science, she proposes that, where a hazardous substance is concerned, plaintiffs need only show that it was capable of inflicting a harm, and that the harm was foreseeable by virtue of the dangerous nature of the substance (ibid: 446-447). This would shift the burden from the plaintiff's need for scientific proof to the manufacturer's negligent conduct founded on the principle of deterrence whereby notice of the potential hazards of a substance duly should be given to users. It is an adaptation of the strict liability proof of negligence.[103] This radical proposal lacks scientific awareness that cause-effect chains are not proved by the simple association of a hazard with an observed effect, even though it might appear direct, nor is it likely that Wagner's prescription can be generalized to all risk situations. Relationships can be complex and care must be taken to qualify them in terms of background, other influences and possible confounding factors. In the continuing debate over the association between overhead power lines and childhood cancer, Draper *et al.*

---

[103] See Fleming (1992).

(2005: 1292) found that children living from birth within two hundred metres of high-tension cables were more at risk of leukaemia than those living six hundred metres or more away. Children living at between two hundred and six hundred metres distance also had a slightly increased risk but the magnetic fields thought to be responsible would be too weak at that range to account for the incidence of illness. Draper and colleagues therefore presume the apparent correlation at two hundred metres is due to chance or confounding influences.

Wagner counsels that rules of evidence and procedure are incompatible with the capabilities of trans-science (1986: 436). The support she presents for this strong statement goes to the heart of the distinctions of trans-science. Judges are forced to discriminate finely between theories generally accepted by the scientific community and those that are controversial. In trans-science, it is precisely such questions that the scientific community cannot answer through lack of an acceptable or reasonable basis for substantiating the finding of a causal connection (ibid: 439). The author's concern actually is for the admissibility of evidence as a distinct issue for the courts but her remarks are confined to those of the United States. When engaging with the discourse of American commentators, it has been found essential in this evaluation of trans-science to maintain awareness of differences of procedure between the American and English jurisdictions. These impinge importantly on what is understood by use of the term trans-science, and it is evident to this study from this and other discussions that its meaning is not universal and sometimes is misappropriated. This troubles explanations and analyses, occasioning the need for careful differentiation of facts in descriptions. Wagner's text alludes to the task for judges when disputes over admissibility of evidence centre on *the scientific validity of vying hypotheses* (ibid: 440). Italicisation here is to emphasize the operational parts of the statement that concern also the pivotal factors in judges' considerations. Wagner conjures the scenario of the judge-turned-scientist *locum tenens* in respect of admissibility of evidence. As if to buttress the notion she opines that 'if lines must be drawn', that is—if there is obligation to choose between contradicting hypotheses, it will be by '...judges who often ignore the inherently limited capabilities of scientific research' (ibid: 442).

In the American jurisdiction, evaluation of evidence according to Federal Rules governing admissibility (and similar state rules) is prioritised (Freeman 1998: 3). These rules and the actions of judges in accordance with them function as 'gatekeepers' or 'filters' to exclude unsatisfactory evidence, to avoid potential confusion of the jurors who give decisions in civil matters in the USA.[104] Subsisting in this account is suggestion of a codifying or formulaic approach to procedure to reduce issues explored in the forum and to expedite decisions. Where it is possible that evidence needs assessment according to the criteria of Federal Rules, it is subjected to a preliminary hearing.[105]

---

[104] See Warren (1998: 177).
[105] See the Oral Argument before the Supreme Court of the United States in *William Daubert, et al. v Merrell Dow Pharmaceuticals, Inc.* (1993) US Trans Lexis, 148. [cont.]

By contrast, in the English jurisdiction a pragmatic style of procedure allows the court to evaluate all evidence openly in determining the merits of the case. There is no jury and it is the judge who concludes on the evidence. In *Ventouris v Mountain (No. 2)*[106] Balcombe LJ said, 'The modern tendency in civil proceedings is to admit all relevant evidence, and the judge should be trusted to give only proper weight to evidence which is not the best evidence.' On the effect of rules of evidence, Sir Richard Eggleston comments that in some cases judges may exclude material that would, if admitted, have undue bearing on the assessment of probabilities (1983: 33).

Procedure in the USA that bowdlerizes evidence precludes some of the adversarial 'sparring' that advertises the strength of belief held by the parties to a dispute in their evidence or opinion that the judge takes into account. In the English jurisdiction, stress in evaluating opinion evidence is placed on the credibility and reliability of expert opinion witnesses judged by a combination of professional standing, their demeanour as witnesses and behaviour under cross-examination (*Loveday v Renton*)[107] rather than total dependence on the substance of their submissions (Jones 1996: 162, 163; Reynolds and King 1992: 23). Raitt considers reliability as an explicit criterion for admissibility of evidence in the United Kingdom (1998: 168-169). Judgments in the following cases include the demeanour of expert witnesses that presiders took into account in reaching their decisions, some showing their appreciation of good witnesses (*Bolitho v City & Hackney Health Authority*;[108] *Nixon v FJ Morris Contracting Ltd*[109]), and others deprecating their poor self-conduct (*John Amos Hill v William Tompkins Ltd*;[110] *Mary Curran v John Finn*;[111] *Dingley v The Chief Constable Strathclyde Police*;[112] *Christine Perry v The Post Office*;[113] *Re: The Oral Contraceptive Group*[114]).

Weinberg's original formulation is nuanced by possible consequences realized through Wagner's discourse on standards of scientific evidence. From it can be considered whether American judicial gatekeeper functions are capable of excluding trans-science from the courts in litigation. Wagner's loose interpretation of trans-science is as poor science unrecognised on which law unknowingly may be called upon to pronounce. Gatekeeper functions are of no avail if unable to discriminate between reliable and unreliable forms of scien-

---

For a useful explanation of the effect of the Federal Rules of Evidence, see Sales and Shuman (2005).
[106] [1992] 1 WLR 887 at 899.
[107] [1990] 1MLR 117 per Stuart Smith at 125.
[108] [1992] 13 BMLR 111 CA via *Casetrack* Transcript.
[109] [2000] All ER Official Transcripts QBD. 21st December 2000.
[110] [1997] QBD.
[111] [1998] IEHC 54.
[112] [1998] SC 548.
[113] Case No. HQ 0100348 QBD 18/10/2001.
[114] [2002] EWHC 1420 QBD (Lawtel).

tific evidence. For instance, at a different point in her critique she asserts that the findings of animal studies cannot be extrapolated to humans (1986: 440). So Wagner attaches the expression trans-science not to reducing scientific infiniteness, believed here to be its progenitor's conception, but to puzzles of science that have been attempted but poorly answered. Sometimes, evidence that proves unreliable in an action simply might mean that it was not adequately brought. Coincidentally, the term 'puzzles of science' was used by Kuhn (1970) to describe the activity of science that accumulates knowledge between paradigm shifts of understanding.

The implications of Wagner's observations are that courts are responsible for trans-scientific decisions unknowingly when evidence is of a poor standard. In this study, decisions made under those circumstances would be called 'sub-scientific'. It signifies that science cannot answer its own questions but has left them unwittingly to legal determination, leaving a question over justice. In the United States, gatekeeper rules are meant to exclude poor evidence, but Wagner contends that sometimes this imposes an impossible burden on judges and the rules are not infallible. In the English jurisdiction, an inadvertent excursion into trans-science could have a better outcome because the court can decide by hearing all relevant evidence and making its own judgment on it. Errors are not impossible but all opinions will have been exposed to cross-examination without any being withheld. If any legal decisions are in reality trans-scientific, in the English jurisdiction, openness and pragmatism in procedure reproduce more closely the conditions of trans-science, even when unaware of it and with less potential harm to law itself.

It is not manifestly clear whether Weinberg considered this utilization of the principles of trans-science in his formulation, though tort was not his starting-point. There is ambiguity in the visualization of fora or tribunals for trans-science. Tribunals involving science as only a part of the evidence in a legal question are created automatically by litigation and adversarial procedures are in any case axiomatic to Anglo-American practice. The occurrence of tribunals convened to hear trans-scientific issues through adversarial procedure are denied by experience. Matters commonly are non-litigative and in the United Kingdom are subjected customarily to inquisitorially-styled procedures such as those of Public Inquiries, Royal Commissions, House of Commons or House of Lords Select Committees, with the same kind of framework being adopted in risk and policy determinations.

Thus, Weinberg's depiction of resolution of questions that science cannot answer either could lie in utilization, by mistake, of adversarial procedure in litigative situations, or in some form of constructed inquiry that eschews inquisitorial methods for the sake of engaging the power of cross-examination. These options are not always exposed to eclecticism but any permitted exercise of choice should include measures to allow expression of conflict of expert opinion and acknowledgement that adjudication of disputes will need to take cognisance of it. Disagreement among experts can add to confusion but current states of knowledge are unlikely to be able to unlock important truths without testing opinions openly. Weinberg's advocacy is for adversarialism to be utilized constructively so that the best insight to reality can be determined through argument.

The exigency of policy formulation and the seizing of trans-science

Possibly overlooked in the need to procure some form of pronouncement on trans-scientific issues is the effect of the finalization of legal determinations. Throughout this work law has been depicted not only as presider over decisions involving science but as a time-limited arbiter of truth that guillotines discussion, even when those truths are known to be provisional. If Weinberg did not realize the conclusory nature of legal determinations, perhaps he imagined issues would be revisited when scientific knowledge improved. In principle there could be no objection to such an idealized process and it might be possible eventually through continuing research for science to have learned sufficiently to be able to answer its own questions. In the meantime, in environmental policy and regulation, trans-science often is characterized by an extrapolatory gap between the findings of short-term research and their predictive value, or pressure to predict from them. This is attributed to a freezing of the investigatory process by trans-science compared to the continual refinement of hypotheses by experimentation and observation normal to traditional science (Wagner 1986: 432-433). In the WTO, gaps in the best scientific evidence on which to found decisions in assessment of risk and formulation of policy can be bridged by *default inference rules* based on non-scientific considerations, propelled by the responsibility of regulatory government to act expeditiously, regardless of sometimes deficient scientific knowledge of consequences and vague or conflicting policies (Walker 1998: 252).

It is desirable to ground risk regulation in the purest possible scientific evidence, but limited knowledge in some circumstances obliges risk assessors to resort to models other than those of empirical science. Commonly, these are science policies that operate on a principle of protecting human health that belong, not to the canons of science, but are reflections of the goals of risk regulation (ibid: 260-261). A 'scientific doctrine' can be invoked in the political and social sphere where a type of scientific justification is used to advance programmes such as the psychological detriment occasioned in minority groups in society by educational deprivation (Weinberg 1972: 214).

Types of scientific evidence and their legal value

A digest of several leading legal disputes involving scientific presentations with difficult proofs will elicit the kinds of evidence relied on and the value placed on them by inquiries in assisting their conclusions. This will illustrate further that legal and quasi-legal fora can mistake issues of trans-science for those of science or oscillate between them. The analysis then can probe the limitations of science in order to locate its boundary with trans-science. It will explore also the relative strengths of various kinds of evidence presented in 'standard science' so that an impression can be gained of the task for law in relatively uncomplicated issues for comparison with the elusive and complex nature of issues belonging to the domain of trans-science.

Recognition that law should equip itself with mechanisms enabling it to distinguish between legitimate science and its 'meretricious look-alikes' sometimes has led to misconceptions that formulaic solutions like rules and the appointment of expert panels to inform the courts can perform the task, overlooking the contingencies that govern the production of scientific evidence (Jasanoff 1998: 84). Amid the disparity of imposed normativity that would be given by the operation of legal rules of evidence and the poor confidence underlying trans-science, judges frequently are called on to make delicate determinations of causation in conditions of uncertainty using rules designed for more determinable situations (Wagner 1986: 422). The judicial frame of mind sometimes is unable to accept that scientists not only can disagree on how to interpret the facts but on the facts themselves (Jones 1994: 46).

Matters in toxic torts are never either comprehensively or unfailingly matters for trans-science, whereas the chemical structure of a substance has a known harmful effect and whether the exposure of a complainant to it caused the injury or disease may be a trans-scientific question (Wagner 1986: 433). Different 'degrees of uncertainty' are created by determining whether a disease is specific to a particular substance or could have arisen naturally. While mesothelioma is specific to asbestos exposure, the link therefore being a matter of science, medical conditions that could be attributed to radiation, atmospheric pollution or hazardous wastes may have other causes and issues then are considered trans-scientific (ibid: 433, n.26). In early asbestos litigation, strict scientific proofs of causation were difficult since epidemiological data usually was not available (ibid: 433, n.26). A medical research aspect of epidemiological study explores the correlation of effects and their possible causation by accumulating sufficient data using strict scientific method to estimate statistical significance for their claims.[115] In diseases such as asbestosis, the interval between exposure to the substance thought to cause the harm and appearance of malignant tumours is so long that many subjects are lost to the study and therefore epidemiological data cannot be obtained (ibid: 433, n.26).[116]

Though toxicologists are accustomed to uncertainty in their science, its presentation in legal contexts confuses rather than informs and decisions are regarded as trans-scientific, being made in conditions of doubt (Brennan 1989:

---

[115] To understand evaluation of published research in medicine, see Greenhalgh (2001).

[116] For the legal effect of this, see Wagner (ibid: 433); and for the opinion that epidemiological evidence should be privileged in matters of toxic tort and product liability, see Edmond and Mercer (1997).

44). The American litigation of *Vann v City of Woodhaven*[117] concerned allegations that the death of a child had been caused by the spraying of insecticide. In the absence of epidemiological studies of the effect of the substance, the parties could rely only on existing case studies, animal studies and short-term tests, none of which were unequivocal (ibid: 48). The case was decided for the defence, possibly because the jury found the exposure data insufficient and they did not believe the causation evidence (ibid: 47).

In legal circles, the last two decades at least of the twentieth century witnessed significantly increased litigation in areas of toxic tort and product liability. Tort cases were over harm caused by industrial, agricultural and other substances, and many concerned pharmaceutical preparations that complainants claimed either had adverse effects, or else failed to achieve their stated purpose, accompanied by adverse consequences. The list of actions taken is long and it would be disproportionate for this study to attempt to examine them all. A rapid scan of literature elicits issues achieving public notoriety such as harms caused by the pesticides used on crops, personal injury claims in tobacco litigation, the linkage of asbestos with pneumoconiosis, harm from industrial effluent, food additives, and liability for pharmaceutical products such as thalidomide, *Opren, Debendox, Myodal*, neomycin, benzodiazopine, the Combined Oral Contraceptive, *Depo-Provera, Bendectin* and from silicone breast implants. Edmond and Mercer (1997: 667; 2000: 255-266) summarize the 'litigation explosion' as involving asbestos, *Agent Orange*, EMF (electricity pylons), oral contraceptives, tobacco, the effects of passive smoking and silicone breast implants.

In evidence-based or epidemiological medical studies, the relative risk of a harm being caused is the ratio of the probability of an event occurring in a group exposed to a conjectured harm versus that of a non-exposed group (see, for example, Badenoch and Henegan 2002: 16). When the ratio is in the order of unity (1.0), the difference in results is considered insignificant; a ratio of two (2.0) or more signifies the difference is higher than that attributable to chance. Where the stakeholders are members of the public, it is likely they could be satisfied with a lower standard of *relative risk* than two (2.0), as vindication of their fears concerning harm to health that it would provide. A concern for society then would be whether conclusions in trans-science were constructed quasi-legal outcomes of little real utility. Over-reaction to any suspected hazards resulting from this policy change would have severe economic consequences and succeed only in elevating perceived risk to such a level that it is never evaluated objectively.

---

[117] No. 84 425 092 NI (Wayne County Cir. Ct. Mich. June 12, 1988). Discussed in Brennan (1989).

Case study: Bendectin

The Bendectin litigation in the USA was a mass tort against the manufacturer, Merrell Dow Pharmaceuticals, by a large number of children claiming harm consequent upon their mothers' ingestion of the drug. Frequently, a difficulty in such cases is inadequate scientific proof of the harm (its causation), decisions turning on interpretation of scientific evidence and the prominence it is accorded in proceedings. *Bendectin* was beset by problems and influences that became common in that class of litigation at the time, chiefly attributed to 'sociologies of error' in which problems of law's operation were located in 'distortions of scientific evidence by the political pressures of the legal-regulatory context' (Edmond and Mercer 2000: 266). Analysis of this dispute consulted by the present study relates to disregard by law for the weight of evidence that properly conducted epidemiological studies represent amid other forms of scientific evidence.

Bendectin shines as a beacon for exploring issues in legal presentation of trans-scientific issues worthy of detailed attention, where not only is scientific knowledge tested in law but also where analysts of its proceedings rank evidence according to weight and certainty, to which law should attend. Rather than permitting themselves distraction by trans-science and entering a debate about whether its matters are real, coherent, reducible or resolvable by adversarial procedure, its critics centre their study on the mutual constitution by law and science of knowledge in legal contexts (Edmond and Mercer 1997: 2000). They are chary of the epistemological status of trans-science, implying its consideration in proceedings as a class of uncertain evidence that must be accepted is falsely premised. Their view is that law can negotiate its conclusions with scientists by identifying sound evidence and that legal functions need not be usurped by what might be trans-science, either in the form of its indeterminacies or its externalities such as political influence.

Research in the present study has given rise to a credible view that labelling indeterminate science or science 'under duress' as trans-science, can appear to legitimate it as a science of its own by the act of its naming. The entire concept, including resolution of conflict by adversarial procedure, then becomes 'respectable' as knowing that we do not know but turning that into a virtue. Edmond and Mercer disabuse us of that notion in their analysis of scientific presentation in Bendectin litigation and substitute firm alternative proposals. Their idea is unique and contradicts a common expectation of science in legal settings that law should seek affirmation of belief concerning the meaning of knowledge construction through scientific consensus. A problem is caused for law when there is no consensus in science and then it is cast in the rôle of adjudicator amid conflicting opinion. In toxic torts in particular, further difficulty ensues for courts if they become pre-occupied with evaluating the types of study offering the evidence, '[I]indeed these were the very controversies which the courts were called to resolve throughout the Bendectin litigation' (1997: 674), accounts of proceedings indicating they had no yardstick or other tool with which to accomplish this. In the same critique, they show that failure to privilege evidence of higher inherent reliability potentiates imperfect understanding.[118] In a prescription that acknowledges scientific provisionalism and, unusually, attributes a similar quality to legal decisions incorporating science, Edmond and Mercer recommend the following. Rather than attempting an artificial construction of scientific consensus, it is preferable to be able to assess the outcome as the co-production by scientists and lawyers of a precarious and incomplete politically (legally) enforced closure that is itself prone to further deconstruction and reconstitution in future law-science settings (ibid: 676). No elaboration of this pronouncement is provided and the last part seems ambiguous. It is accepted that closure by law is mandatory but, if a sense is being conveyed that decisions could be revisited in the light of fresh understanding of evidence or a shift in political background, then problems of managing this are introduced. If such an understanding is too literal, perhaps the line of reasoning it contains is that it can be recognized that adjudicating skills in toxic torts as a continuum of cases might mature over time in the light of better understanding of the value of scientific evidence, as well as acknowledgement of the social and political influences that produce it.

Analysis of single though complex disputes like *Bendectin* would fail to elicit other dimensions of science-law interaction in different toxic torts or environmental inquiries. It might not be appropriate to privilege epidemiological evidence in all circumstances, for instance, the extreme difficulty of establishing harm from passive smoking and from high electromagnetic fields around electricity pylons would tend to favour *in vivo* studies (ibid: 705) but adjudicators would need to be apprised of the reasons in order to avoid error. That there is no systematic method of educating decision-makers about such distinctions, contingencies and inter-case disparities, abandons the nature of outcomes to reliance on the experience of individual adjudicators or, in some civil jurisdictions, to a jury.

It is not believed the aim of Edmond's and Mercer's analysis is totally to discredit or invalidate the process of trans-science as an exigency when science cannot answer its own questions. However, caution is urged that a too-willing acquiescence to its precepts that might be deemed over-liberal with regard to science and assimilation of social, legal and political influences on outcomes, can impair legal integrity in science-law settings. The account is critical of other analysts who 'fail to provide a more refined image of the ambiguity and blurring of boundaries between scientific research and legal knowledge in such contexts' (ibid: 705-706) and incorporates a proposal that the conditions of trans-science can be evaded by a disciplined approach to scientific evidence.

Even more importantly, and connecting the strands of this discourse in a paradox, the assertion is made that the rational conclusion from authoritative epidemiological study that Bendectin was not harmful, would have concluded the tort simply but, in so doing, would have obscured the contingent and

---

[118] This and the above description illustrate what can be called the 'unknowing forum'.

constructed nature of science in the actual closure (ibid: 705). This suggests that the properties of trans-science and attempts at their mediation render service to law by bringing attention to the conditions of closure in toxic torts as well as in other science-law collisions that, in the estimation of Edmond and Mercer, bestow on them a 'secret life'.

Case study: Proving relative risk: *The Oral Contraceptive Group*

Epidemiological study is invoked as the most powerful recourse to proof in toxic torts, a contention supported by Edmond and Mercer but, if it is difficult for science to prove an association between an effect and a conjectured cause, then law cannot accept its evidence simply for that reason. Affirmation of causation in toxic torts for perceived harm is by showing the incurred harm was at least twice the magnitude of that of the normal background level (Wagner 1986: 436-437). If this can be determined with certainty the issue is no longer trans-scientific but this can be difficult even in 'regular' science-law encounters.

Concerning *Re: The Oral Contraceptive Group*,[119] a group action against the manufacturer of an oral contraceptive by women claiming it had caused them thrombosis, experts estimated the relative risk of harm to be raised by between 1.9 and 2.2, even for studies that the judge had not rejected for poor scientific method. This showed '...the claimants have at the outset a perilously low margin of error given their acceptance of the level of the threshold over which they have to climb, namely a true relative risk figure measurably in excess of 2[.0].'[120] The plaintiffs failed due to insufficient evidence of causation. The judge warned of the risks of relying on epidemiological evidence because it produced inconclusive results,[121] whereas in the opinion of the present study it was not the method of determining the evidence that was at fault but the simple fact that the mass of research undertaken did not support the assertion that thrombosis was associated with administration of the oral contraceptive.

In hearing this action, the judge questioned whether he was expected to become a kind of super-scientist in order to evaluate the many studies offered in evidence.[122] He undertook the task most competently, both through his willingness to comprehend the underlying science and in exercising his legal judgment. The judge eliminated several studies from the evidence owing to poor study design and for revealing the fundamental flaws and kinds of bias sufficient to discredit them. For the plaintiffs, success never seemed to have

---

[119] (*XYZ & others v Schering Health Care Ltd & others*). [2002] EWHC1420 (QB); [2002] All ER (D) 437.

[120] ibid: per Mackay, J., at 32.

[121] ibid: at 32.

[122] *Re The Oral Contraceptive Group* per Mackay J., at 34.

been much in promise as the studies estimating relative risks in excess of two that would have helped them were discarded for their poor science, and the better-designed inquiries were inconclusive. Amid the confusing, conflicting and inconclusive evidence the case was well managed by a wise choice of judge who was well matched to the case. Were a different judge less inclined to assimilate so much science, the outcome would be a matter of conjecture.

The issues in *Re: The Oral Contraceptive* Group bordered on the sub-scientific that others might term trans-scientific. It is evident the prior odds of the plaintiffs' success must have been very low but in this instance the question was settled by legal procedure using in-built normative standards.

LAW TAKES CHARGE AS TYRO IN TRANS-SCIENTIFIC ISSUES

Societal exigencies can oblige law to conclude on issues in the absence of convincing scientific evidence. As a common thread in the present study, this comment is by now unremarkable but the examples that follow illustrate procedures enacting the principles of trans-science, each with widely differing outcomes.

The Whooping Cough vaccine

The National Childhood Encephalopathy Study[123] was set up to resolve the controversy of whether the Pertussis Vaccine against whooping cough caused brain damage in children, as had been reported. It concluded that it could do so for one in one hundred thousand children, signifying an extremely low risk. In *Loveday v Renton and The Wellcome Foundation, Ltd.*,[124] Stuart Smith LJ declared himself not satisfied that the vaccine caused permanent brain damage. The plaintiff had called nine expert witnesses and the defendants ten, but the judge was more impressed by the 'quality of evidence and reasoning' of the ten experts called by the manufacturer than by the mechanism of injury proposed by the plaintiff's nine. He also concluded that examination of the data compiled by the *National Childhood Encephalopathy Study* failed to show that brain damage was caused by the vaccine and could be due in some cases to an underlying condition. Earlier, in *Kinnear v Wellcome Foundation Ltd.* (unreported), a case concerning entitlement to legal aid, an expert witness for the plaintiff admitted several errors in his evidence on cross-examination. He felt that the vaccine could cause brain damage in children but that he was in a minority among his peers in holding this view. His research papers had been turned down for publication (Dyer 1988: 1189-1190; British Medical Journal

---

[123] *Whooping Cough. Reports from the Committee for the Safety of Medicines and the Joint Committee on Vaccination and Immunization.* Department of Health & Social Security. London: HM Stationery Office, 1981.

[124] [1990] 1 Med LR 117

[125]1986: 1264-1266). Bowie (1990: 397-399) is critical of the scientific basis of the *National Childhood Encephalopathy Study*.

Curiously, a no-fault compensation scheme was established for vaccinated children exhibiting lasting neurological impairment under the *Vaccine Damage Payments Act* 1979 to parents who had been able to show, on the balance of probabilities, that it was the vaccine that had caused a disability in their children. This was awarded on the basis that marketing of medical products may be justified by their general utility and that those who suffer damage should be compensated because they bear the brunt of a scheme that is intended to benefit the population (Jones 1996: 416). In this confused outcome, law dismissed causation but set up a means via legislation to compensate those who could determine proof individually, provided admission of liability was not sought.

The Measles, Mumps and Rubella (MMR) vaccine

Amid the MMR controversy, Sumner J overrode a mother's objection to her daughters, Child 'C' and Child 'F', receiving the vaccination because he perceived the evidence affirming its safety was 'clear and persuasive' (Alleyne 2003; Tait and Timmins 2003). The law had intervened because the girls' parents disagreed between them over vaccinations and the judge had to act in the children's best interests. By the time the cases were heard it was felt by the medical community and government health agencies that the vaccine was safe but the public debate was continuing. In this instance the matter was concluded by legal decision and law was the only arbiter that could act in that capacity.

Gulf War Syndrome

Combatants returning from the first Gulf War began to complain of illnesses that they attributed to vaccines given them as protection from chemical, biological or other agents that the enemy might use. Sufferers, their families and support associations sought damages from the Ministry of Defence (MoD), which denied a causative link. Medical science has not yet proved the existence of a 'syndrome.' Some veteran combatants, being disabled by their condition and no longer able to work, sought compensation from the MoD in the form of disablement pensions. The Ministry of Defence denied liability and therefore refused their applications. In the instance of *Ministry of Defence v Rusling* [126] Newman J did not deliver a definitive verdict on whether Gulf War Syndrome was a distinct condition or 'single disease entity' but, importantly for the veterans, he did not close off the possibility. He said 'A claimant who bases his

---

[125] Legal Correspondent.
[126] 13th June 2003. Financial Times, London (UK), June 14th 2003.

claim for entitlement on the condition will carry the onus of proving its existence on the balance of probabilities'.

In the decision in *Rusling* the judge distinguished the lack of medical consensus over a syndrome of illnesses and the ability of a plaintiff to base his
claim for pension entitlement on his own proof on the balance of probabilities.
Here, law seems to have conferred liability for compensation on the MoD
without proving the existence of the syndrome. Although an idiosyncratic
conclusion, the tacit assumption that 'something' led to the illness, on the basis
of which individual claims could be made, appears, superficially at least, to
have been a trans-scientific pronouncement.

LAW TAKES CHARGE AS EXPERT: ITS VERY PECULIAR DISCRETION IN MEDICAL NEGLIGENCE

Idiosyncratic *Bolam*

English civil procedure embraces a legal tradition concerning medical negligence that is reminiscent of Weinberg's schema of trans-science, but also has
important differences. The similarity is in the use of adversarial procedure to
deal with difficult matters of science. It does not concern fact so much as
opinion in the way that courts rely on expert evidence. The purpose of experts
appearing in court often is to interpret the meaning of scientific facts, but in
the Bolam Test of liability for medical negligence arising from the leading case
of *Bolam v Friern Hospital Management Committee*.[127] The law separates
breaches of the *duty* of care, on which it can adjudicate unaided, from infrac-
tions of the *standard* of care, for which it is reliant on the opinion of the
medical profession to conclude. Law has no direct means of deciding whether
the practice of a defendant clinician was negligent but looks to the medical
profession to advise on what is acceptable. Inevitably, professional opinion
arises from a conflation of scientific fact, medical knowledge and experience. In
trans-scientific inquiry, viewed from Weinberg's perspective, fact, knowledge,
experience and opinion on the part of experts might be conflated similarly. By
definition, a trans-scientific inquiry would lack requisite facts, so expert opinion would be likely to form the basis for conclusions.

Settling issues in medical negligence sometimes is complicated by uncertainty and conflicting expert opinion, which exercises law's discretion strenu-
ously. Often, there is no single medical opinion about acceptable practice,
therefore no universally 'right' approach to care. Though this can indicate lack
of certainty among the medical community, it remains for law to decide which
opinion it prefers and to provide reasons for that choice.

The debate over whether this typifies the legal conclusions of trans-science
might never conclude, but examining the evolution of *Bolam* evinces striking

---

[127] [1957] 1 WLR 582; [1957] 2 All ER 118.

indications of the way in which law is able to conclude on matters of indeterminable science, irrespective of whether this concerns interpretation of fact or acceptable practice, as the following will show. Although *Bolam* is criticised for its idiosyncratic approach and is felt by some in legal circles to be unreliable, it exhibits a strange coherence among its decisions, a characteristic that trans-science might not be able to claim.

The Bolam Test is concerned with identification of liability and it has been shown that it is an inappropriate test for causation.[128] Judges are reluctant to attribute liability in medical negligence using their own unaided judgment because of the complexities of medicine and the contingencies of practice. In *Sidaway v Board of Governors of the Bethlem Royal Hospital and the Maudsley Hospital*,[129] Lord Donaldson described the inexactitude of medical science, saying that in it 'all things are uncertain or nearly all things are uncertain' and in an almost sociological comment, 'that knowledge', referring to uncertainty, 'is part of the general experience of mankind.'[130] In *Thake v Maurice*, Lord Nourse said that, 'of all the sciences, medicine is one of the least exact',[131] and in *Maynard v West Midlands Regional Health Authority*, Lord Scarman said: '...Differences of practice exist, and will always exist, in the medical as in all other professions. There is seldom any one answer exclusive of all others to problems of professional judgment.'[132]

Bolam situates the question of a practitioner's contended negligence in conformity with the standards of 'reasonably competent medical men at the time' (Jones 1996: 94),[133] so the criterion of acceptable practice is that decided by 'a responsible body of medical men skilled in that particular art.'[134] Brazier captures this idea by advising that courts must ascertain the standard of skill that a practitioner should have met by asking the doctors (1992: 121). This explains finally that the procedure handed down by *Bolam* to the courts hearing actions for medical negligence, is that the judge will assess liability in medical negligence by hearing testimony from practitioners in the same specialty as the defendant called as expert opinion witnesses. The Test is rooted in the 'Reasonable Man' standard residing in the law of torts that assesses practice by determining what a 'man of ordinary prudence' would do (Fleming 1992: 106). Bolam-type determinations in tort may be compared with those of *res ipsa loquitur* and strict liability that pertain more to circumstance and foreseeable risk.[135] With regard to tests of reasonable competence, Teff assigns

---

[128] [1993] 4 Med LR 381 per Simon Brown LJ (dissenting) at 390.
[129] [1985] 1 All ER 643, 649.
[130] [1984] 2 WLR 772 at 778, 782.
[131] [1986] QB 664 at 686–687.
[132] [1984] 1 WLR 634 at 638.
[133] Concerning the dictum of McNair, J. in *Bolam* (*op. cit.*) at 122.
[134] In *Bolam* (*op. cit.*) at 122.
[135] See Fleming (ibid).

Bolam a normative standard juxtaposed, if not conflated, with a descriptive one (1994: 184).

Medical negligence is a complex aspect of the law of tort and the brief description of it given here is to meet the purpose of this part of the study only. By no means is it intended as a comprehensive evaluation of the intricacies and refinements of *Bolam* and the development in common law that it fostered.[136] Judgments in *Bolam* acknowledge there are one or more perfectly proper standards of care (Jones 1996: 94). In *Hunter v Hanley*, Lord President Clyde indicated the scope for genuine differences of opinion among medical practitioners in diagnosis and treatment, saying that negligence is not necessarily attributed to the differing conclusions of one, nor because he has displayed less skill or knowledge than others.[137] In *Bolam*, McNair J. advised that a practitioner will not be found guilty of negligence '...if acting in accordance with such a practice merely because there is a body of opinion that takes a contrary view.'[138] This labyrinthine statement is better understood in the dictum of Robins J. in the Canadian jurisdiction of Ontario, in *Holmes v Board of Hospital Trustees of the City of London*,[139] that Jones (1996: 98) offers: 'Where, in the exercise of his judgment a physician selects one of two alternatives, either of which might have been chosen by a reasonable and competent physician, he will not be held negligent.'

The courts recognize that opinions proffered in Bolam-type procedures are actual evidence, though sometimes they are all that is available to guide decisions. There is also justification for changing the stress of the previous observation to read that expert opinions are no more than evidence. They may not be conclusive or sufficient, for example a common practice itself may be negligent (ibid) and, though an indicator of appropriate action in a test of negligence, opinions are not determinative (ibid: 95; Teff 1994: 184). These are crucially important distinctions because they preserve the ultimate responsibility for decision-making for judges, not experts.

Greater than the critical task for adjudicators in cases following *Bolam* of evaluating conflicting expert opinion is the manner in which such opinions influence decision-making and the means by which judges come to prefer the evidence of some experts to those of others. Judges make inferences from evidence in reaching their conclusions. It is not the case that evidence determines conclusions. Nor is the preference limited just to two diametrically opposing views. In controversial treatments there can be several general differences of opinion and variations with regard to particular aspects within

---

[136] Exploration of issues in medical negligence and the application of *Bolam* can be found in Francis and Johnstone (2001), Jones (1996), Kennedy and Grubb (1994), Brazier (1992). Legal aspects of the Bolam Test are evaluated exhaustively by Teff (1994).

[137] 1955 SC 200, 204-205 (paraphrased).

[138] In *Bolam* (*op. cit.*) at 122.

[139] (1977) 81 DLR (3d) 67, 91, per Robins J. (Ont. HC).

each. When considering Weinberg's idea of a forum, the expectation of conflicting evidence being received introduces problems for judicial types of determination in that, according to some kind of parameter or yardstick, it is necessary
to accept one or other belief as sufficient for today's conclusion. A rationality
founded on common sense and reliance on a sense of reasoning from legal
experience would be helpful, no doubt, but then not only would decisions risk
the lack of inter-dispute coherence, but also the reasons that adjudicators gave
for decisions would lack cogency as they would differ from case to case. Judgments in cases following *Bolam* show development of standards that confer
coherence among decisions on this special aspect of judge-made law, as will be
shown next.

Were there to be divided expert opinions it would be expected that any
single view indicating departure from common practice would be sufficient for
the plaintiff to succeed. But in its contemplation, the Bolam Test provides that
where there is more than one common practice, compliance with one of the
practices will normally excuse the defendant (Jones 1996: 99). The proposition
was fully reversed in *Bolitho v City and Hackney Health Authority*.[140] On
appeal, the decision of the lower court that had been based on one of a number
of accepted practices asserted by several experts was overturned. It was
determined that it was not sufficient for a defendant to produce evidence from
a number of experts that his opinion accorded with medical practice in order to
escape liability. The court had to be satisfied that the exponents of medical
opinion relied upon could demonstrate that such opinion had a logical basis
(Harpwood 2001: 1). Browne-Wilkinson LJ said with regard to assessment of
risk concerning medical treatment in *Bolitho* that '... if in a rare case it can be
demonstrated that the professional opinion is not capable of withstanding
logical analysis, the judge is entitled to hold that the body of opinion is not
reasonable or responsible.'[141] Thus the ruling in *Bolam* that the standard of
medical practice was a matter entirely for expert opinion was weakened by
Bolitho, returning it to legal judgment. Although the standing of expert medical
witnesses usually attests that they are unlikely to give opinions that are unsup-
portable in logic (ibid: 2), the courts now may exercise the option of disregard-
ing it. This narrative will show elsewhere that egregious error on the part of
experts that should have been detected as 'failing in logic' by the courts was
actually accepted. Harpwood's report on the effect of *Bolitho* concludes with a
reminder that expert witnesses should give reasons for their opinions, which
allows the judge to scrutinize them for coherence, rationality and logic (ibid).
This moves proof of liability in medical negligence closer to an objective
standard.

---

[140] [1997] 39 BMLR 1; [1998] 1 Lloyd's Rep Med 26; [1998] AC HL (E) 232.
[141] [1988] AC (HL (E)) at 243.

Exemplifying legal preference of expert opinion:
Swift v Bexley

The reasons judges give for preferring the evidence of certain expert opinion witnesses sometimes can be exquisite and even a minority view among experts found acceptable. In *Swift v Bexley and Greenwich Health Authority*[142] it was claimed by a patient that a clip to repair an aneurysm in an artery at the base of her brain was the cause of her blindness, because placement of the clip had damaged nerve fibres in her optic chiasma—a structure that was very close to the artery in question. This unreported case follows the spirit of *Bolitho* and demonstrates a fine appreciation by the judge of the weight to give particular evidence where it conflicts. It is instructive in the best discretion of the judiciary in cases of conflicting opinion from specialists. There was an impressive array of expert witnesses for both plaintiff and defendant but Mr Justice Gage privileged the evidence of a clinical academic, though he had performed the type of operation concerned only once, against that of a more experienced neurosurgeon. The reason he gave was that, although the neurosurgeon giving expert opinion evidence had far more clinical experience of repairing such aneurisms, using a defined surgical approach, the clinical academic expert medical witness demonstrated 'a great deal of knowledge of the anatomy of the area involving the optic apparatus and the cerebral arteries gained from his interest in lesions around the optic chiasma'. Gage J found the witness whose opinion he preferred to be 'a very impressive witness' and 'knowledgeable and moderate in the expression of his opinions.' He found for the plaintiff. Although surprising in his preference of expert opinion, the judge's reasons withstand logical analysis in prioritising knowledge over experience. Greater understanding of the relationship of structures at risk in the operation by the academic indicated the degree of care incumbent upon the neurosurgeon and was highly apposite to the plaintiff's claim.

Harpwood enunciates a concern in both legal and medical circles that judges lack ability to comprehend medicine and that only judges trained and experienced in medical negligence or who have medical knowledge should be allowed to hear complex cases involving such disputes (ibid: 3). Lack of ability will be construed here as meaning without training. This is irrefutable as an argument but two mitigating factors emerge. First, although examination here has been restricted to selected leading cases and errors are apparent in many others, or this thesis would not need to have been written, judges are seen not only to comprehend principles of medical practice if adequately explained but also to employ reasoning satisfactorily in order to conclude. The judgments in *Bolitho* and *Swift* attest this and they make a strong point for law.

Second, retraining judges as scientists, an idea that has common currency, instead would involve them in scientific disputes (Jasanoff 1995: 209). It

---

[142] 25th May 2000 (unreported).

should not become their task to arbitrate which among scientific opinions is more convincing of the truth. The law would lose its essential autonomy were this to occur. Rather than turn judges into 'referees in scientific disputes', greater benefit would be conferred on legal decisions if judges were to learn pertinent aspects of the philosophy of science, so that they appreciate the limitations of scientific capability, together with the sociology of science and of scientific knowledge. There might be greater utility in this approach than, say, the efforts in the United States to create reference manuals of scientific and psychiatric evidence (Federal Judicial Center 1994; American Psychiatric Association 2000).

NEGOTIATING THE MEANING OF SCIENCE: THE EXEMPLARY PROCEDURE OF THE AMERICAN FOOD AND DRUG ADMINISTRATION

American Food and Drug Administration (FDA) procedures for settling issues of scientific uncertainty with regard to licensing medical products for sale contrast those of litigation, the ramifications of the method of concluding being of great interest in the present study. It represents a regulatory-style resolution of scientific issues and therefore law operating 'at arm's length'. A single case is taken for illustration in which the manufacturers of a pharmaceutical preparation sought FDA approval for its use in preventing breast cancer. Tamoxifen had been administered as a chemopreventative drug for thirty years to women treated for previous breast cancer to inhibit its recurrence, in which it had been highly successful. The manufacturer proposed its application be extended as a preventative to women who had not had breast cancer but were identified as being at high risk of it due to genetic and other predisposing factors. A licence was requested for this use in the United States, and the hearing to be described shortly formed part of that consideration. Trials had been conducted but medical opinion was divided as to whether proof for the envisaged new use of tamoxifen was conclusive. In its approved rôle, the drug showed reduction of mortality and morbidity among women five to eight years post-treatment. A problem for trials was that they needed to be conducted over periods of at least this duration for meaningful evaluation.

To consider the application a meeting was held of the Oncologic Drugs Advisory Committee (ODAC) of the Department of Health and Human Services of the Food and Drug Administration's Center for Drug Evaluation and Research, in Bethesda, Maryland, on September 2nd 1998.[143] The Committee comprised eleven ODAC Members of whom eight were medical scientists and three were consumer/patient representatives. There were also four medical consultants, five medical expert guests and ten scientists employed by the FDA. Lay participants were 'breast cancer activists and survivors.' Procedure com-

---

[143] Miller Reporting Company Inc., Washington D.C.

menced with conflict of interest declarations by all participants. There were open public hearings in which prepared statements were given and letters read out. Sponsors from the applicant manufacturer made their presentations and the Committee put questions. An ODAC member led the presentation on behalf of the FDA and discussion followed. The characteristics of the trials were discussed and arguments for and against the application produced on the basis of the evidence. Adverse effects of tamoxifen were noted, among which was a trend towards increased mortality and morbidity among post-treatment subjects after five to eight years of continuing drug administration, compared with those who discontinued it after that time. Its effect on other cancers was also considered. Social implications of licensing the drug as a chemopreventative were included, for instance a lay participant felt that guaranteeing tamoxifen as a breast cancer preventative would convince high-risk asymptomatic women that they need no longer undergo routine screening for detection of the disease. Another lay participant indicated the tendency in modern times to treat risk as if it were a disease.

It is believed the examined transcript constitutes only part of a chain of processes considering the licence application and therefore that conclusions reached in this instance may not reflect the whole of the FDA procedure concerning use of tamoxifen as a chemopreventative. In order to conclude at that stage, the Committee tendered a number of propositions framed as questions encapsulating problems associated with the application. Negotiation over the language of each question ensued until agreement was reached as to its form. Only the first four are reproduced here, the remainder concerning warnings about adverse effects and advice to be given in product information over the need for women taking tamoxifen to continue with screening. The four questions ran as follows.

1. 'Is NSAPB P–1 (the principal trial proffered in evidence) an adequate and well-controlled trial demonstrating the efficacy of tamoxifen in reducing the short-term incidence of breast cancer in women entered in this trial, which could be all or some?' A vote was held among the eleven Members and the proposition in the question accepted unanimously.

2. 'Does the NSAPB P–1 demonstrate that tamoxifen has a favourable benefit-risk ratio for the prevention of breast cancer in women at increased risk as defined by the study population?' There was a unanimous vote against this proposition. After discussion, the next was offered as a modification of the previous one that had failed.

3. 'With the limited follow-up available, does NSAPB P–1 demonstrate that tamoxifen has a favourable benefit-risk ratio for decreasing the incidence of breast cancer in the patients in this study population?' Votes were nine in favour and two against. And then,

4. 'Should tamoxifen be approved for risk reduction in the short-term incidence of breast cancer in women at increased risk as defined by the study population?' Here there were nine votes in favour and two abstentions.

Portable Decision-making

It can be seen that ODAC worked progressively towards agreement by a staged series of carefully stratified and qualified propositions. All the participants at the hearing contributed to discussion but only the Members had authority to vote. Decisions were reached by deconstructing the single general proposition of the licence application and obtaining agreement to limited use of tamoxifen in prescribed circumstances that in the trial were indicated as efficacious. As a construction of reality by ODAC, it was a negotiated form by virtue of the substitution of more acceptable propositions for the less acceptable, distilled by evidence and discussion. Few other tribunals exhibit such a systematically-negotiated outcome. Procedure accounts for decisions, which lessens the need for appeals or re-hearings. The outcome cannot be taken to mean anything that evidence and procedure cannot show.

As a forum for trans-scientific resolution of issues, ODAC procedure is partly inquisitorial in that the parties submit their case and it is the tribunal that consults the experts. Opportunities for cross-examination do not appear to exist *de facto*, unlike in Weinberg's description of practice to obtain a licence for the construction of a nuclear reactor in the USA (1972: 214), but instead a tempered procedure allows democratic representation of opinion, negotiation of issues and shared decision-making, and has an informal style. This creates a working atmosphere conducive to a non-adversarial form of discussion that would not be alien to alternative dispute resolution, amplified by the negotiated character of settlement. There is a conciliatory tone in that propositions move the need to agree with the general contention concerning the efficacy of the drug that the trial did not support to more specific assertions that the trial endorsed, which the Committee felt comfortable in accepting. There is further resonance with alternative dispute resolution in that, certainly in this instance, all parties emerged as winners—not outright winners but each was rewarded with territorial gains. The applicant won a licence to market the drug for certain purposes, users would benefit from the therapeutic effect of the drug and were protected from misleading representation of prophylaxis. The FDA obtained assurances that the appropriate use of the drug had been decided.

The primary function of the FDA is national regulation in an area of social importance and the statutory framework under which it operates is not built on voluntarism. However, the work of ODAC represents a type of proceduralization of law in that it operates under statute but law itself does not mediate outcomes directly. In its markedly hybridised form, FDA procedure has other quasi-legal aspects in that the Committee seeks the best estimate of truth in the propositions that it frames, and hence minimization of risk.

It is not inevitable that ODAC should contend only with uncertainty. Some licence applications will be supported by conclusive research but its procedure facilitates restriction of decisions to those where conviction concerning evidence can be signalled by voting. It exemplifies the collaboration of science and government in reduction of risk but evaluations are made principally by scientists, even though within a regulatory framework. This is not true to Weinberg's pure form to resolve trans-scientific issues but perhaps is a more honest method of deciding the truth than that offered by adversarialism in such situations, where sometimes the strength of argument rather than the strength of facts govern the success of a proposition.

The FDA method is appropriate when at least some facts are available but contended, and Weinberg's where they are unavailable or speculative. FDA/ODAC procedure contains some of the elements of trans-science in that the members vote on their understanding of what the evidence means, like a jury returning a verdict by majority. A difference from trans-science is that the 'jury' is comprised mainly of scientists, although nothing in Weinberg's idealization suggests judgments would be the exclusive responsibility of lawyers. It emulates a kind of specialist court, though differing from proposals for these by not being held directly under the auspices of law. It also signifies a procedure that scientists could use to negotiate the *meaning* of uncertain science, though in this guise the issues would be more epistemological than trans-disciplinary. Nonetheless, a negotiated agreement on the meaning of uncertain science would offer to law a firmer foundation for its conclusions and reduce the risk of error in interpretation.

PROVIDING ASSURANCE IN REGULATORY DECISION-MAKING

Analysing risks: A National Agency for Science and Health—an institutional approach

Trans-science manifests as a potential mediative resource in the incommensurability of science and law in legal contexts. The preceding characterization is as a contingent medium for resolving contingent problems. This could banish trans-science to a realm of well-intended but unsuccessful measures; poorly-conducted inquiries would confirm that impression. Regardless of outcomes, truth represented by science would be a construction limited by current scientific achievement. Trans-scientific procedure then would become a surrogate for knowledge production with which society might be content, if the wisdom and experience of law or law-like deliberation were seen to be applied to important problems that science could not immediately resolve.

Never far from the debate in this work is the issue of public concern over the MMR vaccine and its possible effects on children. It is plain that parental concern and the failure of government health departments to provide satisfactory reassurance over the safety of the vaccine when the controversy emerged (Horton 2004: 38) added psychological factors that overrode scientific proof as determinant of its acceptability. Viewed dispassionately, the vaccine appears never to have posed the imagined risk but parents still remain unconvinced, as shown by the increased prevalence of measles since the option of the triple vaccine was declined by so many (see Bedford and Elliman 2002). In the pure sense of Weinberg's prescription, science actually has proved adequate on this occasion to answer its own question, so strictly the MMR issue is no longer one of trans-science. But the crisis is typical of many in modern society in that, in psychosocial respects, science is regarded as inconclusive by a section of its stakeholders. This relocates scientific proof firmly in the social domain which then interposes a further hurdle, that of settling disquiet in the public view. This can re-attach the trans-scientific label even if undeserved, and 'transcendent' thereby acquires a new prominence; as Horton indicates in *MMR Science and Fiction: Exploring the Vaccine Crisis*, '...the lack of any reliable institutional mechanism to allow differing points of view to be heard, discussed, challenged and, to the extent that they can be, resolved into a single consensus opinion' (2004: 61). He remarks earlier that society knows little of the way individuals, families and communities reach decisions about the acceptability of medical products (ibid: 59).

Horton devises a remedy—a 'National Agency for Science and Health'—as an independent body to judge the health effects and ethical implications of new science and technology.[144] The MMR vaccine issue appears in Horton's list of exemplified topics similar to those given elsewhere in this chapter, where public concern is attributed to scientific uncertainty that government agencies seem powerless to reduce (ibid: 62). The projected 'Agency', to be led by a prominent and scientifically literate public figure but not necessarily a scientist, would have a multidisciplinary structure and draw on the expertise of national and international centres of scientific excellence. It would have considerable lay participation and operate by means of committees inquiring into areas of concern. Its *raison d'être* would be assessment of risk, upon which it would embark prospectively, not reactively, and a principal aim would be avoidance of short-term flares of public concern driven by marginal scientific opinion and media-induced hyperbole (ibid: 62-63).

Horton also envisages the notion of a 'gain and loss account' in risk estimation that the 'Agency' could inculcate whereby, in the MMR debate for example, the undesirable outcome of children contracting disease by parental refusal of vaccination would be set against the theoretical risk of a rare and disputed complication (ibid: 64). Although grounded more in inquisitorial procedure than adversarial, Horton's inspired vision comes near to that of a 'National Agency for Trans-science', which the present study can imagine.

Horton makes no suggestion of procedures to negotiate the meaning of science and he appears unconcerned with adversarialism. Weinberg is a scientist but it is conceivable that other scientists, like Horton, perceive the adversarial contest of opinion as neither necessary nor proper when discussing science. If scientific evidence is sound then the objective investigation of inquisitorial procedure would be appropriate and productive, but crises of public confidence can cause questioning even of reliable verification. Imagining a vociferous lay membership participating in the business of the Agency seeking to champion the cause of an anxious public, the need can be foreseen

---

144 In effect, an agency dealing with public fears.

quite readily for the ability to cross-examine experts that adversarialism affords. Horton's proposal then needs this restructuring but its philosophy would remain intact. Such a 'National Agency' also would constitute a regularized forum presently lacking for hearing issues in trans-science. It would avoid inquiries in areas of both conventional science and trans-science suffering from the effects of being held under different auspices and according to different rules. For trans-science it would mitigate its greatest disadvantage perceived in this work that it might operate under procedures set up *ad hoc.*

Anticipating risks: participatory processes

Löfstedt's approach to resolving scientific controversies aims at their pre-emption, while Horton's, though prospective, can act only when a problem materializes. Visualizing broad participatory processes involving the public in matters of uncertain or 'risky' science, Löfstedt emphasizes the benefit of appropriate risk communication. Horton's approach is institutional. It imagines the conclusions of its specialist panels will be acceptable to the public, who will not have been consulted and for whom the best methods of communication will not have been considered. Löfstedt's anticipatory vision accords with approaches to problems of philosophy revealed elsewhere in this study that *dissolving* rather than resolving them is preferable. It is considered later whether this represents a promising framework if adopted for mediation of science-law disappointments. Löfstedt's prescriptions could apply equally to science as to trans-science and would be of greater benefit in trans-scientific matters where doubt and risk are more strongly characterized.

Encouraging greater public and stakeholder participation in the policy-making process, either via citizen panels, 'juries' or by having stakeholders participate in a policy-making round table, Löfstedt treats scientists as just one of several stakeholders (2004a: 338). With regard to communication of food risk, he recommends the establishment of a 'platform of scientists' to take the matter forward (2004b: 4). Issues of public trust in risk communication are confronted, Löfstedt believing in employing open-ended face-to-face interviews among random populations where an issue has been raised, using the results to develop a communications programme and acting accordingly (2003a: 427). Risk communication strategies are essential for allaying public concerns but they must be apposite and well-managed. Löfstedt cites the example of the extraordinary disquiet caused by precipitate warnings about high levels of acrylamide in cooked high starch foods in Sweden that transpired to be an over-estimate of danger (2003b: 432). The rôle of Non-Governmental Organisations should be expanded to represent and interpret the precautionary principle, which Löfstedt *et al.* attach among others to problems of genetically modified organisms (2002: 386).

INTUSSUSCEPTION OF LAW AND SCIENCE

The following account is of the ethnographic study of the French Adminis-trative Court—the Conseil d'Etat—that was conducted by Latour and published in the French language as *La Fabrique du Droit: Une Ethnographie du Conseil d'Etat* (2002).[145] The version relied on here is the web-based version in English of *Objets des Sciences, Objectivité du Droit*, translated by Pottage, A., as *Scientific Objects and Legal Objectivity (Portrait of the Conseil d'Etat as a Laboratory)*.[146] 'Intussusception' means the sliding of a tubular organ into another portion, a kind of 'infolding', and is borrowed from medicine where it describes a condition of the bowel needing surgical correction or, in botany, where a cell wall grows by inclusion of particles within it.[147] In *La Fabrique du Droit*, Latour claims to draw the culture of science into that of a special court of law and then considers the court behaving as if it were a laboratory. This is typical of Latour's interdisciplinary form of study in which, because he asserts there is less organisation of intellectual life in France, he declares a freedom to define himself without reference to intellectual boundaries (Crawford 1993).

This brings new and interesting perspectives to this study but it is less concerned with the transformation of microprocedures that Latour explores in his study than the unique manner in which science can be interpreted in a special legal setting. This raises the possibility of a new framework to consider in alleviating science-law difficulty. In the description, emphasis is on scientific evidence presented 'legally' and the contrasts with science's normal presenta-tion that that evinces. However, the idea of intussusception is preferred here because the impression gained from Latour's chapter is more that of the two cultures having 'slid into each other'.

The focus of interest for the present study is the increasing detachment from the evidence achieved through a series of addresses by court officials and the way in which legal argument develops from scientific facts. Latour links scientific research and legal cases through their common reliance on texts—the laboratory record book and the legal case file—and that, for both, these replace the external world. Latour's ethnographic studies are better known in the English-speaking world from his study with Woolgar, *Laboratory Life: The Construction of Scientific Facts*. From it was deduced that scientific facts emerge from a cycle of productivity involving 'literary inscription', that is, the recording of measurements, writing reports and scientific papers (Latour and Woolgar 1986), hence a return to reliance on texts in the work under consid-eration.

---

[145] An ethnographic study of a court also has been carried out by Rock (1993).

[146] Posted on the Bruno Latour Website (2004). See Bibliography.

For an analysis of the functioning of the Conseil d'Etat as part of the executive, not the legislature, see Hamson (1954).

[147] Encarta World English Dictionary (1999) London: Bloomsbury Publishing Plc.

It is believed here by the present author that the exercise conducted in La-tour's 'Portrait' relies on his imagination of the way in which scientific evidence could be brought into a court for decisions concerning its meaning and impli-cation for law; that is to say, he reconstructs the procedures of the Conseil d'Etat as a model way for determining legal implications protested by science, not that the claims necessarily require the support of science.

Hearings in the court consist of oral readings of prepared written state-ments. Experts do not appear and so they are not examined. To open, the Rapporteur presents to the court two contradictory drafts of decisions—'projets du jugement'—which the court debates and, after hearing them, the President can demand preparation of a third if the court accepts neither. A séance d'instruction will have preceded the case in which arguments are rehearsed before submitting them to colleagues. In the next stage the Réviseur re-presents the Rapporteur's note of the case. The Réviseur transforms it by altering the respective proportions of fact and law, placing more emphasis than did the Rapporteur's note on strictly legal questions. The claimant and his/her representative lawyers have the deepest interest in facts. Rising through progressive stages of presentation and the hierarchy of the court, an increasing interest in law is adopted by the Rapporteur and the Réviseur, culminating in total concern with law by the Conseillers, or judges. (It is implicit also from Latour's description that the Conseil d'Etat hears appeals against lower judg-ments).

The Commissaire du Gouvernment, another court official, is a kind of quality controller who retraces the course taken by the participants in the case and tests claims for coherence with accumulated administrative law. (French administrative law is a corpus of case-based law and different from the code-based systems that deal with private and criminal affairs). The Commissaire remains silent in proceedings except for reading conclusions and gives the participants the occasion to doubt properly rather than accept any precipitately reached solution or 'cheaply bought consensus'. Through Pottage's translation, Latour characterizes the Commissaire du Gouvernment as 'an airtight chamber for the avoidance of uncertainty, a kind of injunction to avoid agreement, an obstacle placed along the length of the path of judgment, an irritant'.

Intussusception, with respect to the Conseil d'Etat in Latour's visualiza-tion, would afford the opportunity to compare the representation of science within science with the proffering of scientific matters to law, in conjunction with the distancing of law from science in successive presentations. Such trans-formations are intended to achieve thoroughly legal conclusions. In scientific debate, there is no parallel to the Rapporteur's preparation of two or more distinct draft outcomes. Perhaps scientists should be asked always to present their conclusions and their potential falsifications side-by-side in a manner of which Popper would approve.[148]

---

[148] See Popper (1972).

In the laboratory, every effort is made to connect the material of the study to what is being said about it, but in the Conseil d'Etat similar effort is made to distance the final determination from the particulars of the case. In science, a sound theory can generate a fact through inference. This retrodictive path does not exist in law where, once a point of law is grasped, there need be no further reference to the facts.

As the case ascends the hierarchy of judgment, it is dealt with by people who have decreasing knowledge of the facts. In science, Latour likens this to seeking the advice of people with fewer and fewer competences in the subject to allocate claims about controversial discoveries. The scientist is characterized as passionate about his research; the succession of disinterested presenters in the Conseil d'Etat ensures any passion for results is left behind.

Science has no equivalent of the Commissaire du Gouvernment who gives the opportunity to doubt, unless referring to the diffuse form of self-regulation exercised by the scientific community. Science is preoccupied with reasons for certainty. In other courts, judges might be provided with opportunities to doubt, but errors in law are left to resolution by appeals. There is no contemporaneous scrutinizing of procedure.

Most conspicuously absent from these procedures is the opportunity to examine experts whose facts are incorporated in the lower level presentation to the Conseil d'Etat. No means is available therefore to prevent misunderstanding. In mitigation, the separation of experts' involvement in material from points of law and legal argument approaches the ideal that should characterize law's conclusions in any situation. Assumed is the ability of the Rapporteur to make an adequate assessment of the evidence so that legal points arising from it are properly identified by the Réviseur.

PART C. TRANSCENDENT MEDIATIVE RESOURCES: SURPASSING EPISTEMOLOGICAL SEPARATIONS

Chapter V. The Possibility of Alternative Rationalities in Resolving the Central Problem

PROBLEMS AND LIMITATIONS OF THE EPISTEMOLOGICAL APPROACH

Epistemologically based tensions in tribunals still create the potential for misunderstanding and can place truth at risk. In seeking to reduce such tensions, early recourse often is made to their epistemological foundations. It would be imagined that comparison of the ways in which they construct reality would yield possibilities for amelioration of difficulty. Using this route, the science-law disjunction is confronted directly, which mirrors that encountered in dispute resolution, policy-making and regulation.

In the analysis of mediative resources, it must be asked whether utilizing precisely the nature of the problem as the tool for obtaining reconciliation reasonably can be expected to be productive. After all, it is admitted that different epistemologies create different constructions of reality that in the case of science and law have proved incommensurable. Mixed or hybrid approaches, either through procedures or epistemologies introduce other problems, as was seen in the American attempt to institute science courts (Weinberg 1972; Martin 1977; Christiansen 1979; Brennan 1989),[149] the creation of 'lawyer-scientists' or 'science counsellors' (Jasanoff 1995: 220). Though posed as rational expedients, these mixed approaches seemingly cannot avoid a weakening of law's function in the final outcome due to the tendency for science to move up as the arbiter of truth.

Expectations that sociology would yield a unique perspective with some kind of interpretive capability were disappointed, even though a special new rôle was found for it in the sociology of the epistemic trap. Also considered have been both transcendent and transformative vehicles that import or export

---

[149] For a comprehensive bibliography of science courts, see Cavicci (2003).

their epistemological constructions for contemplation by other fields, as well as inviting decision-making by them, of which Weinberg's trans-science and Latour's ethnographic studies are examples respectively. Through these studies, modification of procedure can be seen to offer respite but not radical solutions, indeed some schools of philosophy indict epistemology with having failed.

Revealed in the literature are new provinces of thought circulating beyond the constraints of epistemological comparisons. These reside in critical and cultural theories and in those emanating from Continental philosophy. They represent radical departures from the kinds of ideas this study has considered so far and offer new frameworks from which to consider resources of potential in the mediation of law's disappointment with science as collaborator in evidential contexts.

EPISTEMOLOGICAL COLLISIONS IN THE LEGAL FORUM: ORIGINS IN THE KANTIAN PHILOSOPHICAL TRADITION

Throughout this work, it has been claimed that the legal forum represents the site not only for exposure of, and argument concerning, scientific issues inhabiting law's decisions—but also as the locus of difficulties in communication and understanding. The problems experienced can be summarized according to the following attributions of cause, mention of which is made at various points in this work. In no order of importance, they are failure of communication in that law does not comprehend fully the meaning it should attach to offered science and science does not possess the facility to express it meaningfully to law; science and law have disparate ways of constructing reality; the historical and epistemological foundations of science and law are different; their perception of truth differs and sometimes law demands a certainty from science that cannot be assured. To these can be added the general caveat that science and law have divergent societal purposes affecting the way they utilize information. In addition to the inherent difficulties posed by the classes of problems just described, others are created by the customs and practices of tribunals and boards of inquiry. While there is insufficient space here to conduct a thorough examination of these—and an interesting research is held in prospect—certain aspects have important bearing on issues in this study and will be indicated briefly.

Until this point, the present study has prioritised the way knowledge is acquired, assigning it to the root of science-law disjunction in legal settings, emphasized by the historiographies of the two knowledge fields as they moved into modernity. In this treatment, philosophy arrived at a watershed with Kant's distinctions of truth, morality and aesthetics in his seminal *Critiques* that are generally acknowledged to have provided the modern philosophical foundations for the institutions of science, law and art (Barron 2002: 1036). Returning to Luhmann's reflections on functional differentiation, in Kant's philosophy can be detected its eighteenth century origins that Luhmann so radically characterized. Even away from pure systems theory, the separations appear stark.

Kant's incentive that produced these delimitations was the reconcilation of the antagonism between empiricism and rationalism that existed in philosophical thought in his time and to create a rôle for metaphysics without recourse to religion.[150] Cognitive functions were distinguished as the basis for science through the *Critique of Pure Reason* (1787/1964). Morality was differentiated as the basis for law through *The Moral Law. Groundworks of the Metaphysics of Morals* (1785/1991) and the *Critique of Practical Reason and Other Writings in Moral Philosophy* (1788/1993). Aesthetics was discerned through *The Critique of Judgment* (1790/1987).[151]

An ungenerous view might be that the epistemological distinctions afforded by the *Critiques* uniquely defined the point where the difficulties for science and law in communicating began. It would be as if in creating order in philosophical thought, instead Kant bequeathed modern society a perverse legacy in devising a remedy for empiricist-rationalist tensions, substituting only new disparities. Taking inspiration here from the sociologist Jürgen Habermas, the theories of whom in relation to this study are presaged and, borrowing his language momentarily, it is as if Kant finalized the project of modernity, as he perceived it, via the theses of his Critiques. It is evident from life's experience that the separations ordained by Kant's thesis, though mediated through the perception of the human being as a rational agent characterized by free will, exhibit great verisimilitude in relation to questions central to this study. 'Watershed' is a term used here as standing for what was perceived by some as the end stage of an Enlightenment philosophical narrative accounting for the divergence of science, law and art as fields of human understanding. Used negatively it could connote curtailment of progress once a zenith in thinking had been attained; regarded positively it could be interpreted as a catalyst for continuation of thought and activity but, importantly, in new directions. Description of the entirety of Kant's comprehensive philosophy of human reason is not possible here.[152] For the current discussion, concern is for his exploration of the limits of pure and practical human reason that led to circumscription of the intellectual spheres of truth and morality.

In assuaging Enlightenment disharmony, Kant retained the conscious subject as the locus of knowledge acquisition (how the subject knows the object—principally an epistemological consideration), but so characterized perception as to provide the basis on which it would be possible to surpass the watershed of modernity. It would open a preliminary nexus to philosophies that have decentred epistemology as a resource for understanding. For example, his

---

[150] See Magee (1998: 135).

[151] For a critical and analytical reading and interpretation of Kant's three *Critiques*, see Caird (1889).

[152] For a synoptic account see Felicitas Munzel (2003), and for critical analysis Cassirer (1918/1981).

notion of the object existing only through the subject's awareness creates a signpost for the prominence of human agency, characteristic of several strands of post-Enlightenment thought.

Therefore, Kant is perceived here to have accomplished an ultimate eminence for epistemology through his analysis but to have invited new fields of study generating progressive ideas with which to examine the problems owned by this study. Thus 'watershed' is rejuvenated as 'springboard'. From this point there follows a progression in philosophical thought on which Kant would have been on the brink had he considered the corollary of his theory of the subject-constituted object, which is expression of that knowledge by means of language.[153]

Failure of epistemology at the level of procedure

It is apparent that current attempts in procedure to alleviate the problems of science-law disjunction in legal contexts continue to depend on means of reconciling their disparate knowledges. Reasons for asserting failure of the epistemic approach considered in the light of procedure are offered as follows.

Making a presumption for the moment that the proposition is acceptably premised, it is possible to characterize current procedure in legal tribunals where science has an important bearing as pursuing unreal ends by unreal means. This emphatic statement can be challenged, for it cannot be asserted that never have there been fruitful interactions of science and law or that all legal decisions inherently were misguided.

It must be qualified, though, by stating that any isolated local successes are not generalizable. For instance, if scientific evidence is plain and acceptable, then legal decisions will not be difficult but this is not always so. Following *Bolitho* a judge can decide whether expert opinion has a basis in logic that should result in a 'correct' conclusion, but still a decision must be made as to which evidence to draw on if all the conflicting opinion is logical. The unpredictability of this forms one of the most serious criticisms of *Bolam*-type cases (and, to some extent, of *Daubert*-based cases in the United States, where different 'gatekeepers' are allowed to draw conflicting conclusions).[154] Jasanoff recounts that procedure offers only incremental solutions to the massive structural problem of science-law disjunction (1995/1997: 222). Dependent on reconciliation of disparate epistemologies, it can be recognized that some judges are competent in science, as perceived in *Re: The Oral Contraceptive Group*,[155] but this quality is unknown until the trial is commenced. Persistence

---

153 See, for example, Horkheimer's invocation of Kant, *in order to claim that the world we perceive is partially the result of the work of our understanding*, and of Cassirer, *in order to argue for the rôle of language in affecting what we perceive* (Stirk 2000: 63-64).

154 See, for example, Graham (2000: 322).

155 [2002] EWHC 1420 QBD (Lawtel), [2002] All ER (D) 437.

with the epistemological approach under these circumstances can seem like pushing harder at a door already firmly locked.

Earlier in this account, comment was made that English court pragmatism admits all but irrelevant or prejudicial evidence into proceedings, compared to American 'gatekeeper' rules of evidence (when used) that pre-assess scientific information to determine its admissibility. The effects of these two radically different approaches were compared. The merits of cross-examination in adversarial procedures have already been cited (Jasanoff 1995/1997: 52).[156] The findings of the present study accord with that pronouncement—and an instinctive impression is admitted that English court pragmatism is fairer than any other system of considering evidence, through openness towards expert opinion that allows the court to appraise all available material. It is acknowledged in alleging this opinion that error is potentiated by poor scientific evidence or the failure of decision-makers to comprehend its significance.

By contrast and in extremes, the American Federal Rules of Evidence[157] that filter evidence before admission into proceedings actually can prevent a case from being heard. For instance in the Agent Orange litigation,[158] the judge ruled that so much of the evidence he reviewed pre-trial was inadmissible that it would be a waste of judicial time and cost to hear the remainder and the case was struck out.[159]

While adversarialism is admired by Jasanoff, it is criticized in its treatment of evidence by some of the professionals who offered opinion to the House of Commons Science and Technology Committee on Forensic Science (Stationery Office 2005). This is because of the nervousness it can produce in expert opinion witnesses, the combative style of counsel, possible bias of expert opinion-givers in favour of the party calling them, and the deference of less experienced experts to the opinions of those of elevated rank or reputation (ibid: 63-64). None of these criticisms is new or surprising, indeed there are others of similar negativity, but lawyers accept that such practices, including the discrediting or distinguishing of witnesses in order to vindicate an argument, is an integral and inescapable part of litigation.

The last points divert the present argument into courtroom behaviour, which is significant in its ability to influence outcomes. Lest it should seem that this narrative has wandered off the point, it is important to show its use in illustrating that missing from such manoeuvres is the concept of truth understood as an immanent reality that a tribunal aims to uncover—that is supposing

---

157 Federal Rules of Evidence (2005), St. Paul, MN: West Publishing Co. Since the Federal Rules were promulgated in 1975, many of the individual states have adopted similar codifications of their evidence law, and in particular have largely followed the amended Rule 702 on expert witnesses and the 'gatekeeping' process recognized in 1993 by the U.S. Supreme Court in *Daubert*.

158 *Re Agent Orange*, 611 F. Supp. 1223 (EDNY 1985).

159 See Wagner (1986).

these manœuvres were the sole means by which conclusions were reached. What would emerge from an unrestrained process of this kind would be a constructed version of truth determined by the success of a legal team in utilizing adversarial procedure to advantage. Though not intended cynically, the foregoing could demonstrate that procedure has the ability to subvert truth as well as affirm it. Regardless of the methods and tactics used in settling disputes or negotiating agreements, the issues of the inability of science and law to exchange meaning productively, differences in their construction of reality and law's disenchantment with science at its incapacity for certainty, all remain obdurate.

Failure of the epistemological approach as manifested in procedure was apparent in recent cases of egregious errors in courts occasioned by evidence proffered as authoritative that transpired to be false but was unchallenged by courts. These were the Sudden Infant Death cases referred to in, for example, *R v Clark*[160] and *R v Cannings*,[161] in which mothers were accused of murdering their children and convicted on subsequently discredited medical evidence. Discussion of the behaviour and responsibilities of expert opinion witnesses in these types of trials potentially is extensive but for which there is insufficient space. Instancing the uncertainty of medical evidence for the purposes of legal determination, in cases of suspected Shaken Baby Syndrome assertions (associated with Sudden Infant Death) that the classic forensic pathology signs of a baby having been shaken violently are unique to that form of injury—indicating cause of death incontrovertibly—are equivocal and further research is required. Proceeding on this basis leads to the anomaly at trial that there may be no proof of murder in the way that autopsy normally concludes, yet parents indicted for homicide sometimes are convicted. Trials of this kind therefore attempt concomitant proofs, as contained in the tormented syllogism that *iff*[162] the death of an infant was caused by shaking, *then* the parent with the opportunity is culpable. This is too much for law because its tasks are conflated and it looks for the help of science that science cannot provide, and it is too much for science to shoulder the burden of proving the guilt of the defendant. Each carries the burden of the other's doubt. Paterson characterizes this as a situation that not only is *trans-scientific* but also is *trans-legal* (2003: 530).

Modernity and the status of epistemology

Critically observed, methodology in the present study has regarded 'epistemology' as the philosophically-oriented study of the nature of knowledge. Also, there has been a more pragmatic interpretation of what it means to science and law to have their knowledges. Reasons for the divergence of science and law in modernity can be given as an epistemological account. Better

---

[160] [2003] EWCA 1020.
[161] [2004] 1 WLR 2607.
[162] The standard abbreviation in a syllogism meaning 'if and only if'.

understanding of knowledge is achieved by considering its formation, use and supplementation as an epistemological study, though it is admitted that sometimes this narrative concerns knowledge *per se* when describing science used in evidence—and understanding when considering how law regards it.

Enlightenment philosophical perspectives prioritise independent conscious thought and the way the subject can know the object. This could be regarded as a universal principle because in itself it is not reliant on the type of knowledge sought but increasing specialization characterizes these knowledges as so different from each other that they become mutually incompatible. The subject knowing the object in science then has no territory in common with the subject similarly occupied in law. In one reading of Kant, understanding in science and law are differentiated by cognition and morality, yet the legal forum attempts to level these as part of reaching informed decisions. A trap for the present study thus is presaged, that of seeking resources mistakenly for unification of the already un-reunitable knowledge fields through an epistemological route because its approach is more analytical, which might appear to suggest that a tool exists.

Further, the recently indicated categorization of epistemologies shows in modern times that the inquiring subject penetrates deeper into the chosen object field exclusively and can learn about another only by transferring attention. The epistemological foundations of multiple specialties cannot be examined *tout ensemble*, nor will one yield information about another. The epistemological approach to resources to mediate science-law incommensurability therefore fails at a philosophical as well as at a procedural level. So success in identifying new resources for mediative potential must lie in frameworks that repossess some kind of universality. Soon it will be seen that such frameworks begin with decentring the conscious subject as the key to understanding and substituting alternative forms of rationality.

Kant's own epistemological revolution

The *Critique of Pure Reason* is acknowledged as providing the basis for the institutionalization of science. In it, Kant shifted the focus of contemplation concerning the way in which the inquiring human subject can know objects in the world from reflection on an independent reality and the 'being' of real things to the subject's cognitive capabilities. It is to such capacities that objects have to conform if they are to 'appear' at all (Barron 2002: 1043). These cognitive capacities Kant describes as the five mental faculties of sensibility, imagination, understanding, judgment and reason.

This theory sometimes is understated as simply that humans can know the world only through their senses, which is banal but, when fully expounded, the theory has far more significance in suggesting the way the world is understood. Prior to Kant, inquiry into how the world could be known was through the subject regarding the object, but his recondite philosophical reconstruction saw the subject constituting its object through being active in knowing it and posing the subject-constructed object as the only kind of reality to which we have access (ibid: 1041-1043).[163] Though this and other aspects of Kant's philosophy were significant for the development of theory that was to come, his proposition of the subject-constituted object nonetheless was unshakably epistemological. As was signalled earlier, developments in philosophy sought an escape from the restrictions of subject-centred consciousness. The inception of the linguistic turn opened up a wealth of possibilities for examining how meaning and understanding can be conveyed by language.

REPUDIATING THE EPISTEMOLOGICAL ENTERPRISE

The philosophy of modernity has been criticized comprehensively and in some instances harshly. In his radical treatise *Overcoming Epistemology*, Taylor observes that, traditionally, its centre was the theory of knowledge wherein science was its gatherer and philosophical reflection concerned its validity claims (1997: 1). At its heart was a vain belief in a foundationalism that through the sciences created 'a rigorous discipline that could check the credentials of all truth claims' (ibid: 2-3). According to Taylor, epistemology has come under close scrutiny in both Anglo-Saxon and Continental cultures (ibid: 1). He credits Rorty with crystallizing thought and accelerating a trend towards repudiation of the whole epistemological enterprise (ibid: 2).[164] He indicates a new orthodoxy impugning the whole enterprise from Descartes to Kant that characterizes the pursuit of nineteenth and twentieth century succession movements as a mistake (ibid: 2). Taylor advances an 'epistemological construal' over-determined by the ideals of science (ibid: 6).

Taylor's strong argument for the dismissal of epistemology was encouraging to the present study in seeking the thesis he would offer as a substitute in situating knowledge. It was hoped that such bold and uncompromising critique, appearing to relegate a science on which the world had for so long relied, would make suggestions for alternative footings. In that sense, the work was unproductive, though displaying a commonality with the present study in that it proposed and examined frameworks through partial perspectives that could lead to provisional conclusions. Its tenor was anthropological, taking as its theme the essential virtues of the ideal foundational scientist and their undermining by modern arguments. Prominent among the offered themes were 'intentionality'—ideas of subjects that are of or about something and the agent-centred knowledge of subjects effectively engaged in the activities of perceiving and getting to know the world (ibid: 10, 11).

---

[163] Barron used the term 'recondite', meaning obscure. Though Kant's concepts can be difficult to understand, in another view perhaps they might be perceived as 'revolutionary'.

[164] This is a reference to Rorty, R (1979) *Philosophy and the Mirror of Nature* (Princeton, NJ: Princeton University Press).

The demise of scientism, the dawn of critical reflection and emancipatory perspectives

The philosophical tradition has been criticised because, in seeking the nature of knowledge, it became inextricable from science and thus grew into a theoretical inquiry into the conditions under which scientific knowledge was possible (Critchley 2001: 4-5). Thus, modern society was over-dependent on scientism for all its explanations and guidance, so believed scholars of Continental philosophy, who claimed that science and technology alienated human beings from the world (ibid 2001: 111). In *Knowledge and Human Interests*, Habermas recognized that 'scientism represented only science's belief in itself so that no longer could we understand science as just one form of knowledge but rather were made to identify knowledge with science' (1971/1986: 177).

By contrast, Anglo-American philosophical interpretations, having a pronounced kinship with analytical philosophy, approved of Kant's aims in separating science, morality and art. Earlier in the present study, Kant was portrayed almost as an oppressor responsible for closing down philosophy. Two readings, though, may be had of his work. In the second, Kant created a 'springboard' into Continental philosophy by virtue of the emancipatory effects of his transcendental inquiry,[165] insofar as it sought to defend the concept of human freedom (Critchley 2001: 112). The stultifying effect of the 'empirical' reading of Kant therefore was lifted. It was not until nineteenth century idealism had run its course that it seemed worthwhile to consider the task Kant had set himself, which was making the transition through reflective judgment from thinking about nature to thinking about freedom (Gregor 1987: xvi). The linguistic turn also had been recognized as dominant in considering new resources. In common with cultural theory, language was foregrounded as the foundations of any possible experience of, or action in, the world (Barron 2001: 1038). From the 'emancipatory' reading of Kant it was seen that the inflections given his Critiques, especially the *Critique of Judgment*, generally could be attributed to the linguistic turn (ibid: 1063). Both cultural theory and Continental philosophy carried the conviction that Kant's 'phenomenal world of appearances' was constituted through and through by language (ibid: 1063).

THE PHILOSOPHICAL SHIFT TO A LINGUISTIC APPROACH

Analytical philosophy and the rôle of language

Analytical philosophy evolved from the studies of the British philosopher Russell through his concern with the logic of mathematics and partly as a reaction to nineteenth century 'high Hegelianism' of obscure writings and ambivalent views (see Russell 1912: 91; Shultz 1992: 608). Schopenhauer had

---

[165] See also Scruton (2001): 33, 55, 105.

denounced Hegel as a 'scribbler of nonsense' and implied he resorted to obscure, unclear language in expressing his theories (Weiner 1992: 29).

Russell subscribed to the Vienna Circle, composed mainly of scientists and mathematicians, concerned to establish the philosophical foundations of a scientific worldview, using an analytical style centred on rigour and clarity in philosophical thought to resolve its identifiable problems. The movement came to be known as logical positivism.[166] In common with enlightenment contemplation, it pursued ultimacy of meaning through objectivating methods with which a scientifically-trained student could identify but its aims were frustrated by its inability to complete its own project. Russell had sought a rational demonstration of the certainty of his knowledge (Hylton 2003: 277) by applying techniques of logical analysis to ordinary claims of knowledge that were developed collaboratively with Whitehead and Frege. Feeling that epistemology could not inform human understanding of the world if events and phenomena were independent of consciousness, instead Frege had interposed logic as its correct basis (Glock 2003: 89). He conceived logic as tasked with breaking the tyranny of words over thought by illuminating the almost unavoidable confusions inherent in the use of language (Waismann 1997: 4).

Russell's view of ordinary grammar was that it could provide an ideal language for the purposes of science that would avoid ambiguity, vagueness and referential failure and truth-value gaps (Glock 2003: 90). His quest in logic had been to demonstrate the correspondence of 'things' with words describing them but he realized 'things' were mere words or symbols that signified nothing (Monk 2001: 335), and hence his abandonment of that project. With Whitehead, Russell's task thus was transformed into one to construct a 'proper logical language' of symbols for particulars and propositional functions (ibid: 336)—a shift from ontology to semantics—from questions concerning the existence of things to those of what it makes sense to say (ibid: 333).

In Britain, analysis of statements was being conducted in terms of the ordinary language of common sense, not by the criteria of scientific or technical logic but through exponents of the linguistic philosophy or linguistic analysis. Among these was G E Moore,[167] the approach being more thoroughly developed through the intermediacy of J L Austin.[168] The linguistic analysts accused the logical positivists of mistakenly trying to force the straightjacket of scientific standards on all forms of utterance. They claimed there are many discourses making up human life, each with its own logic. The preoccupation of linguistic analysis therefore was with clarification of philosophical thought by unpicking the conceptual confusions that arise when a form of utterance appropriate to one discourse is mistakenly used in the context of another.

---

[166] See Ayer (1936); Joad (1950); Russell (1980).
[167] See Baldwin (1993).
[168] See Austin (1976).

In *History, Theory, Text: Historians and the Linguistic Turn*, Clarke attributes the aims of linguistic philosophy as being to solve or dissolve philosophical problems either by reforming language or achieving better understanding of its ordinary use (2004: 29). The transition of the analytical tradition from a single-minded pursuit of an ideal conformity to acceptance of informality, pluralism and proliferation of forms is charted by Sluga who comments that, as an archetype initially of modernist sensibility, analytical philosophy has acquiesced to the pliability of the postmodern (1996: 12). Amplifying this theme and drawing a marked contrast with the analytical school that aimed at closing down uncertainty, and in contextualizing the burgeoning linguistic approach to developments in philosophy, Barron comments that the contemplations of modern cultural theory and Continental philosophy shared a suspicion of the heritage of the Enlightenment and its 'systematic' philosophy (2002: 1037), adopting an ambivalent attitude towards modernity and its associated forms of rationality (ibid: 1038).

Cultural theory is a contemporary multidisciplinary field of inquiry concerned with the production and deconstruction of meaning embracing semiotics, literary theory, psychoanalysis and other sources (ibid: 1035-1036).[169] Continental philosophy is bounded by the conventions constituting the discipline of philosophy and the texts and arguments that have pre-occupied philosophers in modern Europe, especially those of France and Germany (Barron 2002: 1036).[170] Cultural theory has been particularly influenced by the linguistic turn in Continental philosophy, which foregrounded language as the foundation of any possible experience of, or action in, the world (ibid: 1038). The traditions of both cultural and Continental philosophy carry the conviction that Kant's phenomenal world of appearances is constituted through and through by language (ibid: 1063) and regard the linguistic turn as having its awakenings in Kant and arguably completed by Wittgenstein (ibid: 1063).

In the linguistic turn and its development is presaged, for the first time in this study, the possibility of a nexus of philosophical contemplation, and legal procedure. Evaluation of communication and language as the basis of a rationality that is not centred on epistemology would be worthwhile in attempting to discover ameliorative frameworks. Wittgenstein locates language, meaning, agreement and truth in social practice. On examination, his philosophy falls short of the requirement for a mediative resource, even though it presents useful insights into understanding. Habermas's unity of reason that overcomes the limitations of the epistemological categorizations of science, law and aesthetics, advances Wittgenstein's concept from expression of thoughts into the validity of expressions. The last represents the foundations of a theory that the present study appreciates as the most promising resource of all those examined.

---

[169] And see, for example, Osborne (2000); Smith (2001).

[170] And see, for example, Kearney (1994); Critchley and Schroeder (1997); Solomon and Sherman (2003).

Wittgenstein's linguistic philosophy: language embedded in social practice

Wittgenstein joined those engaged in the study of linguistic philosophy. Initially, his ideas were formed from the beliefs of Russell and Frege. These philosophers were contributors to a movement in philosophy aimed at solving or, by preference, *dissolving* its problems, by means of language.[171] Wittgenstein's approach was in stark contrast to movements in the twentieth century that sought to reconstruct philosophy in a scientific manner (Sluga 1996: 25). After Wittgenstein, early versions of linguistic philosophy associated with the Vienna Circle that emphasized a rigorously scientific analysis of language 'acquired a softer Wittgensteinian hue' (Clarke 2004: 29). Urmson confirms that the classical concept of analysis had for long exhibited a sterility outside logic and mathematics (1967: 296).

For those engaged in psychology, anthropology, theology and other fields outside academic philosophy, Wittgenstein represented the voice of dissatisfaction with the intellectual culture of the twentieth century and its overestimation of the value and power of science (Garver 1996: 164). In regarding science as representative of that independent world, he perceived it was not constant and shifted its ground according to advancing theories. No longer was it a 'given' that could be used as a firm anchor for thought. Wittgenstein then, not only sought a new constant in the world as a reference point for a reformed philosophy, but also a fixed place from which to take a new perspective. He identified humanity as representing that solid base, with its use of language rooted in diverse human purposes and differing forms of life (Magee 1997: 146). Wittgenstein felt he could justify substituting language for science, because he opened the criteria of his method to criticism (*TLP*: 654).[172] Being unconnected with knowledge, Garver (1996: 164) calls attention to it as a more radical break with the epistemological tradition in philosophy than that of Kant.

The seminal work of Wittgenstein's early period of contemplation was the *Tractatus Logico-Philosophicus* (1921/1974).[173] The force of this work was the

---

[171] For Wittgenstein's earlier contemplation of language in relation to logic, mathematics and science, see Sluga (1996: 13); Hacker: (2003: 317).

[172] Note: for the sake of brevity, in the following narrative the *Tractatus Logico-Philosophicus* will be referred to as *Tractatus* and cited statements referred to as '*TLP*' and numbered according to Wittgenstein's system. The paragraphs of *Philosophical Investigations* will be referred to by the abbreviation '*PI*' and using the system of numbering from Wittgenstein's text for Part I, except where statements have a common theme on a page and then the entire page will be cited by its number. Section and page numbers for Part II will be employed since it does not use a system of numbered statements.

[173] Wittgenstein's work is divided into his 'early' and 'late' periods. After *Tractatus Logico-Philosophicus*, Wittgenstein felt he had achieved all he could in philosophy and turned to other pursuits. Later, he returned to Cambridge and philosophy, retracted the

theory of what could be expressed by propositions, for example by language and thought (Sluga 1996: 9). His intention in *Tractatus* was to show that philosophy rests on a radical misunderstanding of our language (ibid: 9). Later, the notion of truth and falsity residing in propositions that was the mainstay of thought in *Tractatus* was relocated in *Philosophical Investigations* (Wittgenstein 1953/1972) in human agreement about it in the language used by participants, in what Wittgenstein referred to as 'forms of life' (Scheman 1996: 386, *PI*: 241). These were entities perceived by Wittgenstein to inhere in the agreement within a community about rules, meaning and use of language. 'Forms of life' resemble medleys or garlands of practices that support or complement each other, not in relation to individual performers, but in a requirement for a community that shares practices, uses and institutions (Kober 1996: 418).

These notions were interesting to the present study and justified time spent in their exploration. The interaction of different 'forms of life' as various speech communities, exemplifies the kinds of communicative problems experienced by science and law. The relevance of Wittgenstein's philosophical thought to the present study subsists principally in the *Philosophical Investigations*, for the reason that it can be shown, tentatively, that the concept of language-games that it explores, connects with issues of different practices, customs and institutions that underlie the science-law conflict. The purpose in examining the work was to see if the idea of the language-games and forms of life could be used to illuminate problems of understanding in social and legal contexts.

In *Philosophical Investigations*, Wittgenstein holds that an expectation forms from the use of language in everyday social situations as a frame of reference that is not created by epistemological approaches, since they are concerned with an 'inner world' of knowledge. Language is immediate and within both the ordinary and shared experience of humans in the course of engagement with the world (*PI*: 241, 569). It is represented, not as a unified structure, but as comprising a multiplicity of simpler structures or language-games (Sluga 1996: 17), or a medley of discursive practices (Wittgenstein 1969: 274; Kober 1996: 418). The term 'language-game' is meant to bring into prominence the fact that speaking a language is part of an activity, or a 'form of life.' (*PI*: 23). Wittgenstein sees language as a medium of communication [174] that is woven in with social practice (*PI*: 23). Black points out that Wittgenstein used the label 'language-game' both for a 'language' of communication and for the activities within which such a language is interwoven (1979: 342). Monk (1991: 330) recounts Wittgenstein's description of language-games, as being language that is indivisible from the use to which it is put. Language-games are perceived by Lyotard as the method of legitimating post-modern knowledge, in which observable social bonds are composed of language 'moves', where

---

central precept of *Tractatus* and substituted the thoughts of *Philosophical Investigations*.

[174] See also Waismann (1997), Chapter XII.

speaking is participation in the game whose goal is the creation of new and ever-changing social linkages (1979: 10).

Wittgenstein identifies the problems of understanding caused by using the terms of one language-game mistakenly in another.[175] Magee emphasizes that the meanings of words derive from the language-game in which they are used, whether that is philosophy, science, art, religion, academia or ordinary conversation (1997: 148). For instance, in considering understanding of the term 'evidence' he illustrates the variety of meanings attached to hearsay in law, history and science, where for judges its admissibility in court may be questionable,[176] but for history it may be all that can be relied on as fact and for science it has no legitimacy whatsoever (ibid: 148). To use the term in one language-game without appreciating its changed meaning when used in another would be a source of confusion (*PI*: IIxi, pp.188, 216).

Magee counsels that it is the 'family resemblance' character of meaning that allows this mistake (ibid: 149). Consensus as to meanings of words would be essential. None other than a language-game emphasizes more conspicuously that the rules are the object of a contract, explicit or otherwise (Lyotard 1979: 10). Similarly, and in the context of the present work, there is not a shared meaning of 'proof' in scientific and legal communities: its understanding is as different as the way the term is used in mathematics and logic. A scientific expert opinion witness in court frequently gives empirical data as the basis of proof; for lawyers the criterion applied to the witness is 'what is the strength of your conviction?' In an optimised legal forum, they would converge in a single language-game, but in actual procedure, they are understood differently.

Forms of life and language-games are not arid intellectual concepts and illustrations of their occurrences can be seen. The practice of medicine involves consultations between physicians and patients in which a very specific form of language-game is used. Consulting a doctor lies within the sense of Wittgenstein's 'form of life' and this is confirmed by McGinn's elucidation that a form of life comprises 'historical groups of individuals who are bound together in a community by a shared set of complex, language-involving practices' (1997: 51). The language-game of the patient would be based on a grammar aimed at obtaining explanation, advice, and reassurance, which is both petitioning and compliant; that of the doctor at giving a 'medical' explanation that is authoritative, pedagogical, professional and satisfactory. In Wittgenstein's philosophical reflection, these problems would be 'dissolved' by reducing disparate language-

---

[175] See Urmson (1967: 296) for useful clarificatory answers.

[176] The 'hearsay' rules of evidence are now more relaxed in the English jurisdiction. The admissibility of hearsay evidence in criminal proceedings is set out in §§ 114-136, Part II Criminal Justice Act 2003, and applies to all criminal proceedings begun on or after 4th April 2005 (§ 141 Criminal Justice Act 2003). (See Crown Prosecution Service Guidance, at http://www.cps.gov.uk/legal/h_to_k/hearsay/). In the United States, in federal courts under Rule 801 of the Federal Rules of Evidence and in state jurisdictions applying similar evidentiary exclusions, hearsay rules and exceptions continue to be detailed and enforced.

games in medical consultations to a single common grammar.[177] Black speaks of lying as a 'sophisticated' language-game (1979: 341) and it will be seen later that Habermas recognizes the problem with respect to validity claims in human speech acts. Naffine (2002: 73) demonstrates language as embedded in practice in a gendered legal community, valorising feminists as one community of language users able to influence the male-dominated profession, by bringing terms describing detriments to women into public consciousness. Schapin (1994: 123) offers proposals concerning the influence of 'gentlemanly codes of conduct' on a language-game of seventeenth century reporting of scientific discovery. It was conducted within a paradigm of the 'gentleman whom one could trust to speak the truth'; [178] 'recognition of truthfulness within a culture of honour'; [179] and that of 'the English gentleman in the rôle of reliable spokesperson for reality'.[180] Schapin questions whether in modernity the seventeenth century gentleman's integrity and virtue has been replaced by the specialist's expertise.[181]

The procedure for approving a licence application to market a drug for a particular purpose, undertaken by the Oncologic Drugs Advisory Committee (ODAC) of the Food and Drug Administration (FDA) in America, consists of language-games aimed at concluding by consensus.[182] Wittgenstein's form of intersubjectivity, that he expresses as consensus over meaning, and the new idea expressed here of balancing incongruent personal perspectives means FDA/ODAC procedure can be interpreted as representing a near-ideal form of language-game.

Failure of metaphysics and the inception of critical theory

Similar in sentiment to the movement expressing unease with epistemology was that of critical theory emanating from the Frankfurt School of lawyers, sociologists, psychologists and political scientists. According to Adorno, 'Philosophical terminology gains a decisive significance where firm philosophical schools form' (Stirk 2000: 1), and this sage remark holds equally for the Frankfurt School, the Vienna Circle or Continental philosophy. The Institute for Social Research of the University of Frankfurt—hence The 'Frankfurt School'—represented an academic political movement inclined towards Marxism contextualized in social developments peculiar to Germany in both

---

[177] Doctors are now trained in communication skills, in which not only do they explain medical terms in a language better understood by patients but they solicit from the patient the kind of explanation they require.

[178] ibid: xxvi.

[179] ibid: xxvii.

[180] ibid: xxviii.

[181] ibid: xxxi.

[182] See Chapter III of the present work.

the periods of National Socialism and in post-war democracy. Its founders had been Horkheimer and Marcuse and included Adorno. On its reconstitution after the Second World War, its membership was extended to Habermas.[183] The School exhibited a proclivity for interdisciplinary research. There was a general sense in which critical theorists strove to break down institutionalized disciplinary barriers and made moves to put back the 'whole man' in place of the abstraction that was offered by other philosophical theories as a route to analytical rigor (Stirk 2000: 5-6).

The 'high Hegelianism' to which Russell and Moore objected in their formulation of analytical philosophy was constituted by epistemological theories relying on the *a priori* reasoning of metaphysics and a doctrine of idealism insisting that reality ultimately is non-material and founded on mental or spiritual concepts. Advocates of critical theory denied the position of metaphysics and idealism as able to claim a rational order to the world, even proposing that the progress of philosophy itself had culminated in the contemplations of Kant and Hegel (ibid: 31). Kant's theories of reason mediating the tensions between empiricism and rationalism in his separation of phenomenal and noumenal worlds still were judged by critical theory to overstress metaphysics. 'Critical theory is directed against conceptions of philosophy...which have disdained entanglement in the contingency of the empirical world in favour of some supposed higher reality' (ibid: 8). Horkheimer objected to the 'bifurcation of the rational person' caused by Kant's juxtaposition of will and reason in his *Critiques* (ibid: 40).[184]

Rehabilitating the project of modernity

This undertaking is attributed by Rasmussen to Habermas (Rasmussen 1990). It entails the disappointment of Habermas and Adorno with western civilisation over its failure to prevent the Holocaust, which signified to them a need for a new rationality (Devenney 2004; Roderick 1986: 20-21). Barron speaks of new forms of domination overshadowing the freedoms celebrated by Kant's enlightenment that compromised the possibilities for collective self-determination, alluding to the influence both of technocracy and the political and economic systems of capitalist economies and the centralized state (2002: 1079). Habermas is critical also of the twentieth century welfare state for detracting from the autonomy of will and reason of the individual that the emancipatory themes of the Enlightenment were supposed to afford (Deflem 1996: 7). Among the 'new themes' of Habermas's project were the desire for a systematic approach to modernity, concern with the paradigm shift from the philosophy of consciousness to the philosophy of language, solving the problematic of rationality and rationalization, and establishing an approach permit-

---

[183] See Stirk (2000: Introduction and Chapter 1) for a fuller historical account of the development of the Frankfurt School).

[184] Reference to an untranslated paper in German.

ting forays into discourse ethics, literary theory and the critique of postmod-
ernism (Rasmussen 1990: 2). Habermas holds that the defects of the Enlightenment only ever can be made good by further enlightenment (1985: xvii).

As a political scientist, Devenney casts Habermas's ambitions, of which the
following represent a selection, as providing an orientation for emancipatory
politics without reference either to an intrinsic universal human rationality or a
divine being beyond humankind, and to determine the means of a communicative rationality founded on language implying intersubjectivity and binding
individuals to the social collective (Devenney 2004). For Habermas the familiar epistemological construction of the subject knowing the object excludes
other rationalities and for Taylor it implies missed social action and meaning
not understood (ibid: 2004). Habermas considered the classical subject-object
relationship should be replaced by that between the self and others, suggesting
that a new form of rationality could be established by humans between themselves and others (Habermas 1984/1986: 296-298).

In giving account of the apparent overthrowing of epistemology as Taylor
describes it and the failure of metaphysics in Stirk's characterization of critical
theory, it would be thought simple to draw clear distinctions between theories
in which the conscious, cognitive subject is decentred and those in which *a
priori* knowledge is denied, and alternative rationalities displacing them. With
epistemology and metaphysics thus relegated, it is as though modernity itself is
similarly consigned, *ergo* that which replaces it must represent the post-
modern. In hazarding this interpretation, the method is not so much simple as
simplistic for the philosophy of Habermas is firmly rooted in finding acceptable
revisions of modernity in which he can conserve the humanistic values of
science, morality and aesthetics (Rasmussen 1990: 3). The disparity between
the traditional elements of Habermas's programme and his ideas on the
philosophy of language are emphasized in Rasmussen's elucidation (ibid: 4),
conjecturing that Habermas rehabilitates the project of modernity by his
reconstruction of it within the context of a theory of communication involving
communicative action and reason. The dilemma is recalcitrant, though, when
contemplating that the subject in the philosophy of modernity is repudiated
absolutely in the philosophy of language (ibid: 4). Habermas himself criticizes
those whom he calls the detractors of modernity—the 'anti-modernists'—
(Barron 2002: 1078) and attacks them vehemently for their negative attitudes
to instrumental reason (Habermas 1996: 53).

Acceptability of the above perception depends on opinion concerning the
possibility of paradigm shifts in philosophy. Taylor speaks of the 'corpse of
epistemology' (1997: 61), a dramatic expression that should be regarded
cautiously. Reversing the temporal sense of Kuhn's hypothesis regarding
science, if a paradigm shift has occurred, then post- and pre-paradigmatic
theories will be incommensurable. For Habermas, completing the project of
modernity means regaining moral values impaired by historical events, his
thesis involving a reconstructed dialectic of enlightenment rather than a total
critique of it (Habermas 1985: xv). This is redolent of the revolt against what

would now be regarded as the 'scientism' of seventeenth century world rejection of the Newtonian mathematico-mechanical model of the world that gave no scope for morality (Barron 2002: 1047). For a total paradigm shift to have occurred, all past ideas would be invalidated and there would be no points of correspondence between present and previous assertions. In his new form of rationality, Habermas prevails over Kant's epistemological separations in his own form of linguistic turn, while in doctrinal terms holding inconsistently to reconstructing enlightenment dialectic. His agile surmounting of these antinomies disdains many of the stylistic and would-be paradigmatically shifted approaches to the problem of failed epistemology and metaphysics. On the strength of Rasmussen's observation of Habermas's schema, it is concluded here that the abrupt discontinuities of the paradigm shifts experienced in science are not widespread in the history of philosophy and that it is possible to regain, reshape and re-apply ostensibly pre-paradigmatically shifted-out ideas.

COMMUNICATIVE RATIONALITY

The linguistic theory of Habermas moves this chapter of the present study onward from consideration of the use-oriented approach to meaning of the later Wittgenstein to a connection between language and a sense of validity in utterances.[185] It offers a framework for evaluating statements made by individuals in science-law discourse, resolving disputes as to meaning and reaching agreement via an ethically grounded procedure.

The concept of validity resides, *inter alia*, in Habermas's theory of communicative rationality that 'refers to the rational potential of action oriented towards understanding' (Habermas 1976/1998: 21), such rationality being 'implicit in the everyday linguistic practices of modern societies' and 'located in idealizations guiding communicative action to the extent that everyday communication is connected with validity' (Cooke 1997: 131). Validity claims are universal conceptually to everyone who speaks the language, indicating a non-biological kind of species competence (McCarthy 1982: 60; Roderick 1986: 77).

The theory of communicative rationality is multi-layered in the sense of fullness of meaning, the number of its constituents and their relationships. This research has found that attempting a systematic explanation of this involuted but engrossing theory turns into a recursive process owing to an intimate interconnection of its constituents but taking different paths through them in producing the plurality of its assertions. In the co-dependence of constituents, meticulous disaggregation of concepts is required in order to explain them, point them at the issues of this study and evaluate their potential.

Claims to validity have multiple modes and means of expression nested within each other that Habermas synthesizes in his total theory (1998/2002).

---

[185] See Cooke (1997: 131) for comment on Wittgenstein's 'localized' conception of validity compared with the universal interpretation of Habermas.

Each has subtly different emphasis and depends on the aims of speakers in performing speech acts, the context in which speaking occurs and the relationship of participants (ibid: 22). These will bear importantly on forthcoming discussion about the nature of proffered statements and the intentions of experts bringing evidence or opinion into science-law exchanges.

In communicative rationality, the structure of action oriented towards understanding is revealed in Habermas's formal pragmatic investigations into everyday language that emerge as his universal pragmatics of communication (Cooke 1997: 29). In Habermas's theory, the act of a person speaking to another makes a commitment to them, entering a bond in the form of a claim in which both validity and content inhere, and in order to be taken seriously the speaker must be able to defend claims in a formal structure (Devenney 2004). Cooke explains defence by a speaker as supplying reasons in support of a validity claim if challenged by the hearer, who in turn must provide reasons for accepting or rejecting the claim, concluding that communicative rationality is tied to a process of argumentation (1997: 29). Communicative rationality is not a substantive conception of reason but is defined procedurally by way of purely formal characteristics—a formerly defined procedure of argumentation (ibid: 38).

The goal of reaching an understanding between communicating parties involves agreement culminating in the intersubjective mutuality of reciprocal understanding, shared knowledge, mutual trust and accord (Habermas 1998/ 2002: 23). Achievement of these is by vindicating or 'redeeming' four obligatory conditions of validity or idealizations in the act of speaking that depend upon comprehensible expressions, the innate truth of propositions by virtue of which parties can share knowledge, choice of utterances that are right so that agreement can be reached with respect to a recognized normative background, and an intention of truthfulness so that mutual trust is assured (ibid: 24-25). Lest this idealized situation should be taken as representing insubvertible reality, Habermas cautions about the possibility of 'incomprehension and misunderstanding, intentional and involuntary untruthfulness, concealed and open discord' (ibid: 23). While it would be improvident of this research to fashion unconvincing connections between aspects of theory that seem conveniently to address its central problem and the recognized situations of procedure in which they occur nonetheless, on its face, Habermas's theory of communicative rationality resonates with the so-called witness demeanour with regard to the validity of scientific expert opinion proffered in legal encounters. 'Witness demeanour' echoes also with Wittgenstein's concept of language-games, where issues of motivation in speaking and intersubjectivity in understanding assume great importance.

In developing his schema, Habermas revisits Austin's categories of speech acts and re-invokes the notion of illocution signified by use of words conveying warnings, promises, requests and others of that class that suggest an action-response in the hearer (ibid: 85). Hence, those acts conveyed by utterances establish a relationship between interlocutors, the force of which determines the manner in which speech acts are to be understood. In communicative action then, the plans of individual participants are coordinated by means of the illocutionary binding effects of speech acts, thematizing the relations into which speaker and hearer enter through interactive use of language, whereas it is the content of utterances as propositions concerning something occurring in the world that are thematized in the cognitive use of language (ibid: 75, 77). Thus the establishment of interpersonal relations and representation of content are essential for the performance of a successful speech act, though Habermas points out that irrationality in validity claims can be avoided because the cognitive component of utterances can be checked (ibid: 85). Therefore, Habermas can posit that illocutionary speech acts mutually influencing participants in discourse are connected to cognitively-testable validity claims through reciprocally rational bonds, and that the speaker adopts different modes of communication in appealing to thematically-stressed universal validity claims (ibid: 85-86).

Speech acts, validity claims and the cognitive/social relations they characterize are nested in the following way. In a validity claim, comprehension is grounded in the grammar of speech acts and is presumed by competent participants; *truth* is conveyed by a constative speech act constructed as a proposition and affords a rare glimpse in Habermas's theory of the epistemological subject-object relationship because it relates to facts; *rightness* is a regulative speech act relating to normativity and promoting intersubjectivity and *truthfulness* is an expressive speech act made as an avowal and is characterized by sincerity (ibid: 88, 142).

Misgivings have been expressed in this study that, in applying abstract theory to real life situations, examples tend to be mundane. A particularly pertinent account is elicited through universal pragmatics concerning the attitudinal behaviour of communicators making validity claims that is evocative of experts' conduct in legal settings. Albeit perhaps unknowingly, experts enter into a bond with other participants, reproducing the conditions that Habermas outlines. The issuing and recognition of validity claims is pivotal to erection of conditions for a successful bond constituted by four different speech acts. The first, making comprehensible expressions is assumed. The others put forward in interpersonal relationships refer to propositional truth, the rightness of norms relied on and the willingness of a subject to assume responsibility in speech acts, that collectively indicate obligations within an ethical framework to provide grounds or to prove trustworthy in utterances (ibid: 86). These can be examined in turn and compared with expert opinion brought before law's consideration but prior to this an impression is required of the kinds of validity claims with which it must deal.

In everyday communication, claims to validity arise in ordinary speech of which a banal example might be that today is Tuesday. This would raise little controversy and both substantiation of the proposition and the motivation of a speaker in uttering it would occasion scant intellectual effort. On the other hand, statements in medico-legal disputes and forensic science that post-retinal haemorrhages are incontrovertible signs of a baby having been shaken; that the probability of two or more infants in one family dying suddenly from natural causes is vanishingly small; that multiple sclerosis is an inevitable consequence of soft-tissue or 'whiplash' injury to the neck; that the MMR vaccine causes autism in children, and other strong assertions of this kind, raise validity claims that challenge, not only the accuracy of research, but also the right of experts to claim them and the sincerity of their intentions.

In the legal forum, an expert exhibiting 'reasonable' demeanour will justify assertions, be prepared to defend them against challenge and reconsider them if a conflicting opinion is better founded.[186] In a constative speech act, in evidential terms pertaining to opinion, universal pragmatics dispenses that it will contain an offer 'to recur if necessary to the experiential grounds from which the speaker draws the certainty that his statement is true' (ibid: 86). This indicates that an expert should make recourse to published peer-reviewed research to substantiate a factual statement and symbolizes that the substance of constative speech acts can be checked. The right to make validity claims in a regulative speech act in everyday communications inheres normatively in a moral right to issue the statement (ibid: 142).

An important new perspective on the theory is introduced in the present study that is cognate with its central theme, and pertains to the presentation of expert opinion evidence in the legal forum. It contends that, in utterances, moral rightness for experts in making a validity claim inheres in observation of the normative standards of their specializations. Even though these have been questioned systematically in this study, scientists subscribe to those standards, such as the Mertonian norms, as the moral foundation of their assertions. Translated via Habermas's vision, a scientist will rely for illocutionary force on the institutionally bound speech acts emanating from the scientific branch of learning, its methods and assumptions (ibid: 88). This is distinguished from the institutionally unbound speech of a layman, who will rely purely on the consequences of speech acts connected with each other on the basis of reciprocal recognition of validity claims (ibid: 23). This perception of the Theory of Communicative Action repositions it usefully in the context of the present analysis without disturbing its foundations.

The currency of expressive speech acts is truthfulness in which sincere relationships between experts and the legal forum is established.[187] 'Witness credibility', used by judges in speeches to convey a general impression of the authoritative opinion given and the reliable and flexible behaviour of an expert,

---

[186] See, for instance, comments about the reliability of expert witnesses in the judgment of MacKay, J. in *Re: The Oral Contraceptive Group Litigation* (*XYZ and others v Schering Health Care Ltd and others*) [2002] EWHC 1420 (QB); [2002] All ER (D) 437 (July) (Approved Judgment).

[187] See ibid: 80.

approximates to the sense of trustworthiness and sincerity inhering in this mode of speech.[188]

Problematization of the undertakings of participants in constative, regulative and expressive modes of communication is perceived as follows. Problematic constative speech manifests in experts whose research is flawed or skewed so that the factual basis of assertions cannot be relied on. In challenges to regulative speech acts concerning scientific evidence, the right to issue a claim refers to the normative context convincing the expert that the utterance is correct.[189] An expert's claim that retinal haemorrhaging is evidence of a baby having been shaken violently invokes the normative standard of forensic investigation permitting that conclusion. With more difficulty, it is the underlying norm that is questioned if a doubt remains about the rightness of a statement. In the failure of forensic science adequately to distinguish retinal haemorrhages as indicating shaken baby syndrome from other possible causes, the assumptions of science or the scientific method would be confronted.

This stratification of the legal evidential standard is tenuous because it is not certain in the prosecutions to which this example refers that the fault did not lie with the scientists' own conclusions; however, it serves usefully to illustrate the basis on which both scientists and science itself are challengeable. Habermas's resolution of lingering doubt over a validity claim in regulative speech is by practical discourse, a mediative resource in the interactive use of language,[190] an idea suggested by the model of negotiation in the FDA/ODAC regulatory body in the United States. In expressive speech, problems can arise from the misperceptions of experts concerning their own responsibility in relation to legal purposes that can put truthfulness at risk. Often it is outside the scope or skill of law to verify or challenge these discrepancies or sometimes even to recognize they have occurred. In *R v Clark (Sally) (Appeal Against Conviction) (No 2)*,[191] the claim of an expert opinion witness concerning the statistical chance of two sudden unexpected infant deaths occurring in the same family being natural was outside his expertise, but the court of first instance did not detect it.[192]

PRACTICAL DISCOURSE

Habermas's notion of employing discourse to resolve doubt in validity claims is organized around the socio-politically expressed ideals of freedom

---

[188] See ibid: 64.

[189] See ibid: 53-54.

[190] See ibid: 86-87.

[191] [2003] EWCA Crim 1020; [2003] 2 FCR 447; (2003) 147 SJLB 473 CA (Crim Div), Digested CLY 04/73. The case is discussed in text at note 42 above.

[192] See also *R v Cannings (Angela)* [2004 EWCA Crim 1, [2004] 1 WLR 2607, [2004] 1 All ER 725, [2004] 2 Cr App R 7, [2004] 1 FCR 193, (2004) 101 (5) LSG 27; (2004) 148 SJLB 114, Times, Jan 23 2004 CA (Crim Div), Digested CLY 04/1458.

and equality for participants (Barron 2002: 1081), or as 'discourse and social interaction orientated towards truth, freedom and justice' (Habermas 1970: 372). These constitute an idealized, ethically founded discourse practice in communicative rationality but which is distorted in reality and results in 'impoverishment' of the 'lifeworld'. Habermas's perception of the 'lifeworld' is discussed in more detail in the section on 'Expert Cultures' that follows. Chiefly responsible are the institutionalizations of knowledge, practice and power (Cooke 1997: 135) that have come to be known as 'expert cultures', for instance economic and administrative sub-systems and the mass media (ibid: 142), that militate against freedom and equality of speech and action (Doyal and Gough 1991: 76-77; Roderick 1986: 34).

Three worlds are emphasized and thematized variously in practical discourse as facts, values and inner experience, connected to Kant's domains of knowledge, morality and feeling, and—examined more pertinently here—truth, normative rightness and truthfulness (Roderick 1986: 27). Habermas's sentiments about modernity contextualize his contemplations in morality. An abiding impression is given from a reading of his discourse ethics that, at its heart, it is aimed at resolving moral argument using an ethical framework. For the present study it is appropriate to emphasize normative rightness in the situation of science in collaboration with law and to pose as reasonable reconception of it as the scientific counterpart of morality in that the values of science are its guiding inspiration. Failure to conform to its normativity would constitute moral turpitude, though Habermas makes space for the argument that underlying normative values themselves can be subject to question (Cooke 1997: 114). Nothing in the foregoing proposition should threaten the utility of practical discourse in resolving doubts arising in constative speech acts but rational resolution of knowledge is effected by acceptance of empirical assessment, of which controlled trials of medical therapies are examples (Doyal and Gough 1991: 122), and the communication skill of 'hermeneutic understanding', coined by Habermas as necessary to apply empirical methodology and to discuss its outcomes (1971: 176). In expressive speech acts, Habermas proposes that the truthfulness of utterances can be checked only against the consistency of the speaker's subsequent behaviour (1998/2002: 87). In ordinary life the means of achieving this appear vague and would rely on observation of a speaker for long periods, but it translates very well in legal contexts as witness demeanour and the skill of counsel to test a series of statements or answers for consistency.

Adversarial procedure in the legal forum would perceive practical discourse as culturally alien, since it engenders little sense of negotiated consensus over the meaning of scientific evidence. There are echoes of Habermas's themes of practical discourse through the challenging of normative rightness in cross-examination of experts by testing the strength of their convictions. Asymmetrical power structures and the adversarial style of the courtroom, though, deprive this discourse of its full potential. Habermas's notion of withstanding criticism by providing justification via his three speech act domains is present too in challenges to expert opinion, but the harsh partisanship of the legal environment can overwhelm the liberality of his practical discourse. Preceding discussion demonstrates also that the legal system sometimes is unable to discriminate between experts' protestation of normative rightness in their evidence and the potency of the underlying norm so that, for example, a prosecution for murder is allowed to proceed where science offers empirical evidence, which is not convincing that a death actually was the result of homicide (see *R v Clark (Sally)*;[193] Batt 2004: *passim*). Clinical research continues in attempts to clarify whether certain findings in forensic evidence are indicative of violence (Geddes *et al.* 2001a, Geddes *et al.* 2001b). In the meantime such convictions must be characterized as conclusions that are at the same time trans-legal and trans-scientific (see Paterson 2003).

The present debate returns to the conjectured repositioning of science as having capacity for causative explanations but which cannot produce them reliably. In an ideal world, Habermas's practical discourse would identify and discuss these issues until consensus about meaning was achieved, which would have the virtue of better informing legal tribunals but for which in real life there is no time.

With inquisitorial procedure there might be thought more opportunity for practical discourse in the absence of partisanship and with examination led by the arbiter but much would depend on judicial attitude to experts, their evidence and the extent of scientific understanding, none of which has reason to be different from that found in adversarial situations. Both procedures are constrained by the need to conclude, so elaborate, protracted argument usually is not feasible, but the style evident in some other legal, para- or quasi-legal settings is more conducive to negotiation that is evocative of Habermas's imagined practical discourse.

Conspicuous among procedures examined previously is that of the manner in which pharmaceutical licence applications are heard by the *Oncologic Drugs Advisory Committee of the Food and Drug Administration Center for Drug Evaluation and Research* (FDA/ODAC) in the United States. This has been described extensively in Chapter IV. It employs a unique type of internal democratic discourse that narrows progressively the issues in the application by agreement between its voting members and those that they consider attested by the scientific evidence before them. Proponent and opponent experts as well as affected participants provide the basis on which argument is made. This is achieved by means of a series of recessive propositions submitted to the *Committee*, the detailed construction of which is negotiated by them prior to the ballot. Through Habermas's practical discourse, FDA/ODAC deliberations can be depicted in the following way. Amid a procedure from the transcripts of which little tension is apparent, the *truth* of constative speech acts is checked

---

[193] [2003] EWCA Crim 1020; [2003] 2 FCR 447; (2003) 147 SJLB 473 CA (Crim Div), Digested CLY 04/73.

by reference to the empirical data of the trials. The regulative *rightness* to issue claims is confirmed intersubjectively by the members and is embedded in the Committee's evaluation of the clinical trial methodology that guides their conclusions and, in case of doubt, that the normative assumptions of science underpin. As the style of the *Committee* is informal, issues of *truthfulness* in experts' expressive speech acts that can be clouded by adversarial procedure can be seen more readily in experts as intentions of sincerity. Of paramount advantage in reaching decisions in the FDA/ODAC licence application procedure is that Committee members and experts all are scientists, only patients' representatives being lay contributors. This enables issues to be better focused upon without the need for legal interpretation of scientific information that introduces the possibility of misunderstanding; indeed the decision to approve the application is primarily a scientific one, albeit overlaid by a moral constraint only to grant a licence to a safe product.

EXPERT CULTURES

In a personal mission, Habermas strives to complete the project of modernity by re-engaging with enlightenment perspectives to rehabilitate the enlightenment culture that he considers twentieth century historical and social developments impeached. Completion of the project that Habermas sees as inaugurated by Kant would be accomplished by reworking the philosophy of his Critiques (Barron 2002: 1079) and when the rationality embedded in communicative practice were recognized and advanced in social interactions (see ibid: 1080). Concomitantly, Habermas acknowledges the deleterious effects on Kant's conception of individual freedom of modern forms of domination in the organisational and instrumental rationality of capitalist enterprise and the welfare state (see, for example, Roderick 1986: 134-135), among which are the 'alienation and atomisation' effects of economic markets and bureaucracy, and the 'dependency and normalization' effects of the welfare state (Barron 2002: 1079). He refers to these as 'systems'.

Habermas mourns the 'cultural impoverishment of the lifeworld' (see Cooke 1997: 16, 133). Barron relays the sense of the lifeworld synoptically as 'the realm of shared norms, understandings and identities' (2002: 1079), Rasmussen very economically as 'the ordinary world of lived experience' (1990: 81) and Cooke more analytically as 'the symbolically and communicatively structured spheres of society—the stock of implicit assumptions, intuitive know-how and socially-established practices that functions as a background to all understanding' (1997: 15). With Habermas's conception of an imperilled lifeworld comes the need to examine the sources of threat and their potential consequences for his theory of communicative action. Perceiving 'systems' as the organic development of structures within society, Habermas characterizes them as impersonal, bypassing the action orientation of individual human agents and coordinating action by the functional interconnection of action consequences (Habermas 1987/1989: 117). Systems coordination is distinguished analytically from lifeworld coordination that takes place by means of personal communicative action and depends on the orientation of individuals in society (Cooke 1997: 5).

At the systemic level, Habermas sees a form of instrumental rationality that is sophisticated and effective (Barron 2002: 1079). When systems imperatives superimpose themselves over lifeworld imperatives, a distortion of the lifeworld occurs (Ramussen 1990: 45). Devolved from a Weberian interpretation of society as owning the traditions of scientific theories, moral and legal beliefs and aesthetic productions—culturally expressed as truth, justice and taste—its questions are answered increasingly by experts and given an institutionalized form (Cooke 1997: 41). Cooke recognizes these from Habermas's description as the three increasingly esoteric 'expert cultures' of science, law and morality, and art, in which questions of validity are dealt with only by specialists (ibid: 17). Habermas typifies the control exerted by various experts in society as ranging from the courts to therapists and social workers (1987/1989: 321).

Modernity therefore is seen as a radicalization of the divisions of philosophy propounded in Kant's *Critiques* that in part represent a quasi-institutional process in which experts in the relevant area develop specialized languages and criteria (Stirk 2000: 44). The European Enlightenment thus can be viewed here historically as comprising two distinct chapters, in the first of which it gave rise to the divergence in 'earlier modernity' of religion, science, morality, and feeling and, secondly, in 'later modernity' to Kant's inculcation of reason that inspired the tripartite institutionalizations of science, law and art. In Habermas's attempt to rescue modernity, to his depiction of the lifeworld as distorted by functional rationality is added the emergence of expert cultures that serve further to entrench distinctions that are manifest in legal contexts, investigation of which justifies embarking on this study. A negative perspective might persuade that these distinctions are irrevocable (see also ibid: 38-39).

The task for Habermas then is to re-unify the spheres of reason divided through Kant's affirmations and amplified by expert cultures. He justifies his claim to success by recursion to the assertions of his theory of communicative rationality, displaying an intellectual versatility that has come to be associated with him uniquely. For the current work, this presents an inviting opportunity to examine and engage with a framework offering potential for a 'master precept' that might overcome science-law disjunction more comprehensively and completely than others studied so far.

UNITY OF REASON

Habermas depends for his solution on the proceduralization that underlies his theory of communicative action to avoid recourse to the metaphysics that might capture him in attempts to reunite the differentiated spheres of reason into a substantive totality (Cooke 1997: 41). The form a credible metaphysical solution to incommensurabilities would take that would be of utility to a legal forum is unimaginable. Cooke refers to the differentiation of validity dimensions that are most developed on the level of specialized and formalized argumentation in science, law and morality and aesthetic discourse respectively (ibid: 92) but here 'validity dimensions' is presumed to relate to those by which each explains the authority for its claims, namely what is peculiar to scientific, legal, moral or artistic justification for its contentions. Coincidentally, Cooke articulates precisely the goal of the present project by declaring that the need for productive interpenetration is most urgent in these three spheres but adds there is no metadiscourse to show the manner in which participants in argumentation in one sphere of validity can bring to bear arguments from another (ibid).

This is the embodiment of the incommensurability problem, but ways of elucidating the impasse are legion and nothing can be gained by their recitation. Habermas overcomes it, *deus ex machina*, by adopting a *tentative notion of a formal unity of reason* (ibid: 41) that he uses to make 'transitions between worlds' (ibid: 91). The potential basis for such success is enunciated by Cooke as the interpenetration of spheres of validity (such as truth, rightness and truthfulness) that allow productive insights to be gained through argumentation in one sphere (for example, science) to be re-applied to problems in other spheres (such as law or aesthetics) while respecting the distinctive logic of each (ibid: 41).[194] In Habermas's terms, 'the unity of reason must be conceived in the plurality of its voices' (ibid: 42). Reification of the formal unity of reason would offer for the first time in this study hope of a prospective framework for successful mediation of science-law problems. His proposal is at the same time ingenious, consistent with his theory of communication and exploits his own version of the linguistic turn advantageously to perceive the solution as inhabiting a new intellectual space. The success of Habermas's idea must be judged here in terms of the genuine relief it affords for the intransigencies encountered by the present work.

The formal-pragmatic underpinning of Habermas's thesis (ibid: 92) lies with the performative attitude of participants in communicative action in which the three validity claims inhere simultaneously in every utterance (Habermas 1984/1986: 330). Cooke clarifies usefully that the matter at issue here is the speaker's ability to consider the validity of an utterance under three different aspects (1997: 93). As described previously, these refer to the constative, regulative and expressive utterances in which subsist truth, rightness and truthfulness but which in Habermas's schema acquire crucial new eminence as universals (ibid: 93; see also discussion in Habermas 1984/1986: 311). The significance of this visualization of unified reason is interpreted in the present study on the presumption of meaning in the argument that follows.

The new insight into reason has liberating consequences. In considering the productions of specializations hitherto, their validity claims have been regarded as context-specific—made in the general normative contexts of their

---

[194] Additions in parentheses are the author's to assist clarity and therefore represent his interpretation.

respective specializations. For instance, in scientific parlance, 'reliability' is understood broadly as the unfailing reproduction of the outcome of a specific study under specified conditions in the same or different locations. A speaker in science therefore can profess truth on the basis of good scientific method; in law a speaker can rely on truth within the principle of justice and in aesthetics on critique. Again, after absorbing Habermas's theory of the universal pragmatics of communication, it appears that such validity claims reside principally in normative rightness, that is, the proper basis as a consequence of which speakers have the right to issue them. Normally, they are confined to the specializations in which they are made and their questions are answerable only by experts. But if validity claims are universal under Habermas's formal concept of the unity of reason, then the speech acts of speakers in *any or all* of the expert cultures inevitably raise the claims to truth, rightness and truthfulness simultaneously (Cooke 1997: 93) and these are context-transcendent.

From the standpoint of this work and inescapable in its 'take', acceptance of the theory of Habermas as revelatory requires especially that it be considered in terms of its effect on proceedings in the legal forum and particularly on utilization and interpretation of expert opinion. It is difficult to imagine a total revolution in traditions and procedures but, without the bifurcation in evidential contexts attributable to the prevailing expert cultures of science and law, the boundaries of contributions to legal judgments could be made more permeable. This would avoid the kind of compartmentalized discussion that locates truth uniquely in the attestations of science and through which sometimes law abrogates responsibility for its conclusions. This perspective impels a strong contention that decisions in law must be made surely on the foundation of validity claims couched in Habermas's universals, so that its assertions—say of causation or liability—raise them simultaneously and that they are essential to explanation and justification.

In a practical sense, dislodging the traditional nature of validity claims inherent in scientific expert opinion and replacing them with Habermas's universals would not be trivial. Total 'de-specialization' not only would be impracticable but also undesirable as it would deny expertise. Nonetheless, a robust interpretation of Habermas's visualization of the formal unity of reason affecting procedure would recommend that law should de-prioritize the validity claims of experts in recognition of their provinciality and substitute the universals, so that claims underscoring its decisions reflect truth, normative rightness and truthfulness that it 'knows', or 'knows that' on its own account after hearing the issues. As illustration, in no longer regarding truth as the sole province of science through its representation as objective fact, it should be recognized that ('known that') even the unprecedentedly high degree of probability of DNA evidence in forensic science that associates defendants with a crime should be understood initially as confirming only that they were present at the scene or that, somehow, traces of their DNA were found at the scene.

Guilt would then be confirmed only by other corroborative evidence (Schklar 1998: 110).[195]

In some instances, regard should be had in legal procedure for its own normative values so that, in a case in point, prosecutions relating to suspicious sudden infant deaths, medical expert opinion is not used to establish perpetration of a crime. Without the embroilment of science in a matter for law, often only the circumstances of parents/child-minders being alone with their infants could be used by the prosecution to infer their culpability, which would be unsafe. In pronouncing an erroneously guilty verdict in such cases, truth—here comprising a premise and conclusion that if homicide had occurred, the accused parent automatically was responsible—would be the first casualty in the validity claims of the tribunal.

The account of the formal unity of reason of Habermas thus far has been slanted, not too self-consciously, towards the way in which science and law can utilize the same rationality to achieve understanding. However, a theoretical objection to the basis of the idealizations has been raised and arises from a circularity produced by direct application of Habermas's arguments for them. The objection manifests in an analysis of trans-science where law is called on to decide questions of fact using its normative capacity, a cause of fundamental philosophical disharmony and a further reason for caution in regarding the procedures of trans-science. The concept of the formal unity of reason was trialled as an escape route from this distortion of law's rôle (Paterson 2003). The circularity emerged from the meaning of the lifeworld and the orientation towards understanding that Habermas construed. The lifeworld refers to the symbolically and communicatively structured spheres of society but more precisely to the stock of implicit assumptions, intuitive know-how and socially established practices that function as the background to understanding (Habermas 1982: 252). But inasmuch as the lifeworld forms a background to the everyday processes of communication, it also functions as a resource—'the reservoir of intuitively certain interpretations upon which participants in communication can draw' (Cooke 1997: 15). Paterson confirms that Habermas locates this rationalization of the lifeworld in the formal world-concepts of truth, rightness and truthfulness that constitute a reference for that about which understanding is possible (2003: 538), in other words the idealizations or 'universals' of the formal unity of reason. In reifying a problem for trans-science no different from that experienced by law generally in circumstances of science-law conflict, Paterson felt that, at the level of the resources in Habermas's theory of communicative action, the familiar incommensurability was made to reappear. Thus in a validity claim, truth appears in the assertions of empirical science, moral rightness in law from a normative reference and truthfulness as a measure of trustworthiness in a communicating participant (ibid: 538-539).

---

[195] See also Wall (2002).

The above contention could signify that Habermas's tentative notion of a formal unity of reason is defeated but, in current context, concern is for the representation science makes to law, so that law's interest in the claims to validity of utterances in science takes priority. However, in order to interrupt Paterson's asserted circularity, when law listens to science, it always should take whatever steps it can to verify that proffered scientific evidence represents the best estimation of the truth currently available. That might imply recourse to rules of evidential admissibility or reliance on adversarial procedure. It should not attempt a critique of the evidence. For science, according to its own tenets, there are no difficulties in accepting the idea of truth claims as dependent upon empirical evidence that can be checked—indeed, law must insist on this checking—but law's primary rôle in judgment is to decide on the significance to accord it. Rightness must be extrapolated from the narrow idea of moral rightness as the exclusive province of law, to include moral rightness to express claims through standards observed in acquisition of knowledge that are applicable to science (or any field). It has already been shown that science has its own basis for regulative statements. Truthfulness inheres in the honesty of experts that adversarial procedure confirms (or should!). This examination shows there is no reason to abandon the universals of Habermas's thesis.

The formal notion of the unity of reason, however tentative, creates a unified approach to rationality for science and law by which law can regard the validity of the assertions of science and which science, too, can apply to itself. Ultimately, law should not avoid fact/value distinctions in drawing its conclusions. Nonetheless, improving the representation of science and law's trust in what it hears safeguards the security of its conclusions without the risk of deflection by either the inflated or underrated influence of science.

THE CONSEQUENCES OF THE CONSENSUS THEORY OF TRUTH

Habermas's incentive for decentring epistemology

The consensus theory of truth of Habermas emerges from his notion of communicative rationality and all its connected themes. Nowhere concisely or specifically expressed, it is presumed from the exercise of his idealizations, particularly the pragmatic theory of meaning, intersubjectivity of understanding and recommendations for discourse to reach agreement. This grounds truth in human action rather than deriving it from knowledge. It entertains neither the correspondence theory of truth, which contends a positive association between theory and reality to which scientists subscribe, nor the coherence theory of truth, which rationalizes theories on the basis of consistency with others to form an acceptable body of knowledge.

As a philosopher of science, Hesse contends that the almost universal reliance on versions of the correspondence theory of truth among analytical philosophers will prove seriously inadequate to resolve current epistemological problems and that a deep challenge to many entrenched assumptions of empiricism must be faced (1980: 206). Stressed is the need to attain new concepts of knowledge and truth that do justice to interpretations in both theoretical and natural science, social science and ethics, while not deviating radically from traditional understandings of these concepts (ibid).

Habermas is motivated in developing his scheme by distrust of scientism. This is the assumption that empirical science is co-extensive with knowledge and is adequate for knowledge of persons and societies as well as things, and that empirical knowledge is sufficient for its own explanation (Habermas 1971/1986: 4). In his critique, he indicts the positivist theory of scientific knowledge for its inadequacy in failing to consider communicative knowledge—the linguistic conditions of personal interpretation—and for being incapable of self-reflection (Hesse 1980: 208). The limitations of what can be understood in the theory of empirical science and the failure of social science to recognize the irrelevancy of ideas like 'truth', 'objectivity' and 'knowledge', in a method that lacks the predictive power of empirical science, inspired Habermas to dissociate 'truth' from 'correspondence' and to relocate it in consensus (ibid: 210-211).[196]

The critical thrust of Habermas's theory of communicative rationality is its reliance on the claims of speakers in discourse that are motivated by the force of the better argument. This might be perceived as leaving truth more precarious and contingent than before, suggesting that the way in which this is avoided must be germane to acceptance of consensus theory as a credible substitute for empirical knowledge.

In this work so far, it has been seen that few avenues for mediating incommensurability issue from the epistemological confrontations of science and law; there is even less likelihood of compatibility through systems and the ideological disposition of its theory. Trans-disciplinary procedures showed their limitations, indeed proving that they were always already an integral feature of the problem for law and contributing to heterogeneity in its conclusions. Not least, critical evaluation of trans-science by Paterson showed the contradiction of resorting to law's epistemology, founded on value, in order to conclude on that of science, founded on fact. In this study, examining Habermas's communicative rationality as the framework for mediating the central problem and, by association, the consensus theory of truth, involved a methodological de-prioritization of epistemology in order to discover the nature of the resultant alternative resources. The consequences of that choice need careful explanation. Preferring Habermas's transcendent(al) proposals confers responsibility for justification of the non-epistemological nature of the consensus theory of truth.

---

[196] In reflecting Habermas's texts, Hesse's account uses 'empirical science' fairly regularly to imply the methods of the natural sciences that generate nomological laws and 'hermeneutical science' to imply the social sciences, which are interpretive.

No pretence is made here that epistemology has in some way been declared obsolete, even though some modern theorists contend that it has. But it is not the point of this study to make that decision; rather it is to emphasize that truth can be proceduralized through intersubjectivity, discourse and argumentation. How that departure characterizes truth without the assurances of a conventional epistemological basis then becomes a natural question. More essentially, what is non-epistemological about Habermas's consensus theory of truth? What would it mean for it to be that? An initial response to this stern challenge to the fundamental nature of Habermas's theory is that, in respect of the present study, it affects principally the representation and reception of science to law as the embodiment of truth. It marks a shift of emphasis from the objectified truth sustained by traditional epistemology that is indeed demanded in the legal forum, to a representation of truth that inheres in communicative acts between persons. Hesse has the way of explaining, most tellingly, what occurs in this change with regard to the statements of scientists. When reflecting on *justification* of their statements, consideration rises to the level of the *logic*[197] of science or epistemology, this being termed discourse by Habermas (Hesse 1980: 208-209). And on the question of where truth now lies, 'truth is no longer a predicate of propositions but a predicate of claims made in speech acts' (ibid: 219). Questions of how truth and reality can be known are relocated in consensus in both empirical and social science, via the suppositions of communicative rationality.

Habermas's ambition is for a pragmatic account of the idea of validity that, potentially, is able to overcome all accepted agreements over definitions and judgments. That an utterance is understood when the conditions of its acceptability are known, is intended to accommodate a notion of a context-transcendent validity that equates to truth within a pragmatic framework (Cooke 1997: 96). Truth itself can be understood as a specification of underlying generic notions of validity. The concept of truth has the same connections with reasons given for its acceptance and the same pragmatic function of eliciting consensus (Finlayson 2005: 45).

The need for certainty

Habermas rejects scientism—the thought that science can provide all necessary knowledge in society.[198] The current influence of science and technology in the world is undeniable; indeed, even mundane matters in society are subjected to scientific analysis. Its methods, even if only crudely applied, have been inculcated into modern culture. The notion of 'scientific' transcends the boundaries of the sciences though, and many fields of knowledge and practice believe a systematic and disciplined approach mandatory in analysis of events

---

[197] Author's emphases.

[198] For an impression of Habermas's rejection of scientism, see Hesse (1980): 211-214.

or in the basis of opinion. The foregoing remarks are broad and generalized but not controversial.

The philosophy of science is absorbed with the study of methodology that examines mean by which certainty can be assured. Even though these can be overturned or questioned, opinion persists that adherence to good scientific method pledges that assurance. This is the rationality relied on by society, notwithstanding its flaws. Habermas's alternative raises questions immediately concerning assurances over its theoretical assumptions and his critics are numerous and vocal. In the present study, this invites two problems and there is tension between them. First is a requirement to show how decentring epistemology opens channels to resources potentiating mediation of incommensurability. The second is common both to this thesis and the problem raised by Habermas's detractors. The methods of science provide society with assurances of certainty and the extent to which those assurances are acceptable can be decided. If, hypothetically, science is to be deprived of that rôle, society requires replacement of the assurances thereby lost, and knowledge of the conditions under which they can be offered. For the positivist, this would require a great conceptual leap.

From epistemology to argumentation: truth, validity, consensus and fallibilism

VALORIZING ARGUMENTATION

Habermas construes 'rationalization' as referring to the development of the internal logic of a particular mode of societal action coordination—his Theory of Communicative Action. Importantly, consensus is identified as its mechanism, which irrevocably is tied both to linguistic understanding and the process of reaching agreement. Argumentation is the process that achieves such agreement (Cooke 1997: 5-9). The comprehension of a linguistic utterance is connected with the evaluation of reasons in argumentation, which by definition is oriented towards understanding (ibid: 96). Whether theoretical or practical, discourses are conceived as ideal forms of argumentation (ibid: 32).

Habermas contends that truth and morality have a special context-transcendent power based on his perception that they are internally connected with the idea of argumentatively reached universal agreement (ibid: 36). Going to the heart of engagement in argumentation, it permits any participant to call into question the reasons that are *accepted as valid* in existing contexts of validity (ibid: 13). The discourse is dialogical in nature: what counts as a good reason for a claim to validity is always in principle subject to critical evaluation by others in dialogue (White 1989: 73). This process-evaluative aspect of argumentation is its paramount attribute.

EXPANDED CONCEPTS—EXPANDED LEXICON OF MEANINGS

In explanations of the consensus theory of truth, important distinctions of meaning emerge that are critical to proper understanding of argumentation and its achievements. Meanings are precise and specific in the theory and apply to Habermas's unique conception of the way truth is understood. There is no negativity associated with distinctions that account for the shift of meaning away from their normal associations; rather, they accentuate the significance of processes involved in argumentation and elevate matters to another level of cognition. Persistent among them are insights that re-characterize truth conceptually, convey new means of its perception and disenfranchise objecti-vating methods of its estimation. In Habermas's form of argumentation, truth claims are criticisable on an intersubjective basis (Cooke 1997: 36), which sharpens the meaning of intersubjectivity from that of general congruence of understanding to a more incisive factor in judgment.

Regarding the perception of agreement reached in discourse as a criterion of truth, Habermas now regards it as merely explicating the meaning of the idea of truth (1982: 232f). In an almost revolutionary way, truth is construed as a regulative scheme, 'the idea of an infinite rational consensus' (ibid) and not owed to epistemology. It is part of the idea of truth through the idealizing suppositions and the dynamics of argumentation that, if a claim is held to be true, equally it is held that every rational person aware of the relevant arguments and evidence must accept it as true, not just now but at any conceivable time in the future (ibid: 277).

TRUTH AS A MORAL CONCEPT

Crucially, operating at the level of reasons in argumentation lends truth a moral connotation or an 'ought' predisposition, placing emphasis on action and de-stressing its epistemological basis in favour of conditions for acceptance of knowledge. This is through reasons that are intersubjectively agreed as valid. If concern for the objectivity of truth as derived fact, over which both science and law are exercised, could be reassigned to the arena of moral justification for its claims, then law would be more naturally equipped to deal with this than in its attempts to attach legal significance to the meaning of scientific evidence and opinion. This would reconfigure the central problem of the present study in that the tension between science and law in legal contexts would disappear.

ACCEPTABILITY

In argumentation, the 'acceptability' of truth is prioritised over 'assertibil-ity', the distinction residing in the conditions of validation. 'Assertibility' suggests that these conditions can be known or 'recognized' as true independ-ently of discussion with others, which Habermas advises is incorrect. To the contrary, he claims the conditions of validation can be produced only through a procedure of discursive justification. These conditions have to be understood in a dialogical and fallibilistic way (Cooke 1997: 99-100). 'Assertibility' also has empirical and epistemological connotations, appearing derived from knowledge of the semantic truth conditions of sentences, whereas 'acceptability' reflects what it is for a speaker or hearer to know the conditions under which the truth conditions would be satisfied (ibid: 99).[199]

Reliance on justification of truth claims is the essence of Habermas's scheme.[200] He puts forward a fallibilistic interpretation of truth, tied to the process of argumentation. It has surprising resonance with the concept of the provisionalism of knowledge in science—a temporal basis to the understanding of truth. Habermas holds that no proof ever is conclusive, for no proof ever is in principle immune to challenge through new evidence or insight; one could say also that no justification of a claim ever is in principle immune to critical re-evaluation on the basis of new information (ibid: 1997: 108). Schematized in consensus theory, such re-evaluation would be entered anew into argumentation. At any given moment, truth is the result of an instantaneous well-grounded agreement. Truth and its justification are distinguished: whereas truth has a moment of 'unconditionality' transcending all spatio-temporal concepts, justification, in the sense of well-grounded agreement, always is conditional (Habermas 1982: 231f).

NO UTOPIAN DREAM

The form of argumentation advocated by Habermas is guided by clearly conceptualised expectations of conduct in the process of argumentation that is aimed at understanding. This takes place amid the idealizing supposition that participants are motivated only by a concern for the better argument. A sceptical impression of communicative rationality might view such expectations as a utopian ambition. This is because participants derogating from the spirit of this form of argumentation could render consensus difficult, if not impossible, thereby making the process a negative experience and affecting outcomes detrimentally. The subversive power of validity claims resides in the tension between the normative promise contained in the implicit strong idealizations and actual occurrences in everyday practices of argumentation (Cooke 1997: 36). The idealizing supposition that participants are motivated only by concern for the better argument produces a critical standard for the assessment of the actual process of argumentation. Allowing criticism of those who unavoidably must profess to, but do not in fact share this motivation, it

---

[199] In formulation of his theory, these distinctions are necessary and are drawn up by Habermas through a need to overcome restrictive aspects of the theory of semantics. These threaten to demolish the pragmatics of his communicative theory. The interested reader will find a full explanation of this in Cooke (1997) Chapter 4: 'A Pragmatic Theory of Meaning: from Comprehension to Pragmatics', 95-130.

[200] The meaning of 'justification' lies in the knowledge by participants of what they must do to redeem discursively a contested validity claim (Cooke 1997: 106-107).

thus provides a standard for the critique of latently strategic action [201] (ibid: 37).[202]

METHODOLOGICAL JUSTIFICATION

Pursuit of Habermas's theory in this work was inspired by the form of rationality that it appeared to offer, that coincided with the methodological aim of seeking what mediative resources for the incommensurability problem would materialize by demoting epistemology as the dominant rationality. This was a tactic and not meant as a judgment of epistemology itself, even though the study found little capital in that domain. To the conservative or ideological theorist, it relocated resources in anthropologicalized virtues of sincerity, openness, good faith, justice, honesty, commitment and so on. Forsaking the safe haven of more conventional contemplation involves not only a risk but also impels an urgent need to discover imaginative solutions with newly recognized potential. Communicative rationality allows criticism, not of arguments themselves, but of the way they are conducted. The basis of criteria for acceptable argument is not the validity of reasons but the way in which they are discussed. Judgments cannot be criticized on the basis of the knowledge they embody but only *on the basis of the way they are reached* (ibid: 161).[203]

Argumentation thus moves dependence on knowledge in resolving the central problem two steps from the focus of consideration. In the judgments that emerge, knowledge already has been subsumed in validity claims resting on anthropological qualities in their making. Validity lies at the heart of judgments but argumentation entails criteria regulating the process by which they are reached. Judgments thus are processually, not epistemologically, created. Epistemology recedes to the background as an influence. It cannot be eliminated entirely, nor should be, because participants in communicative acts cannot eschew personal knowledge in issuing their claims. However, the change of emphasis to the transcendent or sublime form of rationality offers new opportunities for ameliorating law's disappointments with science, which is the reason for its inclusion here.

TAKING STOCK: TOWARDS A COMMON INTELLECTUAL SPACE FOR THEORY AND PROCEDURE

This has been a wide-ranging account of developments from the linguistic turn that has included language, speech communities and action oriented towards understanding. While several valuable points have emerged and been

---

[201] When actions are connected through influence rather than consensus, the agents are oriented towards success rather than towards understanding. They recognize no other modes of rationality than the cognitive-instrumental mode. (Habermas 1982: 247f).

[202] See also ibid: 37, note 27.

[203] Author's emphasis.

discussed in their turn, an important trend has been noticed where the disturbing gulf between theory and experience or theory and procedure detected early in the study appears to be closing. Wittgenstein did not wish his contemplations to be regarded as theory though their abstruseness gave them that semblance. They are situated in everyday social relationships that make it possible to consider them in relation to the central problem of the study albeit by extending them in ways that Wittgenstein did not consider necessary. The Theory of Communicative Action of Habermas concerns interpersonal understandings that can be cast in any human context. A fascinating social theory thus has real life significance.

PART D. PROVISIONAL CONCLUSIONS

Chapter VI. Potential Frameworks for Bridging Law's Disaffection with Science in Evidence

POSTSCRIPT ON METHODOLOGY: THE UTILITY OF THE TRIPARTITE APPROACH AND THE LESSONS OF RESEARCH

At the outset of this work, it was affirmed that approaches to evaluating potentially mediative resources would be categorized as epistemological, trans-disciplinary and epistemologically transcendent, through partial perspectives that might yield frameworks with potential to ameliorate the asserted central problem of law's disappointment with science in evidence. In the design of the study, these were reckoned to be of empirical and critical value. While there was not always a perfect conceptual fit between the frameworks for consideration and each category, they were more than sufficient to select, direct and contain the examinations. Though the approach is not contended as unique or superior, its starting point was the central problem that always returned to disparate epistemologies and the need to ameliorate that impasse. That this approach around a single theme bred fruitful ideas for examination justifies its choice.

The study has not freed itself wholly from the dichotomy of the various expressions of legal theory and the institutions of procedure that present a bifurcated appearance to law. Not accountable to flawed methodology, it was an empirical realization. Abstractions often could not be reified in procedure, except in some important instances where theory itself assumed a different mantle. Whereas in science, theory could be taken to explain phenomena in a direct relationship, attempts to find correspondence in the study of legal theory and procedure usually were not rewarded. For a non-lawyer, conducting the study initially was perplexing. Yet it would have been as counterintuitive to assume legal theory so rarefied as to offer no gain from its contemplation, as it would have been to dismiss philosophy as having no concern with reality. Both can provoke thought, build perspectives and offer different conceptual analyses. Recognizing this and that there was not an easy nexus of thought and procedure was not detrimental to progress, although it necessitated a different understanding. Encouragement was given by descriptions of the association of

175

legal theory and practice by Penner *et al.* stating that jurisprudence explores what is implicit in a lawyer's understanding of law that forms the background assumptions or beliefs when 'doing law' (2002: 4). The distinction also was used as productively as possible through immersion in philosophy, legal and social theory to explore human understanding that would provide insightful reflections on the problem, coupled with the thought always held in the background that the way these might be connected to procedure would provide a reality check.

The tripartite methodology delimited research so that knowledge could be added to a specific realm of scholarship identifiable in such a way as to permit later advancement using the same principles. Research was structured around epistemology as lying at the core of science-law problematization. This probed the disparate knowledges and rhetorics of science and law, examining and characterizing their interactions and imbuing the study with consequent themes for exploration.

Completed, this analysis would then make it possible to evaluate the possibility of frameworks founded on some form of epistemological reconciliation or other mechanism for the interchange of knowledge and understanding. If this were to fail, satisfaction of the research question would need to be sought through a reconfiguration of the inquiry, firstly so that the possibility of frameworks for epistemological transformations in science-law encounters could be reconsidered, and consequently whether a new form of rationality to mediate incommensurability that was not dependent on epistemology existed and could be substituted.

Preferred categories: the 'A List' of Mediative Resources

Central to the methodological approach of this study was the need to engage, ultimately, only with those resources with potential to mediate science-law incommensurability and to improve the teleological relationship that law seeks with science. After examination, inevitably this entailed rejection of some and the 'grading' of others according to their likely success. Chapter V gives account of this process and provides the assessment necessary to value the explored resources for their possible contribution to alleviating the central problem. The account is silent on resources that were de-selected from this process. Those upon which critical analysis is performed, and in which a greater hope is placed for mediative potential, constitute the 'A List' of resources. That is to say, they are a 'preferred category' because they inform the debate more usefully and their realization in concrete form could lead to mitigation of the central problem. It is unnecessary to re-enumerate them all but helpful to refresh the memory about the contributions of the most prominent.

In summary then, the sociology of scientific knowledge emerged conspicuously as a method by which scientists could evaluate their beliefs that is superior to a myopic allegiance to raw scientific method. Systems theory, that concretised incommensurability via the conditions of autopoiesis, was subjected to its most critical challenge through the possibility of reflexive law as *transformable* law. Though the discussion was inconclusive, glimpses were afforded of ways in which transformable law might become a reality without contravening the canons of autopoietic theory. Its study had the effect of rendering Smith's account of 'peripheral contact zones' in issues of child adoption as opportunities for structural coupling as a weak and tenuous proposition, highly contextualized within special circumstances.

The possibility of reflexive law itself as a *transformative* form of mediation was absorbing and clearly exercised the minds of theorists who believed in its possibility. It is not that reflexive law is infeasible; the problem is to discover ways in which it might be consistent with autopoiesis. In regulation of risk environments, that is, of systems and organisations likely to incur risk in their operations, is seen that a principal regulator can become the regulator of the self-regulation of other systems, requiring, of course, that those systems are capable of responsible self-regulation. This much can be salvaged from Teubner and Paterson's conception of reflexive law and suggests the present author's questioning of a transformative law. It is indirect in effect, though, because regulation is carried out at arm's length from law via agencies, albeit often underpinned by statute.

The status of regulation within autopoietic law therefore is uncertain, and it is difficult in the context of the present study to perceive the potential of reflexive law as a mediative resource, even though the possibility tantalizes. As a remarkable discovery among the previously hidden virtues of the much-denigrated Bolam Test of medical negligence, was that its peculiar procedure could be estimated to fall within the *understanding* of responsive law. The reason was that medicine pronounces upon the standard of medical care to which law responds in determining liability. There is therefore a sense in which law takes account of extra-legal contemplations in reaching decisions (though the decisions must forever be those of law).

A fresh analysis of sociology by Luhmann, in the context of risk, provided a means within the compass of systems theory of observing the heteronomy of law's conclusions, over which the present study primarily is concerned. This reconfigured sociology as a second-order observer of communications *between* systems. Although restricted to this special example, sociology could overcome epistemological disjunction by observing the distinction autonomy/heteronomy. The individual system distinctions of true/false for science and legal/illegal for law were implicit in its operations but not brought specifically into play.

The apogee of the study's conclusions is the notion of the unity of reason extended by Habermas, and the method by which it is estimated that epistemological boundaries are transcended by this rationality. Justification for this choice follows through a brief recapitulation of Habermas's scheme, to be followed by concrete examples of its occurrence in the real world.

UNITY OF REASON: A CANDIDATE FOR THE SUBLIME?
EVALUATION OF AN ALTERNATIVE RATIONALITY

Language emerged as a postmodern theme to express thought and meaning that turned epistemology aside and, through critical social theory, was realized the possibility of an alternative rationality. Habermas's Theory of Communicative Action suggested that a tentative notion of a formal unity of science, law and aesthetics—or facts, values and inner experience—was possible through reason. Represented by a new paradigm, its comprehension alone required a new mind-set. Was this a candidate for the sublime or would it prove a too tactical theory in out-manoeuvring Kant's epistemological separations?

The impetus for the social theory of Habermas was the failure of modernity to prevent the holocaust, the restriction of intellectual freedom caused by the perspectives of the Enlightenment, supported by the sacrifice of personal autonomy evident in the welfare state and the colonization of the lifeworld by 'expert cultures'. A new basis for the coordination of social action was required and Habermas replaced the discredited dependence on the development of the conscious self by locating its rational basis in speech acts. Practical and moral knowledge was based instead on the interest of humans in understanding each other (Finlayson 2005: 18).

For the credence of Habermas's proposition of the 'tentative notion of a formal unity of reason' as a framework for examination, the use and sense of his notions of validity in utterances was crucial. Validity claims were implicit in the sense that they were always already understood to have been made in the act of speaking (ibid: 35). This applied to everyday speech and from their explanation the claims to validity that were truth, rightness and truthfulness were not difficult to visualize and reflect upon. Pragmatic meaning embedded in the use of language between speaker and hearer on the basis of shared understanding and intersubjective consensus about meaning, suggested there should be no problems in communicating. In the realms of specialized and formalized argumentation though, differentiation of 'validity dimensions', Cooke said, was the most developed. Providing a reminder of Habermas's 'expert cultures' science, law and aesthetics reappeared therefore as distinct entities and it would be a test of his scheme of universals to see whether they could be applied to utterances in science that law would understand on the same basis of validity. If this answer to the problems of science-law disjunction represented the sublime it required extra vigilance for potential inconsistencies or failures.

One strong theoretical objection perceived by Paterson was in the recourse of Habermas to the lifeworld resources of truth, rightness and truthfulness for his formal unity of reason that attempted the overcoming of expert cultures through context-transcendent claims to validity. In this conception, truth drew on science and moral rightness on law, thereby assigning Habermas's reasoning to a continuous loop. Habermas realized this and proposed a solution dependent upon a daring counterfactual concerning the unproblematic transfer of meaning from the factual to the normative that lay at the heart of the problem for trans-science.[204]

As an escape route from science-law disparity, Paterson did not accept it. In the present study, the circularity was averted by relocating the resource of the moral rightness of science's ability to make a validity claim in the normative standards of science. This attempt at modifying Habermas's notion was not without problems of its own. The previously intact perception of the formal unity of reason as capable of transcending the disjunctions occasioned by expert cultures now was disturbed by reconsidering the effect of science. It has been emphasized several times that the practice of science does not adhere unfailingly to its normative standards. This could represent part of the disappointment that law experiences with science. The Mertonian Norms were consigned in this study as a kind of sociological reproduction of scientific methodology but, at least, respect was earned for the vigilant self-regulation of science and the principle of the general acceptance of conclusions through their approval by the scientific community. The 'Norms' might now appear too gentle or even naïve for today's harsher, more exacting world.[205]

Dissolution of problems by negotiating the meaning of science, protocols that establish what the evidence proves and the sociology of scientific knowledge that can provide scientists with the basis for their beliefs, have the capacity to restore confidence in its normative values. If law as a participant in communication can be given reasons to accept the validity claims of science, then action orientated towards understanding will have been successful.

In the reconfigured notion of the formal unity of reason, the expectation that law presides will not be diminished. Fears that law would be captured by a more cogent science are not justified. In hearing a claim to truth it is law that can send science to verify its empirical findings. It can continue to question the normative standards underlying the rightness to make a claim that Habermas prescribes.

In this unilateral aspect of science-law relations, law can learn reasons to trust science. The circular argument between lifeworld as the background to understanding and resources enabling communication is circumvented in this special context and the case for the acceptability of scientific validity claims by means of a modified Habermasian notion is strong. Paterson's critique cautions against wholesale acceptance of the formal unity of reason and its possibility of success is only by means of the special interpretation given it here. Now it appears less than sublime through this limitation of its scope and perhaps its 'universals' are not truly transcendent as Habermas intended. But an advance has been made in respect of the native problem of this work, in that

---

[204] See Paterson's detailed discussion (2003: 540).

[205] Discussion elsewhere in this study shows that science can have other means of estimating its validity that move ahead of pure norms to include admissibility rules, the philosophy and sociology of science and the sociology of scientific knowledge.

there can be a way for science and law to concur over the bases of claims to validity.

This presents a framework deserving of examination, because next would be required the means by which science and law could be brought to this understanding and the way even a modified notion of the formal unity of reason could transform their interactions in evidential contexts. The factual/normative dichotomy generated by law being pressed into decisions concerning fact might never be resolved but law has shown ability to contend with it and improved representation of science is a key not only to more autonomy in decisions for law but also to safer ones.

A NEW INTELLECTUAL SPACE FOR THEORY AND PROCEDURE

Sometimes research provides answers beyond its original questions. From the beginning of this study, concern was expressed that no nexus in law existed between theory, procedure and legal practice. Exploration of theory gave no help towards procedural resolution of the central problem and the theoretical basis of the difficulty encountered in procedure was opaque. Sociology had been unable to offer resources to connect them.

In investigation of language, speech, discourse, intersubjectivity and understanding via transcendent perspectives, in the work of Wittgenstein and Habermas was perceived for the first time theory abiding in human interactions that could be visualized in relation to procedure. They were not legal theories so that, for example jurisprudence played no part; neither were they theories rooted in science. This study admits to placing high value on language, speech and universal validity claims as the bases of new rationalities potentiating mediation of the central problem and it is satisfying that these forms of social theory can be seen to occupy the same intellectual space as the life situations they describe. The old disparities are gone. Inasmuch as this work did not set out to forge links between theory and procedure deliberately, it must regard this fortuitous outcome as particularly useful.

Exploration of the new intellectual space: sites of occurrence of theory and procedure

No single site has been found for actions conforming to the rationality preferred by the present study that is attributed to Habermas, but its principles are evident in real and proposed alternatives to litigation, in regulation and the formation of policy. None represents the theory underlying Habermas's idealizations of speech acts wholly but, while not established specifically to reproduce them, their characteristics can be seen in several contemporary developments of society concerning democracy, trust and the uncoerced opinions of experts that increasingly are being relied upon.

Those chosen here as examples vindicate Habermas's approach, remembering that his ideas concerning claims to validity are located in the everyday speech of humans and in the lifeworld of shared norms, understandings and identities. Without explanation, some of these can be considered mundane but it is their importance in action orientated towards understanding that Habermas emphasizes. Their recognition and a means of incorporating them systematically in the discourse between science and law would offer considerable potential as a resource for mediating their incommensurability. Reliance is placed upon it by the present study.

The theory of communicative rationality as a metaphor for democracy

The interest of Habermas in reshaping modern society that motivated his theory has been sketched. His concern is for the moral and epistemic values that nourish democracy, namely those of equality, liberty, rationality and truth.[206] Although in his thinking these are applied to broader issues of the public sphere, they are no less important at a detailed processual level and are manifested in the real examples to be examined. The foundational concept of democracy is exalted in the treatment of them, not just in the wider political sense, but particularly in order to valorise its programmes of fairness and equality in communication among members of society and their right to participate in discourse as its stakeholders.

Discourse is initiated with a challenge issued by the hearer to the speaker to make good the validity claims of truth, rightness and truthfulness. It is construed as a highly complex and disciplined practice. The process of argumentation required to clarify the basis of a claim to validity involves following identifiable, formalizable rules. These occupy three levels of principle. The first is situated in logical and semantic rules that require non-contradictory and consistent claims (Habermas 1991: 86). The second, itself in two parts, pertains to norms governing procedure, such as the need for sincerity—participants must undertake to assert only that which they genuinely believe—and for accountability—insisting that participants undertake either to justify their assertions on request or to provide reasons for declining. The third level interests the present study most and incorporates norms that immunize the discourse against coercion, repression and inequality, ensuring that only the 'unforced force of the better argument wins out' (Cooke 1997: 31). These in turn comprise sub-rules allowing the participation of every subject competent to speak and act, permitting everyone to question and to introduce any assertion whatsoever, and allowing all participants to express their attitudes, desires or

---

[206] Summarized in Finlayson (2005: 14f).

needs.[207] No speakers may be prevented, by internal or external coercion, from exercising their rights as laid down above (Habermas 1991: 89).

Clearly, these liberal and right-bearing rules would be out of place in court but, equipped with them now, it will be possible to consider via the examples below the way in which Habermas's construction of rationality can be pursued for the sake of better understanding between science and law. These will be contextualized in legal, quasi-legal and regulative action and the formation of policy. The examples are treated under the general headings of the non-confrontational settlement of disputes, uncoerced expression of opinions and objective facts, and the establishment of mutual trust.

Non-confrontational settlement of disputes

The merits of forms of alternative dispute resolution (ADR) have been extolled at length elsewhere and it is proposed to consider only those of direct bearing on issues in this chapter. ADR procedure is characterized as any among a spectrum of relatively informal procedures that can precede or substitute for litigation. They are noted for their less confrontational culture than that of action through the courts. Their purpose is to reach amicable and symmetrical win-win resolutions of conflict, rather than the usually asymmetrical win-lose outcomes of adversarial procedures. Thereby, the constructive relationships of the parties are preserved for the future.

Prominent in use among ADR procedures, mediation averts the segregation of parties into hostile camps and encourages them to focus on their mutual problems rather than on each other (Liebmann 1996: 163ff). Parties are encouraged to examine their needs and feelings. Mediators can concentrate on the common ground between disputants and the prospect of resolution, not on flaws in their arguments. Mediation provides the opportunity for parties to relate their version of events, to hear and consider that of the other side. Though both will have legitimate concerns and grievances, they are more likely to reconsider their view if made aware of the effect of their actions on the opposite party.

Issues in medical negligence claims are complex and the experience distressing for plaintiffs. Litigation often is endured only because otherwise they cannot obtain satisfactory explanation of harms rendered in an aspect of their medical care.[208] Mulcahy collated the reasons for bringing an action, revealing that they were not concerned exclusively with obtaining damages nor were

---

[207] For an admirable treatise on the nature and expression of human needs in the modern context, see Doyal, L and Gough, I (1991) *A Theory of Human Need*, Basingstoke: The Macmillan Press Ltd

[208] For an analysis of risk management procedures aimed at averting adverse clinical incidents and hence reducing occasions for disputes, see Gilson, C. C. (2001) Risk management strategies in acute NHS hospitals that help reduce the incidence of disputes in medical negligence: preliminary insights, LLM Dissertation, School of Law, University of Westminster.

vengefully motivated (1999/2000: 12). Concerning the adverse clinical event(s) that occurred, their purposes are listed as requiring an admission of fault; preventing its recurrence; instigating an investigation; eliciting an apology; making the defendants understand; receiving an explanation; making the defendants show care; money; improving the quality of care and hearing the explanations of the other side (ibid: 12).

Court cases are protracted, debilitating for plaintiffs and costly, with satisfaction being a rare outcome for either party. ADR procedures have been proposed in an effort to provide a more efficient and less stressful means of resolving medical disputes, mediation featuring highly among those favoured. Mulcahy *et al.* (1999/2000) undertook evaluation of a National Health Service mediation pilot scheme in the UK that had been conducted in April 1995. Several models of mediation are extant but that on which Mulcahy's study was carried out involved a neutral third-party mediator intervening between the parties to facilitate negotiations. The power of agreement to solutions lay with the parties rather than the mediator. Legally, the resolutions were non-binding but, in recompense, mediation operates as a private process seeking to maximise the parties' interests and can offer remedies of which courts are incapable. The procedure is not bound by the rules of substantive or procedural law (ibid: 29). Mulcahy reports that it is often said that mediation is 'interest based' rather than 'rights based'. It is directed commonly towards the *creation* of relevant norms rather than those supported by the formal legal system.[209] Mediators adopt a problem-solving rather than an adversarial approach to conflict, even though mediation often occurs in the shadow of the law and with reference to arguments constructed for use in an adversarial setting (ibid: 29).

Notwithstanding that the present study has noted exhortations of adversarialism, referring chiefly to the effectiveness of cross-examination, the harshness of its culture sometimes can distort truth, because it modifies the behaviour of expert opinion witnesses in court.[210] Away from court, a more relaxed environment pursues truth no less reliably if the participants engage honestly. 'Truths' in ADR can have a depth and quality not obtainable when constrained by court practice. Mediation promises self-determination by allowing the parties to speak for themselves and define the issues at stake (ibid: 29).

In the narrative concerning ADR, 'participation' refers to the physical engagement of the parties themselves in discourse, as distinguished from their representation by counsel in litigation. It was a sufficiently novel feature to a lawyer evaluating the pilot study to warrant her comment.[211] Introducing a new dynamic to procedure, participation is a frequently recurring theme in the other examples giving account of validity claims that follow. Within it, subsist the conditions and possibilities for democratic and uncoerced expressions of

---

[209] Emphasis in Mulcahy *et al.*

[210] See, as examples, Jasanoff (1995, 1998); House of Lords Select Committee on Science and Technology (1993).

[211] That is, Mulcahy herself.

belief and opinion on which the satisfactory reception of science by law must rely for its conclusions. Mulcahy stressed the importance of participation in mediation as follows. She considered it made the settlement process in mediation visible; claimants could put their own case; it made personalized explanations and apologies possible and it facilitated catharsis (ibid: 75). The negotiation process made it possible for one party to understand the point of view of the other—a 'window into the other side's head' (ibid: 74). However, this can have consequences transpiring to be two-edged. In stand-alone and successful dispute resolution outcomes, it will have facilitated mutual respect and understanding; in court-annexed procedures [212] and unresolved instances in mediation, this same understanding might have bestowed strategic importance on information that the parties share.[213]

It is contended in modern negotiation theory that the likelihood of settling disputes is enhanced when a greater number of issues, rather than fewer, are exposed. ADR is credited with this capability (ibid: 97). Court procedures usually narrow issues. There is an ethical element operating within ADR when idealized, which resonates with the ethical dimensions of Habermas's scheme of discourse that, *en passant*, warrants mention in the present study. According to the terms of Pareto-optimal Efficiency, parties in negotiation explore possibilities until a point is reached where no party should benefit from an agreement if it harms the other side (ibid: 97). Applying mainly to financial matters, nonetheless it is equally valid in negotiation of needs.[214]

EVALUATION

Mediation as described here can now be evaluated in terms of Habermas's scheme of rationality and its relevance to the *cause célèbre* of the present study—the reasons and possible remedies for heteronomy in law's decisions. Of prime consideration is the responsibility of speakers to account for their claims to validity when challenged. Alternative dispute resolution procedures constitute no lesser challenge to these values and they are as crucial to the outcome as in adversarial procedure, even if the setting is interpersonally markedly more benign. Through the democracy evident in mediation, parties can claim truth, rightness and truthfulness in their assertions reciprocally in a manner less easily avowed and received amid litigative pressures. The conditions and possibilities for ethical discourse that Habermas espouses are manifestly evident in the setting for mediation.

---

[212] Where a court will instruct mediation to be attempted before initiating proceedings.
[213] The suggestion here is that disclosed information can be advantageous to one or both parties if litigation follows.
[214] 'Pareto efficiency has appeal as a liberal theory'. For discussion of Pareto Efficiency, see Nobles, R (2002) 'Economic Analysis of Law' in 'Approaches to Jurisprudence, Legal Theory and the Philosophy of Law' in Penner, J, Schiff, D and Nobles, R (eds), *Introduction to Jurisprudence and Legal Theory* (2002), p. 859.

Challenges take the form of requests for explanation that the inquirer tries to understand, rather than the attempts to discredit the beliefs of participants in processes to construct truth that are usual in court. There is even freer rein for Habermas's principles, in that the sentiments of ordinary people affected by a materialized harm can be expressed—moreover in terms of everyday speech—rather than being constrained and compelled by the questions that counsel choose to ask in litigation. Here, there are also rôles for both lay participants and experts in that lay participants' claims to rightness will subsist in the normative values of morality, as a 'right-behaving' person in society while, according to the determination of rightness made by the present study, for experts these will lie in the normative values of their field. In appropriate cases, these will be those of medical science and clinical practice. Habermas distinguishes 'naïve' forms of communication—thematization of validity claims in everyday communication practice—and 'reflective'—the development of institutionalized forms of argumentation or expert cultures. Discourse is the reflective form of communicative action in the sense of 'reflective' (Cooke 1997: 14). However, in the need for explanation and the willingness to give it in mediation sessions, there can be a crossover of these values, in that experts can empathize with lay participants through appreciation of complainants' perspectives and removal of the presumed threat to professional integrity that giving fair and unbiased explanations commonly risk. In this can be seen one of Habermas's rules of discourse that the issuing of assertions neither should be coerced nor the result of internal or external influences.

Use of mediation in medical negligence disputes therefore presaged successful dispute resolution, but Mulcahy issued a caveat in her study pertaining to circumstances in which mediation was unsuccessful. She concluded that certain causes of action were suitable only for resolution via litigation. Nevertheless, her (negative) examples served all the more to vindicate and emphasize Habermas's principles of communicative rationality. Among cases cited as unsuccessful were those where high compensation was sought, proof of liability was the sole aim, and where issues were very complex or required forensic investigation. There were instances where a party refused mediation or was not genuine.

The present study translates 'genuine' as 'sincere'. Contextualized via Jürgen Habermas, an insincere party to mediation may subvert truth and so cannot make a claim via constative speech to validity. With neither the normative standards of science as the basis of rightness for experts nor resource to morality for laypersons, a claim to validity via a regulative speech act cannot be made. Misunderstanding can be negotiated by means of an ethical discourse, as Habermas prescribes, but an insincere participant will subvert this effort too. Finally, with regard to truthfulness, no benefit will be gained from an insincere participant and invitations to explain reasons for a claim to validity either will be rebuffed or, if the participant is hostile, the process can slip into one indistinguishable from cross-examination in court.

Rather than demonstrating the limitations to Habermas's idealized scheme, though they are undeniable, the foregoing serves to illustrate the way in which failure to comply with its conditions only underlines the importance of communicative rationality in negotiating disputes.

Uncoerced expression of opinions and objective facts

The next example is set in the context of parliamentary inquiries aimed at clarification of complex scientific matters of both governmental and public concern, so that recommendations can be made that inform policy, regulation and, if necessary, enact legislation. A type of committee of inquiry invites expert witnesses, equipped by virtue of their qualifications, experience, professional distinction and institutional affiliations, to respond to questions put by its members. In reports, these experts usually are referred to as 'witnesses' but there is no legal action in train. The information that experts provide is termed 'evidence' but the procedure is not a trial. The present study suggests that instead experts should be described as 'consultants' and their expert opinion received either as exactly that or 'expert information'.[215]

The degree of voluntariness in responding to the invitation is not known to the present study but it is presumed that neither would it be diplomatic to decline, nor that witnesses would wish to forfeit an opportunity to explain their work and contribute to government policy. The tenor of such debates is that only the issue itself is being investigated and there are no matters over which culpability is sought. The government honestly is seeking resolution of problems and 'witnesses' should not feel intimidated. A cogent explanation of science is expected but, as well as seeking 'evidence', committee members also solicit advice and opinion. The atmosphere is non-hostile and intended to be constructive. In the United Kingdom, inquiries that government conducts are set up under the auspices of the House of Commons and the House of Lords via their Select Committees, which are drawn from their Members. The purpose is formal, incurring a similar degree of formality in procedure, but there is informal discourse inasmuch as experts can answer questions in their own fashion and add any information or opinion they consider important. Members of the Committee seek clarification and amplification of answers where necessary. After deliberation, the Committee compiles a report of evidence gathered and makes recommendations based upon them that the government considers in forming policy, introducing regulation or drafting statute.

The present study has referred frequently to the House of Commons Science and Technology Committee Report Forensic Science on Trial,[216] for the

---

[215] Some Select Committee inquiries (not those of the House of Commons Science and Technology Committee) are set up to investigate irregularities, where court-resembling procedures of the inquisitorial style are used. Those that provide information then really are 'witnesses' in that setting.

[216] *Forensic Science on Trial*, House of Commons Science and Technology Committee (2005).

views of experts on the relationship of science and law in the legal forum, such experts often having experience as witnesses in litigation and other procedures. The Report is relied on now to exemplify aspects of the theory of communicative rationality and the ethical discourse of Habermas. To achieve this it will be necessary here to cite passages from its transcription of oral proceedings verbatim[217] and to analyse their content. This is intended neither as linguistic analysis nor any critical method of examining texts. Examination will be of the mode of speech employed, together with the way questions and responses are formed in terms of Habermas's speech acts and claims to validity. The thrust of the cited inquiry is on the utility and reliability of DNA samples in criminal evidence and, though not examined here, the need for increased regulation of its storage, access and permitted use.

The point chosen is from the session of the Select Committee on 26th January 2005, where experts were drawn from the academic community having expertise in genetics, analytical science, forensic computing, and anatomy and forensic anthropology.[218] The discussion concerns the reliability of evidence afforded by the number of genetic markers used to compare DNA samples gathered at crime scenes with that of a suspect or from a database. A genetic marker is a gene or DNA sequence with a known location on a chromosome that can be used to identify individuals or species.[219] Observations of the text passages are concerned less with the scientific argument than the nature of the discourse in relation to Habermas's values.[220] The point in the discussion was preceded by a general question concerning the reliability of DNA evidence. (Reported speech).

Q385 Dr Iddon[221] (directed to Professor [Alec] Jeffreys): You have been quoted in the media as having said that DNA fingerprinting is no longer foolproof. Is that a true statement or is there media exaggeration?

Professor Jeffreys: It is a true statement but I will get rid of the "no longer": it never was foolproof. There is no such thing as a scientific technology that delivers foolproof answers. I think it is a trivial point but an obvious one.

Questioning then moved to the issue of markers.

Q388 Dr Iddon: It is 10 markers now.[222]

---

[217] This also implies grammatical errors will be reproduced.

[218] Anatomy and forensic anthropology constitutes a single field.

[219] Wikipedia, Sept. 12, 2012. See also Wall (2002).

[220] Conventions over quotation marks and italicised speech have been disregarded.

[221] Dr Iddon is a Member of the Select Committee. His Doctorate may be irrelevant to the inquiry, though Select Committee Members often are chosen because of their special knowledge.

Professor Jeffreys: Yes, and I would argue that is not enough.

Q389 Dr Iddon: You are arguing it should be 15 or 16.

Professor Jeffreys: That is correct. If you look, for example, at the Tsunami disaster, the identification there is done on a 16-marker system and I would argue that the UK should be running at about that sort of number.

Q395 Dr Turner: [223] Could you expand a little on reasons why uncertainties can arise in DNA evidence? Are you saying that it is normally presented in court in terms that there is a one in a million or whatever chance of this being somebody other than the accused, does it affect these probabilities markedly? Are there technical reasons that completely pervert that evidence? [...]

Professor Jeffreys: 10 markers give a chance of a match between two unrelated people of, on average, 1 in 10,000,000,000,000. While this is extremely low, the current size of the DNA database coupled with the very large numbers of speculative searches means that even extremely rare chance matches will arise. [...] *The consequences of even one false match leading to a conviction that was subsequently overturned could be severe for the DNA database and its public acceptability*.[224] My suggestion for increasing the numbers of markers to 16 reflects my views on the numbers needed to trap false matches. An additional six markers would guarantee, with better than 99.9% certainty, that any such false matches would be detected in a given case.[225] [...]

In considering the evidence given in the report, the Select Committee responded as follows. *"We recognise that adventitious matches are extremely unlikely under the present regime. Nevertheless, we find that Professor Sir Alec Jeffreys' warning that 'the consequences of even one false match leading to a conviction that was subsequently overturned could be severe for the DNA database and its public acceptability' sufficiently persuasive to merit a thorough investigation of the benefits and risks of staying within the current 10 marker system and moving to, for argument's sake, a 16 marker system. We therefore recommend that the government commission a cost-benefit analysis for this move"*.[226]

---

[222] A question was implied in the statement.
[223] Like Dr Iddon, a Member of the Select Committee.
[224] Author's emphasis.
[225] *Forensic Science on Trial*, Appendix 23, Ev 170 (*op.cit*. Volume II).
[226] *Forensic Science on Trial* (*op. cit*. Volume I, § 88). Emphasis added by the present author.

ANALYSIS

While some aspects of the quoted interchange could be regarded as mundane, Select Committee procedure and its manner of discourse reveal Habermas's notions in operation. The tenor of this kind of Select Committee work, which is aimed at resolving difficult issues ultimately for societal benefit, may affect favourably the dispositions of those appearing before it, because they perceive it as a constructive and useful process in which they are glad to participate. Undeniably, the procedure forms part of the democratic process at work in the overt political sense, but democracy also is demonstrated in the equality of participants in the inquiry. Though the Select Committee undoubtedly represents officialdom and has Parliamentary authority, experts carry the corresponding authority of their specialty, privileged knowledge and professional status on which the Committee will depend for its recommendations. According to Habermas, participants, here the experts, have the right to make any assertions whatsoever, provided they can give reasons for them.

Though issues are crucial, questioning is not coercive or repressive. Experts have no need to be intimidated by the Select Committee and each relies on their personal knowledge and experience that they bring honestly into the discourse. They respond to requests for scientific facts objectively, any passion evident in expressing a view or concerning the use to which the information could be put is acknowledged and treated neither as bias nor an attempt to subvert the Committee's purpose. Strongly expressed but sincere convictions sometimes are helpful in this kind of inquiry.

In the example, the forum provided a unique opportunity to correct a common misconception about the interpretation of science (Q385). When invited, the speaker declined to make a claim of validity for the notion that DNA evidence was 'foolproof'—rather, the opposite—and disabused his questioner of it firmly and with historical reference.[227] The three idealizations of communicative rationality were in play: the claim to validity concerning truth as verifiable fact; the (moral) rightness to make the claim subsisting in the normative standards of science in conformity with which the conclusion was reached; the speaker being truthful in that he sought earnestly to avoid a misunderstanding about the capability of that branch of science. Compare this to a situation, imagined in court, where the notion that DNA is 'foolproof' is challenged in a prosecution lawyer's cross-examination of a flustered and inexperienced defence witness who, mistakenly, considers it incumbent upon him or her to defend both the accused and the proffered scientific evidence. This would give rise to a typical constructed misunderstanding, itself the refutation of an ethical discourse concerning claims to validity in utterances.

---

[227] The suggestion that the point was trivial though obvious underplays the necessity for law of being able to place confidence in the conclusions of science. For law, the matter is non-trivial.

Q388, Q389, Q395 and their responses were key to assessment of the reliability of DNA evidence. The claim that DNA 'fingerprinting'[228] is not foolproof, and never was, is now understood. More accurately characterized, the reliability of DNA evidence is probabilistically-based. It concerns the possibility of a match between the crime scene sample, that of a suspect and, by chance, with the DNA of one or more persons in a database bearing no relationship to the event. That such a chance match would be possible would threaten to undermine the evidential value of DNA sampling. Professor Jeffreys claimed that more than ten markers, possibly up to sixteen, would be necessary to reduce chance matches to negligible proportions.

By comparison with Habermas's theory, the conditions that allowed Professor Jeffreys to make such a claim subsisted in the normative values of science, against the background of which appropriate research had come to that conclusion. In this instance, it was the resource for rightness in his claim to validity. The conditions under which his hearers, the Select Committee, could accept the possibility of Professor Jeffreys' claim and thus reach intersubjective understanding with him on the point, were that they recognised there were norms of science that would allow him to make such a claim. As a respected researcher, they would accept his entitlement to it. He was being truthful when commenting that identification of bodies in the Asian Tsunami disaster relied on a higher number of markers for accuracy than was standard practice in the United Kingdom.

The remainder of the discourse that has been included here reveals the idealizations of speech inherent in the theory of Habermas in several instances. Significantly, from the analysis of the response to Q395, an outstanding difference is evident between the nature of evidence usually proffered in the legal forum and that permitted in Select Committee procedure. It has been said that Professor Jeffreys averred that even one false match leading to a wrongful conviction would discredit the DNA database and unsettle public confidence in it.[229] The Select Committee was sufficiently perturbed by the remark to include in its recommendations that government should investigate the benefits of moving to a sixteen-marker system.

Two of Habermas's essential rules of ethical discourse are perceptible in Professor Jeffrey's assertion. The first accords him the democratic entitlement to make any assertion whatsoever. But, in speaking of wrongful convictions and public confidence in the DNA database, Professor Jeffreys volunteered an opinion that was, *prima facie*, beyond the bounds of his expert knowledge and so could be considered to have moved into an area of social concern in which he was no more expert than an educated layperson. Conscientious though it was, this aspect of his claim to rightness therefore was founded on a purely moral standard and was not made in conformity with scientific norms. How-

---

[228] A term commonly applied to DNA sampling as being the even more reliable successor to the earlier forensic technique of fingerprinting. It is a misleading term.

[229] See italicised part of the transcript of Professor Jeffreys' response to Q395, *supra*.

190

ever, the second rule engaged allows everyone to express their attitudes, desires and needs, thus Professor Jeffrey's opinion would be received by the Committee as legitimate. This marks a huge departure from that followed in some legal proceedings. For instance, such a volunteered opinion from an expert witness might be ordered to be disregarded as it was closer to public policy than science, might not have been sought by counsel and not considered material as evidence in a criminal prosecution.

Again, although Professor Jeffrey's remark was very general and there was no individual who would be affected by it directly, some expert opinion witnesses have misled courts through egregious errors of fact, unfounded or unqualified opinions. Proffered opinion that is outside an expert's sphere of responsibility can go dangerously unrecognised. Nonetheless, the approach of the Select Committee was to be encouraging to all useful contributors and, as a body of hearers, was accepting towards the utterance as part of the process of communication oriented towards understanding. It bestowed high value on opinion.

EVALUATION

Like other organs of institutional inquiry, The Science and Technology Select Committee operates after the inquisitorial style but seeks information to enable it to provide the best advice on social questions. Ideally constituted, it allows the 'unforced force of the better argument' to win out. Contention or misunderstanding over claims to validity can be put to an ethical discourse for resolution that the Select Committee can stimulate, hear or even join. The analysis shows that the nature of the forum in which issues are decided is crucial to proper understanding. Some fora that are employed are 'wrong' in the sense that they are not conducive to intersubjective agreement. Both mediation and the procedure of Select Committees offer more potential for success as crucibles for these social performances.

The analyses have shown that a common intellectual space for theory and procedure through the communicative theory of Habermas does indeed occur in selected settings and that his concept of rationality offers a constructive approach to the central problem of the present study. But perhaps Habermas's Theory of Communicative Action simply is common sense writ large? That it operates in the domain of everyday speech might make it seem so and analysis of its pragmatics can be considered unremarkable. Yet, his concept relies on the commitment of the speaker and hearer of utterances to one another—a concept that is equally important at the 'higher' or specialist levels of function and at that of everyday human interactions. Common intellectual spaces that occur are can be unplanned as such; indeed participants are unconscious that Habermas's form of rationality describes much of their procedure. Rather than *ad hoc* occurrences of sites though, it is required that such fora should be created deliberately, with operations consciously founded on the rules of ethical discourse. The test of them would be whether they would be sufficient to enable conclusions that, over time, would satisfy the needs of society and embody the conditions in which, according to Habermas, reason may be redeemed. In all but those instances where legal action is unpreventable, it is suggested here that they could.

Issues of democracy, participation and trust

In the regulation of risk, institutional arrangements acquire and process the information required for making decisions in the light of it (Ogus: 1997). This is the basic process at work, for instance, in the deliberations of the House of Commons Select Committee on Science and Technology. The technological approach to risk management requires it to be taken by a group of elite persons, reflecting or relying primarily on relevant expertise.[230] Ogus reports that an excess of political accountability can subvert decision-making away from instrumental goals, for which technical expertise is important (ibid: 150). The sensation that exclusion of lay stakeholders and interest groups from decisions promotes mistrust is strong. In areas of occupational health and safety, Paterson explains that, in a 'top-down' paradigm, responsibility for decisions rests ultimately with elected decision-makers (2002: 8). This implies that employees who stand to be affected are not regarded as stakeholders in terms of their protection, and are excluded from the process. Moreover, it is implied that their expertise and experience also is disregarded. The literature discloses a pronounced trend towards the need for democratic processes in regulatory decision-making.

In their exposition of responsive law, Nonet and Selznick indicate the need for participatory decision-making (1978/2001: 98-99). They speak of a new administrative style that would borrow from the experience and rhetoric of democracy, but primarily to achieve the ends of a more purposive organization, free from the straitjacket of bureaucratic authority. They depict the 'post-bureaucratic organization' as less preoccupied with administrative regularity. Participatory decision-making is understood as a source of knowledge, a vehicle of communication and a foundation for consent, 'the leaven in the bureaucratic dough' (ibid: 100).

Instrumental as well as process values can be accommodated in a shift towards the democratic approach, anticipating lay participation in negotiation of risk management (Ogus 1997: 150-151). Citizen participation can represent lay perception of risk, and the democratic approach can allay feelings of mistrust (ibid). The preferences of interest groups can militate against the democratic ideal in consultations but do not weaken the ideal of expert bodies to be transparent and to articulate fully their reasons for regulatory proposals (ibid: 152). The European Commission's White Paper on European Governance declared the need to 'democratise scientific expertise', particularly in the sensitive area of health and safety (Paterson 1997: 8). This new ethos paved the

---

[230] This includes the natural sciences, statistics, engineering, economics and epidemiology.

way for the shift to a mutual trust approach that would unite the disparate stakeholders within a new grouping. These would be based on common values, and thus the establishment of social trust and the rebuilding of confidence. The revised paradigm would allow responsibility for decisions to be shared among all those involved. In the encouragement of collective learning, The European Forward Studies Unit would need to encourage different stakeholders to explain and justify their accounts of a problem and their proposed answers (ibid: 9).

Science Panels in the United States, comprising scientists, lawyers and concerned citizens, adjudicate on a specific question regarding a technical dispute (Brennan 1989: 10). The expert conclusions of the one-time proposed Federal Toxic Substances Board would be publicised, which would inhibit experts concerned for their professional reputations from 'testifying in a preposterous fashion' (ibid: 62-63). Experts serving on the Board from industry, government and academia, as well as public interest groups, would need to understand that respect for the resultant policy statements would depend on participants' readiness to suppress their institutional affiliations and discuss matters in an unbiased fashion. The Public Agenda Foundation experiment in the United States, which sought to create techniques whereby citizens are enabled to make informed judgments about regulatory policy, found—among several interesting outcomes relating to lay understanding of science—that they would alter their views substantially on being exposed to a complete and balanced discussion (Pildes and Sunstein 1995: 90).

EVALUATION

Situated in the context of democracy, Habermas's ethical values regarding discourse and argumentation again are unmistakable in notions of lay participation in the preceding discussion of risk management. Nonet and Selznick (1978/2001: 100) describe the foundation for consent in the 'postbureaucratic organization', a matter at the root of communicative action in the sense of Habermas's intersubjectivity. 'Full articulation of reasons' by expert bodies shows a desire to be understood and exhibit sincerity.

The European Commission believes in a Habermasian concept of establishing trust and building confidence that fulfils his prescription exactly— 'explaining and justifying their accounts'. Experts on science boards are discouraged from preposterous testimony, which incorporates Habermas's provisions for latent strategic action and untruthfulness. The efficacy of communication between experts and citizens can alter lay views that perhaps were prejudiced, founded on ignorance or fear, and achieve an understanding of issues similar to that of the experts.

Habermasian concepts of communicative action and ethical discourse already are evident in the world. With more deliberation and attention, surely the problem of law's disaffection with science in evidence can be tackled in like fashion?

Bibliography

Diagnostic and Statistical Manual of Mental Disorders, Fourth Edition (DSM-IV-TR) (American Psychiatric Association, 2000)

'Forensic Science on Trial', *House of Commons Science and Technology Committee* (2005). Seventh Report of Session 2004–5 (HC 96-1) London: The Stationery Office Limited, 29th March 2005

'Forensic Science', *House of Lords Select Committee on Science and Technology*, (1993) 6th Report of Session 1992-93, HL 24, London: HMSO

'Investigation of the Possible Increased Incidence of Cancer in West Cumbria', Report of the Independent Advisory Group (1984) Chairman: Sir Douglas Black. London: HMSO

Reference Manual on Scientific Evidence (2nd Edition) Federal Judicial Center, 2000. Available at http://air.f jc.gov/public/f jcweb.nsf/pages/16

'Science in Court', Postnote, Parliamentary Office of Science and Technology, October 2005 (248), www.parliament.uk/parliamentary_offices/post.pubs2005.cfm (last accessed 28/10/2005)

Alleyne, R. (2003) '"Triple Vaccine Ruling MMR Evidence is Persuasive and Clear", says Judge', *The Daily Telegraph*, London (UK) 14th June 2003

American Psychiatric Association (2000) *Diagnostic and Statistical Manual of Mental Disorders, DSM-IV-TR*, Washington DC

Andersen, N. A. (2003) *Discursive Analytical Strategies. Understanding Foucault, Koselleck, Laclau, Luhmann*, Bristol: The Policy Press

Atiyah, P. S. (1987) *Pragmatism and Theory in English Law*, London: Stevens and Sons

Austin, J. L. (1976) *How to Do Things with Words* (Urmson, J O and Sbisà, M (eds.), Oxford: Oxford University Press

Ayer, A. J. (1936) *Language, Logic and Truth*, Harmondsworth: Penguin

Badenoch, D. and Henegan, C (2002) *Evidence-based Medicine Toolkit*, London: BMJ Books

Baldwin, T. (ed.) (1993*) G E Moore: Selected Writings*, London: Routledge

Barnes, B. (1974) *Scientific Knowledge and Social Theory*, London: Routledge

Barnes, B., Bloor, D. and Henry, J. (1996) *Scientific Knowledge: A Sociological Analysis*, London: Athlone

Barron, A. (2002) '(Legal) Reason and its 'Others': Recent Developments in Legal Theory' in Penner, J., Schiff, D., and Nobles, R. (eds.) *Introduction to Jurisprudence and Legal Theory. Commentary and Materials*, London: LexisNexis Butterworths Tolley

Bastide, F., Courtial, J. P. and Callon, M. (1989) 'The Use of Review Articles in the Analysis of a Research Area', 15 *Scientometrics* (5-6) 535-562

Batt, J. (2004) *Stolen Innocence: The Story of Sally Clark*, London: Ebury Press

Bechmann, G. (1992) 'Reflexive Law: A New Theory Paradigm for Legal Science' in Teubner, G and Febbrajo, A, *State, Law and Economy as Autopoietic Systems*, Milan: Guiffré

Beck, U. (1992) (trans. Ritter, M.) *Risk Society. Towards a New Modernity*, London: Sage Publications

Bedford, H. E. and Elliman, D. A. C. (2002) The adverse effects of vaccines—fact and fiction, 12 *Current Paediatrics* 62-66

Bertalanffy, Ludwig von. (1971) *General Systems Theory*, Harmondsworth: Penguin

Black, M. (1979) 'Wittgenstein's Language-Games', 33 *Dialectica* 337-353

Bloor, D. (1981) 'The Strengths of the Strong Programme', 11 *Philosophy of the Social Sciences* 173-198

Boseley, S. (2008) 'How a crisis in confidence in MMR led to the return of a disease doctors hoped was a thing of the past', *The Guardian*, 5th February 2008

Bowie, C. (1990) 'Lessons from the Pertussis Vaccine Court Trial', 325 *Lancet* 397-399

Brazier, M. (1992) *Medicine, Patients and the Law*, Harmondsworth: Penguin Books

Brennan, T. A. (1989) 'Helping Courts with Toxic Torts: Some Proposals Regarding Alternative Methods for Presenting and Assessing Scientific Evidence in Common Law Courts', 51 *University of Pittsburgh Law Review* (1) 1-71

Caird, E. (1889) *The Critical Philosophy of Immanuel Kant Vol I, Critique of Pure Reason; Vol II Critique of Practical Reason and Critique of Judgement*, Glasgow: James Maclehose and Sons

Campbell, D. (2000) 'The Limits of Concept Formation in Legal Science', 9 *Social and Legal Studies* (3) 439-447)

Capps, P. and Olsen, H. P. (2002) 'Legal Autonomy and Reflexive Rationality in Complex Societies', 11 *Social and Legal Studies* (4) 547-567

Cartwright, N. (1999) *The Dappled World. A Study of the Boundaries of Science*, Cambridge: Cambridge University Press

Cassirer, E. (1918/1981) (trans. Haden, J.) *Kant's Life and Thought*, New Haven and London: Yale University Press

Casti, J. L. (1990) *Paradigms Lost. Images of Man in the Mirror of Science*, London: Abacus (Little, Brown and Company)

Cavicchi, J. R. (2003) 'The Science Court: A Bibliography', at <http://www.piercelaw.edu/risk/vol4/spring/bibliography.htm> [last accessed 09.05.2011]

Chalmers, A. F. (1999) *What Is This Thing Called Science?* Buckingham: Open University Press

Choo, A. (1998) *Evidence—Text and Materials*, Harlow: Addison Wesley Longman Limited

Christiansen, D. (1979) 'Science Court Tested', 16 *IEEE Spectrum* 27

Clark, E. A. (2004) *History, Theory, Text: Historians and the Linguistic Turn*, Cambridge, Mass.: Harvard University Press

Cogito (1995) 'An Interview with Nancy Cartwright', *The Cogito Society*, 9 (3) 203-215

Cooke, M. (1997) *Language and Reason. A Study of Habermas's Pragmatics*, Cambridge, Mass. and London: The MIT Press

Cotgreave, P. (2003) *Science for Survival: Scientific Research and the Public Interest*, London: The British Library Publishing Division

Cotterrell, R. (1992) *The Sociology of Law: An Introduction*, London: Butterworths

Cotterrell, R. (1995) *Law's Community. Legal Theory in Sociological Perspective*, Oxford: Clarendon Press

Coyle, S. (2005) 'Two Concepts of Legal Analysis' in Coyle, S and Pavlakos, G (2005) (eds.) *Jurisprudence or Legal Science? A Debate about the Nature of Legal Theory*, Oxford and Portland, Oregon: Hart Publishing

Coyle, S. and Pavlakos, G. (eds.) (2005) 'Introduction' in Coyle, S and Pavlakos, G (2005) *Jurisprudence or Legal Science? A Debate about the Nature of Legal Theory*, Oxford and Portland, Oregon: Hart Publishing

Crawford, T. H. (1993) 'An Interview with Bruno Latour', 2 *Configurations* 247-269

Critchley, S. (2001) *Continental Philosophy: A Very Short Introduction*, Oxford: Oxford University Press

Critchley, S. and Schroeder, W. R. (eds.) (1997) *A Companion to Continental Philosophy*, Oxford: Blackwell

Crouch, D. (1986) 'Science and Trans-science in Radiation Risk Assessment: Child Cancer around the Nuclear Fuel Reprocessing Plant at Sellafield UK', 53 *The Science of the Total Environment* 201-216

Dampier, Sir W. C. (1961) *A History of Science and its Relations with Philosophy and Religion*, Cambridge: Cambridge University Press

De Stefano, F. and Chen, R. T. (1999) 'Negative Association between MMR and Autism', 353 *Lancet* 1987-1988

Deflem, M. (1996) 'Introduction: Law in Habermas's Theory of Communicative Action' in Deflem, M. (ed.) *Habermas, Modernity and Law*, London, California and New Delhi: Sage Publications

Devenney, M. (2004) 'The Universal Pragmatics of Communication, Central Problems in the Philosophy of Science and Social Science', 37th *Essex Summer School in Social Science Data Analysis and Collection*, 12th July–20th August 2004, Lecture notes: 4. 'Habermas, Critical Theory and the Critique of Hermeneutics: a Reconstructive Approach', 15th July 2004. (Much of this discussion now can be found in Devenney, M (2004) 'Between Critical Theory and Post-Marxism', in *Ethics and Politics in Discourse Theory*, London: Routledge, pp. 129-139.)

Dicker, G. (2003) 'Descartes', in Arrington, R L (ed.) *The World's Greatest Philosophers*, Oxford: Blackwell Publishing Ltd 2003

Ditchburn, R. W. (1963) *Light*, London: Blackie & Son Limited

Doyal, L. and Gough, I. (1991) *A Theory of Human Need*, Basingstoke: The Macmillan Press Ltd

Draper, G., Vincent, T., Kroll, M. E. and Swanson, J. (2005) 'Childhood Cancer in Relation to Distance from High Voltage Power Lines in England and Wales: a Case-control Study', 330 *British Medical Journal* 1290-1292

Dyer, C. (1988) 'Judge "not satisfied" that Whooping Cough Vaccine Causes Permanent Brain Damage', 296 *British Medical Journal* 1189-1190

Dyer, C. (2005) 'Court Hears Shaken Baby Cases', 330 *British Medical Journal* 1463

Edmond, G. (1999) 'Law, Science and Narrative: Helping the Facts Speak for Themselves', 23 *Southern Illinois University Law Review* 555-583

Edmond, G. (2000a) *Scientific Evidence and the Construction of Guilt and Innocence*, PhD Thesis, Faculty of Law, St. John's College, University of Cambridge

Edmond, G. (2000b) 'Judicial Representation of Scientific Evidence' 63 *Modern Law Review* (2) 216-251

Edmond, G. (ed.) (2004) *Law's Experts*, Aldershot: Ashgate

Edmond, G. and Mercer, D. (1997) 'The Secret Lives of (Mass) Torts: The 'Bendectin Litigation' and the Construction of Law-Science Knowledges', 20 *University of New South Wales Law Journal* (3) 666-706

Edmond, G. and Mercer, D. (2000) 'Litigation Life: Law-science Knowledge Construction in (Bendectin) Mass Tort Litigation', 30 *Social Studies of Science* (2) 265-316

Eggleston, Sir Richard. (1983) *Evidence, Proof and Probability*, London: Weidenfeld and Nicholson

Federal Rules of Evidence (2005) St. Paul, MN.: West Publishing Co.

Felicitas Munzel, G. (2003) 'Kant', in Arrington, R.L. (ed.) *The World's Greatest Philosophers*, Oxford: Blackwell Publishing Ltd

Feyerabend, P. (1978) *Science in a Free Society*, London: Verso

Finlayson, J. G. (2005) *Habermas: A Very Short Introduction*, Oxford: Oxford University Press

Fleming, J. G. (1992) *The Law of Torts*, Sydney: The Law Book Company Ltd

Fleming, P. J. Blair, P.S. Sidebotham, P. D. and Hayler, T. (2004) 'Investigating Sudden Unexpected Deaths in Infancy and Childhood and Caring for Bereaved Families: an integrated multi-agency approach', 328 *British Medical Journal,* 331-334

Francis, R. and Johnstone, C. (2001) *Medical Treatment Decisions and the Law*, London: Butterworths

Freeman, M. (1998) 'Law and Science: Science and Law' in Freeman, M. and Reece, H. (eds.) *Science in Court*, Aldershot: Ashgate/Dartmouth 1998

Fuller, S. (2006) *The Philosophy of Science and Technology Studies*, Abingdon: Routledge

Garver, N. (1996) 'Philosophy as Grammar', in Sluga, H. and Stern, D. G. (eds.) *The Cambridge Companion to Wittgenstein*, Cambridge: Cambridge University Press

Geddes, J. F., Hackshaw, A. K., Vowles, G. H., Nickols, C. D. and Whitwell, H. L. (2001a) 'Neuropathology of Inflicted Head Injury' 124 *Brain* (7) 1290-1298

Geddes, J. F., Vowles, G. H., Nickols, C. D., Scott, I. S. and Whitwell, H. L. (2001b) 'Neuropathology of Inflicted Head Injury' 124 *Brain* (7) 1299-1306

Gilbert, G. N. and Mulkay, M. (1984) *Opening Pandora's Box: A Sociological Analysis of Scientists' Discourse*, Cambridge: Cambridge University Press

Gilson, C. C. (2001) 'Risk management strategies in acute NHS hospitals that help reduce the incidence of disputes in medical negligence: preliminary insights', LLM Dissertation, School of Law, University of Westminster

Glock, H-J. (2003) 'Frege', in Arrington, R. L. (ed.) *The World's Greatest Philosophers*, in Oxford: Blackwell Publishing Ltd

Graham, M.H. (2000) 'The Expert Witness Predicament: Determining "Reliable" under the Gatekeeping Test of *Daubert, Kuhmo* and Proposed Amended Rule 702 of the Federal Rules of Evidence', 54 *University of Miami Law Review*, 317-358

Bibliography

Greenhalgh, P. (2001) *How to Read a Paper*, London: BMJ Books

Gregor, M. J. (1987) 'Foreword' in Kant, I. (1790/1987) (trans. Pluhar, W. S.) *Critique of Judgment*, Indianapolis/Cambridge: Hackett Publishing Company

Haack, S. (1995) 'Science is Neither Sacred Nor a Confidence Trick', 1 *Foundations of Science*, 323-335

Haack, S. (1996) 'Towards A Sober Sociology of Science', 775 *Annals of the New York Academy of Sciences*, 259-265

Haack, S. (1997) Nelson, J. and Hankinson Nelson, L. (eds.) 'Science as Social?— Yes and No', in *Feminism, Science and Philosophy of Science*, 79-94, Dordrecht: Kluwer Academic Publishers

Haack, S. (1999) 'Defending Science—Within Reason', 3 *Principia* (2), 187-211

Haack, S. (2001) 'Clues to the Puzzle of Scientific Evidence', 5 *Principia* (1-2), 253-281

Haack, S. (2003) 'Inquiry and Advocacy, Fallibilism and Finality, Culture and Influence in Science and Law', 2 *Law, Probability and Risk*, 205-214

Haack, S. (2004) 'Truth and Justice, Inquiry and Advocacy, Science and Law', 17 *Ratio Juris*, 15-26

Habermas, J. (1970) 'Towards a Theory of Communicative Competence', 13 *Inquiry* 360-376

Habermas, J. (1971/1986) (trans. Shapiro, J.) *Knowledge and Human Interests*, Boston: Beacon Press

Habermas, J. (1976/1998) (Cooke, M ed.), 'What is Universal Pragmatics?' in *Jürgen Habermas. On the Pragmatics of Communication*, Cambridge, Mass: The MIT Press

Habermas, J. (1982) 'A Reply to My Critics' in Habermas: *Critical Debates*, Thompson, J.B. and Held, D. (eds.) London: Macmillan

Habermas, J. (1984/1986) (trans. McCarthy, T.) *Theory of Communicative Action, Vol I: Reason and the Rationalization of Society*, Oxford and Cambridge: Polity Press/Blackwell

Habermas, J. (1985) (trans. Lawrence, F.) *The Philosophical Discourse of Modernity*, Cambridge, Polity Press

Habermas, J. (1987/1989) (trans. McCarthy, T.) *Theory of Communicative Action, Vol II, Lifeworld and System: a Critique of Functionalist Reason*, Oxford and Cambridge: Polity Press/Blackwell

Habermas, J. (1991) *Moral Consciousness and Communicative Action*, Cambridge: Polity Press

Habermas, J. (1996) 'Modernity: an Unfinished Project', in d'Entrèves, M.P. and Benhabib, S. (eds.), *Habermas and the Unfinished Project of Modernity*, Cambridge: Polity Press 1996

Habermas, J. (1997) (trans. Rehg, W.) *Between Facts and Norms*: Contributions to a Discourse Theory of Law and Democracy Cambridge: Polity Press in association with Blackwell

Habermas, J. (1998/2002) *On the Pragmatics of Communication*, Cambridge: Polity Press

Hacker, P. M. S. (2003) 'Wittgenstein', in Arrington, R.L. (ed.) *The World's Greatest Philosophers*, in Oxford: Blackwell Publishing Ltd

Hand, Judge Learned. (1901) 'Historical and Practical Considerations Regarding Expert Testimony', 15 *Harvard Law Review*, 40.

Harpwood, V. (2001) 'Bolitho, Expert Evidence and the Rôle of Judges', 6 *Health Law* (10) 1-3

Hesse, M. (1980) 'Revolutions and Reconstructions in the Philosophy of Science', *Habermas' Consensus Theory of Truth*, 206-231) (Chapter 9) Brighton: Harvester Press

Holder, J. and Elworthy, S. (1998) 'The BSE Crisis: A Study of the Precautionary Principle and the Politics of Science in Law' in Reece, H. (ed.) *Law and Science: Current Legal Issues*, Vol 1, Oxford: Oxford University Press

Horton, R. (2004) *MMR Science and Fiction. Exploring the Vaccine Crisis*, London: Granta Books

Hylton, P. (2003) 'Russell', in *The World's Greatest Philosophers*, in Arrington, R.L. (ed.) Oxford: Blackwell Publishing Ltd

Jacob, Sir Jack. (1987) *The Fabric of English Civil Justice*, London: Stevens and Sons

James, A. L. (1992) 'An Open or Shut Case? Law as an Autopoietic System', 19 *Journal of Law and Society* (2) 241-283

Jasanoff, S. (1998) 'Expert Games in Silicone Gel Breast Implant Litigation', in *Science in Court*, Freeman, M. and Reece, H. (eds.) Aldershot: Ashgate/Dartmouth

Jasanoff, S. (1995/1997) *Science at the Bar. Science and Technology in America*, Cambridge, Mass.: Harvard University Press

Joad, C. E. M. (1950) *A Critique of Logical Positivism*, London: Victor Gollancz Ltd

Jones, C. A. G. (1994) *Expert Witnesses. Science, Medicine and the Practice of Law*, Oxford: Clarendon Press

Jones, M. A. (1996) *Medical Negligence.* London: Sweet and Maxwell

Kant, I. (1785/1991) (trans. Paton, H. J.) *The Moral Law. Groundworks of the Metaphysics of Morals*, New York: Routledge

Kant, I. (1787/1964) (trans. Smith, N. K.) *Critique of Pure Reason*, London: Macmillan

Kant, I. (1788/1993) (trans. Beck, L. W.) *The Critique of Practical Reason and Other Writings in Moral Philosophy*, New York: Macmillan

Kant, I. (1790/1987) (trans. Pluhar, W. S.) *Critique of Judgment*, Indianapolis and Cambridge: Hackett Publishing Company

Kearney, R. (ed.) (1994) *Twentieth Century Continental Philosophy*, London and New York: Routledge

Kennedy, I. and Grubb, A. (1994) *Medical Law. Text and Materials*, London: Butterworths

Kidd, I. M., Booth C. J., Rigden, S. P., Tong, C. Y. and MacMahon, E. M. (2003) 'Measles-associated encephalitis in children with renal transplantation: a predictable effect of waning herd immunity', 362 *Lancet* 832

King, M. (1993) 'The Truth About Autopoiesis' 20 *Journal of Law and Society* (2) 218-236

King, M. (2006) 'What's the Use of Luhmann's Theory' in King, M. and Thornhill, C. (eds.). *Luhmann on Law and Politics. Critical Appraisals and Applications*, Oxford and Portland, Oregon: Hart Publishing, 37-52

King, M. and Kaganas, F. (1998) 'The Risks and Dangers of Experts in Court', in Reece, H. (ed.) *Law and Science, Current Legal Issues*, Vol 1, Oxford: Oxford University Press

King, M. and Schütz, A. (1994) 'The Ambitious Modesty of Niklas Luhmann', 21 *Journal of Law and Society* (3) 261-287

King, M. and Thornhill, C. (2006) 'Introduction', in King, M. and Thornhill, C. (eds.). *Luhmann on Law and Politics. Critical Appraisals and Applications*, Oxford and Portland, Oregon: Hart Publishing, 1-10

King, M. and Thornhill, C. (eds.) (2003) *Niklas Luhmann's Theory of Politics and Law*, Basingstoke: Palgrave Macmillan

Kober, M. (1996) 'Certainties of a World Picture: The Epistemological Investigations of On Certainty', in Sluga, H. and Stern, D.G. (eds.) *The Cambridge Companion to Wittgenstein*, Cambridge: Cambridge University Press

Kuhn, T. S. (1970) *The Structure of Scientific Revolutions*, Chicago: University of Chicago Press

La Torre, M. (1997) 'Rules, Institutions, Transformations. Considerations on the 'Evolution of Law' Paradigm', 10 *Ratio Juris* (3) 316-350

Latour, B. (2002) *La Fabrique du Droit. Une Ethnographie du Conseil d'Etat*, Paris: La Découvert. (Republished as Latour, B., Pottage, A. and Mundy, M. (eds.) 'Scientific Objects and Legal Objectivity. Portrait of the Conseil d'Etat as a Laboratory' (2004), in *Law, Anthropology and the Constitution of the Social. Making Persons and Things*, Cambridge: Cambridge University Press, 73-114)

Latour, B. (2010) 'Scientific Objects and Legal Objectivity', in *The Making of Law. An Ethnography of the Conseil d'Etat*, Cambridge: Polity Press

Latour, B. and Woolgar, S. (1986) *Laboratory Life. The Construction of Scientific Facts*, Chichester: Princeton University Press

Legal Correspondent, British Medical Journal. (1986) 'The Law tries to Decide whether Whooping Cough Vaccine Causes Brain Damage: Professor Gordon Stewart Gives Evidence', 292 *British Medical Journal* 1264-1266

Liebmann, M. (1996) 'The Future of Community Mediation' in Smith R. (ed.) *Achieving Civil Justice. Appropriate Dispute Resolution for the 1990s*, London: Legal Action Group 1996

Lingham, R. Simmons, A., Andrews, N., Miller, E., Stowe, J. and Taylor, B. (2003) 'Prevalence of Autism and Parentally Reported Triggers in a North East London Population', 88 *Archives of Disease in Childhood* 666-670

Löfstedt, R. E. (2003a) 'Risk Communication: Pitfalls and Promises', 11 *European*

Bibliography

Review (3) 417-435

Löfstedt, R. E. (2003b) 'Science Communication and the Swedish Acrylamide "Alarm" ', 8 *Journal of Health Communication* 407-432

Löfstedt, R. E. (2004) 'Risk, Communication and Management in the 21st Century', 7 *International Public Management Journal* (3), 335-346

Löfstedt, R. E., Gaskell, G. and Renn, O. (2004b) 'Quo Vadis Food Risk Communication?', *EUFIC Forum*, No. 1, August 2004 (1-5)

Löfstedt, R. E., Fischoff, B. and Fischoff, I. R. (2002) 'Precautionary Principles: General Definitions and Specific Applications to Genetically Modified Organisms', 21 *Journal of Policy Analysis and Management* (3) 381-407

Longino, H. E. (1990) *Science as Social Knowledge: values and objectivity in scientific inquiry*. Princeton, NJ: Princeton University Press

Luhmann, N. (1988) 'The Third Question: The Creative Use of Paradoxes in Law and Legal History', 15 *Journal of Law and Society* (2) 153-165

Luhmann, N. (1987a) 'The Unity of the Legal System', in Teubner, G. (ed.) *Autopoietic Law. A New Approach to Law and Society*, Berlin: de Gruyter 12-35

Luhmann, N. (1987b) 'Closure and Openness: On Reality in the World of Law', in Teubner, G. (ed.) *Autopoietic Law. A New Approach to Law and Society.* Publication Series of The European University Institute, Berlin: de Gruyter, 345-348

Luhmann, N. (1989) 'Law as a Social System', 83 *Northwestern University Law Review* (1 & 2) 136-150

Luhmann, N. (1992a) 'Operational Closure and Structural Coupling: The Differentiation of the Legal System', 13 *Cardozo Law Review*, 1419-1441

Luhmann, N. (1992b) 'Some Problems with Reflexive Law' in Teubner, G. and Febbrajo, A. (eds.) *State, Law and Economy as Autopoeitic Systems*, Milan: Guiffré

Luhmann, N. (1995) (trans. Bednarz, J. (Jr.) and Becker, D.) *Social Systems*, Stanford CA: Stanford University Press

Luhmann, N. (1997) 'Limits of Steering', 14 *Theory, Culture and Society* (1) 41-47

Luhmann, N. (2000) (trans. Knodt, E.) *Art as a Social System*, Stanford, CA: Stanford University Press

Luhmann, N. (2004) (trans. Zeigert, K.) *Law as a Social System*, Oxford: Oxford University Press

Luhmann, N. (2005) (trans. Barrett, R.) *Risk. A Sociological Theory*, Piscataway NJ: Aldine Transaction

Lyotard, J-F. (1979) (trans. Bennington, G. and Massumi, B.) *The Postmodern Condition: A Report on Knowledge*, Manchester: Manchester University Press

Magee, B. (1997) *Confessions of a Philosopher*, London: Phoenix

Magee, B. (1998*) The Story of Philosophy*, London: Dorling Kindersley Ltd

Mahlmann, M. (2004) 'Niklas Luhmann's Theory of Politics and Law by Michael King and Chris Thornhill' (Book Review), 31 *Journal of Law and Society* (3) 421-425

Majone, G. (1989) *Evidence, Argument and Persuasion in the Policy Pr*ocess. New Haven and London: Yale University Press

Martin, J. A. (1977) 'The Proposed Science Court' 75 *Michigan Law Review*, 1058-1091

McCarthy, T. (1982) 'Rationality and Relativism: Habermas's 'Overcoming' of Hermeneutics' in Thompson, J.B. and Held, D. (eds.) *Habermas: Critical Debates*, London and Basingstoke: Macmillan Press 1982

McGinn, M. (1997) *Routledge Philosophy Guidebook to Wittgenstein and the Philosophical Investigations*, London: Routledge

Merton, R. K. (1973) *The Sociology of Science. Theoretical and Empirical Investigations*, Chicago: University of Chicago Press

Monk, R. (1991) *Ludwig Wittgenstein: The Duty of Genius*, London: Vintage

Morawetz, T. (1980) *The Philosophy of Law. An Introduction.* New York: Macmillan Publishing Co. Inc.

Mulcahy, L., Selwood, M., Summerfield, L. and Netten, A. (1999/2000) *Mediating Medical Negligence Claims: An Option for the Future?* London: The Stationery Office

Mulkay, M. (1979) *Science and the Sociology of Knowledge*, London: George Allen Unwin

Murch, S. (2003) 'Separating Inflammation from Speculation in Autism', 362 *Lancet* 1498-1499

Naffine, N. (2000) 'In Praise of Legal Feminism', 22 *Legal Studies* 71-101

Nelken, D. (1998) 'A Just Measure of Science', in Reece, H. (ed.) *Law and Science, Current Legal Issues*, Vol 1, Oxford: Oxford University Press

Neves, M. (2001) 'From the Autopoiesis to the Allopoiesis of Law', 28 *Journal of Law and Society* (2) 242-264

Newton-Smith, W. H. (1981) *The Rationality of Science*, London: Routledge and Kegan Paul Ltd

Nonet, P. and Selznick, P. (1978/2001) *Towards Responsive Law. Law and Society in Transition*, New Brunswick and London: Transition Publishers

Ogus, A. (1997) 'Risk Management and 'Rational' Regulation' in Baldwin, R., *Law and Uncertainty, Risks and Legal Processes*, London: Kluwer International

Okasha, S. (2002) *Philosophy of Science. A Very Short Int*roduction, Oxford: Oxford University Press

Osborne, P. (2000) *Philosophy in Cultural Theory*, London: Routledge

Paterson, J. (1997) 'An Introduction to Luhmann', 14 *Theory, Culture and Society* (1) 37-39

Paterson, J. (2002) 'Truth or Dare: Expertise and Risk Governance', OECD Nuclear Energy Agency (ed.) *Better Integration of Radiation Protection in Modern Society*, Paris: OECD

Paterson, J. (2003) 'Trans-science, Trans-law and Proceduralisation', 12 *Social and Legal Studies* 525-545

Paterson, J. (2006) 'Reflecting on Reflexive Law' in King, M. and Thornhill, C. (eds.) *Luhmann on Law and Politics: Critical Appraisals and Applications*, Oxford-Portland, Oregon: Hart Publishing, 13-35

Penner, J., Schiff, D. and Nobles, R. (2002) 'Approaches to Jurisprudence, Legal Theory and the Philosophy of Law' in Penner, J., Schiff, D. and Nobles, R. (eds.) *Introduction to Jurisprudence and Legal Theory: Commentary and Materials*, London: LexisNexis Butterworths Tolley 2002

Phillips, E. (1994) 'Testing the Truth: The Alliance of Science and Law', in McConville, M. and Bridges, L., *Criminal Justice in Crisis*, Aldershot: Edward Elgar

Pildes, R. H. and Sunstein, C. R. (1995) 'Reinventing the Regulatory State', 62 *University of Chicago Law Review* (1) 90-91

Pinch, T. (1986) *Confronting Nature: The Sociology of Solar Neutrino Detection*, Dordrecht: D. Reidel Publishing Company

Polkinghorne, J. (2002) *Quantum Theory. A Very Short Introduction*, Oxford: Oxford University Press

Popper, K. (1972) *Conjectures and Refutations*, London: Routledge

Pound, R. (1959) *Jurisprudence*, St Paul, Minn: West Publishing Co.

Raitt, F. E. (1998) 'A New Criterion for the Admissibility of Scientific Evidence. The Metamorphosis of Helpfulness' in Reece, H. (ed.) *Law and Science; Current Legal Issues* Vol 1, Oxford: Oxford University Press 1998

Rasmussen, D. M. (1990) *Reading Habermas*, Cambridge, Mass: Blackwell Publishing Limited

Redmayne, M. (1999) 'Standards of Proof in Civil Litigation', 62 *Modern Law Review* (2) 167-195

Reiner, R. (2002) 'Classical Social Theory and Law' in Penner, J., Schiff, D. and Nobles, R. (eds.) *Introduction to Jurisprudence and Legal Theory. Commentary and Materials*, London: LexisNexis Butterworths Tolley

Resnik, D. (2003) 'Is the Precautionary Principle Unscientific?', 34 *Studies in History and Philosophy of Biological and Biomedical Studies*, 329-344

Reynolds, M. P. and King, S. D. (1992) *The Expert Witness and His Evidence*, Oxford: Blackwell Scientific Publications

Rock, P. (1993) *The Social World of an English Crown Court: Witness and Professionals in the Crown Court Centre at Wood Green*, Oxford: Oxford University Press

Roderick, R. (1986) *Habermas and the Foundations of Critical Theory*, Basingstoke: Macmillan Publishers Ltd

Rothstein, H. (2004) Personal communication: Risk and Regulation. Postgraduate Student Conference (CARR/LSE) 16th September 2004

Royal Commission on Criminal Justice. (1993) Cm 2263, Chairman Viscount

Bibliography

Runciman of Doxford, London: HMSO, July 1993

Russell, B. (1912) *The Problems of Philosophy*, Feedbooks

Russell, B. (1948) *Human Knowledge: its Scope and Limits*, London: George Allen and Unwin

Russell, B. (1980) *An Inquiry into Meaning and Truth* (William James Lectures 1940), Reading: Cox and Wymans Ltd

Sales, B. D. and Shuman, D. W. (2005) *Experts in Court: Reconciling Law, Science and Professional Knowledge*, Washington DC: American Psychiatric Association

Sanders, J. (1992) 'The Bendectin Litigation: A Case Study in Life Cycles of Mass Torts', 43 *Hastings Law Journal*, 301-418

Schapin, S. (1994) *A Social History of Truth. Civility in Science in Seventeenth Century England*, Chicago: University of Chicago Press

Scheman, N. (1996) 'Forms of Life: Mapping the Rough Ground', in Sluga, H. and Stern, D. G. (eds.) *The Cambridge Companion to Wittgenstein*, Cambridge: Cambridge University Press 1996

Schklar, J. (1998) 'DNA Evidence in the Courtroom: A Psychological Perspective' in Freeman, M. and Reece, H. (eds.) *Science in Court (Issues in Law and Society)*, Aldershot: Dartmouth 1998

Schultz, B (1992) 'Bertrand Russell in Ethics and Politics', 102 *Ethics* (3) 594-634

Scruton, R. (2001) *Kant: A Very Short Introduction*, Oxford: Oxford University Press

Shanks, N. (2004) *God, The Devil and Darwin*, Oxford: Oxford University Press

Sluga, H. (1996) 'Ludwig Wittgenstein: Life and Work. An Introduction', in Sluga, H. and Stern, D. G. (eds.) *The Cambridge Companion to Wittgenstein*, Cambridge: Cambridge University Press

Smith, C. (2004) 'Autopoietic Law and the 'Epistemic Trap': A Case Study of Adoption and Contact', 31 *Journal of Law and Society* (3) 318-344

Smith, P. (2001) *Cultural Theory: an Introduction*, Malden, Mass and Oxford: Blackwell Publishers Ltd

Solomon, R. C. and Sherman, D. (eds.) (2003) *The Blackwell Guide to Continental*

Philosophy, Malden, Mass and Oxford: Blackwell Publishing Ltd

Stirk, P. M. R. (2000) *Critical Theory, Politics and Society*, London: Pinter

Sudden Unexpected Death in Infancy. A Multi Agency Protocol for Care and Investigation. (2004) The Report of a Working Group convened by The Royal College of Pathologists and The Royal College of Paediatrics and Child Health (Chair: The Baroness Helena Kennedy QC. September 2004)

Tait, N. and Timmins, N. (2003) 'Judge Orders Girls to have MMR Jab', *Financial Times*, London (UK) 14th June 2003

Taylor, B., Miller, E., Farrington, C. P., Petropoulos, M-C., Farot-Maynaud, I., Li, J. and Waight, P. (1999) 'Autism and Measles, Mumps and Rubella Vaccine: no epidemiological evidence for a casual association', 353 *Lancet* 2026-2029

Taylor, C. (1997) *Philosophical Arguments*, Cambridge, Mass.: Harvard University Press

Teff, H. (1994) *Reasonable Care–Legal Perspectives on the Doctor/Patient Relationship*, Oxford: Clarendon Press

Teubner, G. (1983) 'Substantive and Reflexive Elements in Modern Law', 17 *Law and Society Review* 239-285

Teubner, G. (1985a) 'The Transformation of Law in the Welfare State', in Teubner, G. (ed.) *Dilemmas of Law in the Welfare State*, Berlin/New York: de Gruyter

Teubner, G. (1985b) 'After Legal Instrumentalism: Strategic Models in Post-regulatory Law' in Teubner, G. (ed.) *Dilemmas of Law in the Welfare State*, Berlin/New York: de Gruyter

Teubner, G. (1989) 'How the Law Thinks: Towards a Constructivist Epistemology of Law', 23 *Law and Society Review* (5) 727-758

Teubner, G. (1998) 'Juridification: Concepts, Aspects, Limits, Solutions', in Baldwin, R., Scott, C. and Hood, C. (eds.) *A Reader on Regulation*, Oxford: Oxford University Press

Teubner, G., Nobles, R. and Schiff, D. (2002) 'The Autonomy of Law: An Introduction to Legal Autopoiesis' in Penner, J., Schiff, D. and Nobles, R. (eds.) *Introduction to Jurisprudence and Legal Theory: Commentary and Materials*, London: LexisNexis Butterworths Tolley

Urmson, J. O. (1967) 'The Linguistic Turn. Recent Essays in Philosophical Method', in Rorty, R. (ed.) *The History of Philosophical Analysis*, Chicago: Chicago

University Press

Vestergaard, M., Hviid, A., Madsen, K. M., Wohlfart, J., Thorsen, P., Schendel, D., Melbye, M. and Olsen, J. (2004) 'MMR Vaccination and febrile seizures', 292 *Journal of the American Medical Association* (3) 351-357

Viskovatoff, A. (1999) 'Foundation of Niklas Luhmann's Theory of Social Systems', 29 *Philosophy of the Social Sciences* (4) 481-516

Wagner, W. (1986) 'Trans-science in Torts', 96 *Yale Law Journal*, 428-449

Waismann, F. (1997) (ed. Harrè, R.) *The Principles of Linguistic Philosophy*, Basingstoke: Macmillan Press Ltd

Wakefield, A. J. Murch, S. H., Anthony, A., Linnell, J., Casson, D. M., Malik, M., Berelowitz, M., Dhillon, A. P., Thomson, M. A., Harvey, P., Valentine, A., Davies, S. E., and Walker-Smith, J. A. (1998) 'Ileal-lymphoid-nodular Hyperplasia, Non-specific Colitis and Pervasive Developmental Disorder in Children', 351 *Lancet* 637-641

Walker, V. (1998) 'Keeping the WTO from Becoming the "World Trans-science Organization": Scientific Uncertainty, Science, Policy, and Factfinding in the Growth Hormones Dispute', 31 *Cornell International Law Journal* 251-320

Wall, W. (2002) *Genetics and DNA Technology: Legal Aspects*, London: Cavendish Publishing Limited

Ward, T. (1998) 'Law's Truth, Lay Truth and Medical Science. Three Case Studies' in Reece, H. (ed.) *Law and Science, Current Legal Issues*, Vol 1, Oxford: Oxford University Press 1998

Ward, T. (2004) 'Experts, Juries and Witch-hunts: From Fitzjames Stephen to Angela Cannings', 31 *Journal of Law and Society* (3) 369-386

Warren, L. M. (1998) 'Using law to define uncertain science in environmental policy', in Freeman, M. and Reece, H. (ed.) *Science in Court*, Aldershot: Ashgate/Dartmouth 1998

Weber, M. (1978) *Economy and Society*, Berkeley: University of California Press

Weinberg, A. M. (1972) 'Science and Trans-science', 10 *Minerva* (2) 209-222

Weinberg, A. M. (1991) 'Origins of Science and Trans-science' (Citation Classic), 34 *Current Contents/Social Behaviour* 10

Weiner, D. A. (1992) *Genius and Talent: Schopenhauer's Influence on Wittgenstein's Early Philosophy*, New Jersey, London and Ontario: Associated University Press

White, S. K. (1989) 'The Discursive Interpretation and the Demand for Reciprocity', in *The Recent Work of Jürgen Habermas: Reason, Justice and Modernity*, Cambridge: Cambridge University Press, pp. 69-72

Whooping Cough. Reports from the Committee for the Safety of Medicines and the Joint Committee on Vaccination and Immunization. (1981) Department of Health & Social Security, London: HM Stationery Office

Wiethölter, R. (1985) 'Materialization and Proceduralization in Modern Law', in Teubner, G. (ed.) *Dilemmas of Law in the Welfare State*, Berlin/New York: de Gruyter

Wittgenstein, L. (1921/1974) (trans. Pears, D.F. and McGuiness, B.F.) *Tractatus Logico-Philosophicus*, London: Routledge and Kegan Paul

Wittgenstein, L. (1953/1972) (trans. Anscombe, G.E.M.) *Philosophical Investigations*, Oxford: Blackwell Publishers Ltd

Wittgenstein, L. (1969) (trans. Anscombe, G. E. M. and von Wright, G. H.) (ed. Paul, D. and Anscombe, G. E. M.) *On Certainty*, Oxford: Blackwell

Wolpert, L. (1998) 'What Lawyers Need To Know About Science' in Reece, H. (ed.) *Law and Science, Current Legal Issues*, Vol. 1, Oxford: Oxford University Press

Wynne, B. (1989) 'Establishing the Rules of Laws: Constructing Expert Authority', in Smith, R. and Wynne. (eds.) *Expert Evidence. Interpreting Science in the Law*, London: Routledge

Zander, M. (1996) *Cases and Materials on the English Legal System*, London: Butterworths

Ziman, J. (1984) *The Philosophical and Social Aspects of Science and Technology*, Cambridge: Cambridge University Press

Ziman, J. (2000) *Real Science, What It Is, and What It Means*, Cambridge: Cambridge University Press

ABOUT THE AUTHOR

Cedric Charles Gilson, PhD, LLM, MSc, PGDip, is presently Visiting Fellow in Law in the Department of Advanced Legal Studies, School of Law, University of Westminster, London, UK. After a professional career in UK National Health Service hospitals, university medical schools and medical postgraduate institutes, Cedric moved into the study of law via dispute prevention and resolution at Westminster, where he applied his previous working experience and understanding of the intersection of science and policy to his further graduate study. Combining science and healthcare interests with law led to an initial focus on medical negligence, which then expanded into an examination of the interaction of science and law in the context of evidence in the English jurisdiction. This formed the basis of the doctoral thesis that he developed into this publication, in the Dissertation Series edited by Professor John Flood of the University of Westminster.

Cedric currently is studying the rationalities of ethics and law over assisted dying, principally via the medium of systems theory. He is also concerned with the admissibility of expert opinion evidence in English courts with regard to the way in which law understands and uses scientific evidence. He has taught "Regulating Risk Environments" as a module of LLM dispute resolution courses at the University of Westminster.

qp

Visit us at *www.quidprobooks.com*.

www.ingramcontent.com/pod-product-compliance
Lightning Source LLC
Chambersburg PA
CBHW070406270326
41926CB00014B/2729